THE PSYCHOSOMATIC DELUSION

T H E

PSYCHOSOMATIC

DELUSION

Why the Mind Is Not the
Source of All Our Ills

ROBERT DANTZER

THE FREE PRESS
A Division of Macmillan, Inc.
NEW YORK

Maxwell Macmillan Canada
TORONTO

Maxwell Macmillan International
NEW YORK   OXFORD   SINGAPORE   SYDNEY

The Free Press
A Division of Macmillan, Inc.
866 Third Avenue, New York, N.Y. 10022

Maxwell Macmillan Canada, Inc.
1200 Eglinton Avenue East
Suite 200
Don Mills, Ontario M3C 3N1

Macmillan, Inc. is part of the
Maxwell Communication Group of Companies.

Printed in the United States of America

printing number
1 2 3 4 5 6 7 8 9 10

Library of Congress Cataloging-in-Publication Data

Dantzer, Robert.
    [Illusion psychosomatique.   English]
    The psychosomatic delusion :   Why the mind is not the source of all our ills / Robert Dantzer.
        p.   cm.
    Includes bibliographical references and indexes.
    ISBN 0–02–906937–8
    1. Medicine, Psychosomatic.   I. Title.
RC49.D2613   1993
616.08—dc20   93–19682
                                                                  CIP

Illustrations by Laurent Lalo and Rose Marie Bluthé.
Published with the assistance of the Ministère Français
chargé de la Culture.

But let us understand each other: since it is assumed we agree that—and we have constantly repeated this from the first—everything that seems clear and precise belongs in fact to the realm of conjecture, almost of invention. And most of the time the obvious flares briefly and is then extinguished above—or, if you prefer, beyond—what we call words. And to repeat once again, so that everything will be quite clear, even though nothing has changed and it is supposed that we have, from the first, agreed on all points, all of this is only approximate, and if you wish it to be, and in the end, what's the difference!

—JUAN JOSE SAER, *L'anniversaire*

CONTENTS

4. CONFRONTATION / 67

5. THE MISFORTUNES OF INDIVIDUALITY / 119

6. MIND AND IMMUNITY / 155

INTRODUCTION TO THE AMERICAN EDITION

We all believe in the healing power of the mind. The idea seems so simple and appealing that we often cannot resist the temptation of blaming those who become ill and, conversely, applauding those who succeed in fighting such life-threatening illnesses as cancer. Being in harmony with ourselves and our environment is presented as the only way to stay healthy and resist the daily pressures in our lives. It is the subject of many self-help books, which claim to provide information of vital importance to us.[1] If despite all efforts we have the misfortune of becoming ill, still other books and popular magazines teach us how to mobilize our natural healing defenses in the battle against disease. The concept is that we are more than material bodies; we are "beings of light and energy whose quantum power can be manipulated to cure or prevent disease."[2] To develop the healer within, we must revive ancient medical practices based on the harmonious flow of energy between the universe and ourselves.

For those who need to bridge the gap between intuitive knowledge and rationality, these old recipes are backed up by a number of scientifically oriented books that explain how this marvelous machine of a brain, with its myriad neurotransmitters and hormones, is able to maintain and restore harmony within the body.[3] Thanks to the breakthrough discoveries achieved by psychoneuroimmunology—the new scientific discipline that explores the previous unknowns of the relationship between the mind and immunity—we are supposed finally to understand how and why negative emotions can compromise our immune system and therefore increase susceptibility to infections and cancer. However, fortunately for those of us who believe that nature, despite its apparent wildness, is guided by wisdom, we are told that the detrimental effects of negative emotions inside our bodies can be overcome by positive emotions.[4] After all, this should come as no surprise, since we know perfectly well that after having alienated those around us, we can bring them back with happiness and love.

What is fantasy, what is reality in this maverick world? When I was still an adolescent, I was shocked to learn that my younger sister, who had bone cancer, was going to die. In my concern for her, I concentrated all the powers of my mind on the fragile hope of her remission. To decisively win this last battle, I went as far as promising myself that if she were to survive, I would work hard to become a scientist and find remedies for cancer. My sister died, and for many other unrelated reasons I became much later a neurobiologist interested in stress and health, emotions and the brain, mind and body. When I started in this field in the early seventies, I was very much influenced by the nonspecific theory of stress elaborated by Hans Selye, and I was therefore convinced that stress leads to disease by decreasing the organism's resistance to pathogens. This theory had the advantage of making the research task relatively easy since it implied that it was sufficient to study the mechanisms of stress in order to understand how stress-related diseases could develop.

After many years of work, I have realized that it is not so simple, and even more, I have developed some doubt about the validity of the whole concept of stress and disease. That is what this book is about. It is an attempt to show that we have come a long way from the early naive description of the way stress leads to disease to our present understanding of why we feel sick and behave in a sick manner when we are sick. The knowledge gained in the interim puts into new perspective the question of the relationships between psychological factors and health by revealing two important facts:

(1) In the same way that the driver of a car cannot manage to jump over the line of cars in front of him to escape a traffic jam, the power of the mind over the body is not infinite but is very much constrained by the nature of the relationships the brain establishes with bodily processes. This situation comes about because the brain is not connected to the body so as to enable my mind to do within my body whatever I can dream of; rather it is to enable my body to function in real time and anticipation of what is going to happen, to optimize the way I interact with my environment.

(2) There is nothing like a free mind. If my stomach is empty, I may feel aggressive impulses. If I feel sick, I don't feel like joining the party I am invited to. The way the brain can work is profoundly influenced by bodily functions, which means in particular that if I am sick, I do not have the same mental resources as when I am healthy.

This does not imply that the biomedical model, which reduces sickness to organ dysfunctions, is the only viable alternative. There is a profound and legitimate need for a different model that cares for the whole patient; however, to state that "wholeness" is the root of "healing"[5] is of little use if it is impossible to delineate precisely the different components of sickness: the sociocultural, the psychological, and the biological components, their interactions, and their contribution to the disease process. How can we assimilate the enormous amount of information provided by the latest scientific research and at the same time care for the whole patient? This book has been written with the belief that this goal is at hand, provided we are ready to accept complexity and deal with it by adopting a systems perspective of health instead of taking refuge in a fairyland populated with fuzzy concepts such as "stress," "holistic medicine," and "healing powers."

Robert Dantzer
Bordeaux, March 1993

INTRODUCTION

It is true that, thanks to Descartes, the immortal soul has been definitively driven from the body, which leaves mechanics free to explore the brain without interruption or hindrance. But precisely because it was expelled from the ramparts of the body with excessive violence, has not the soul become too noisy?

—JEAN-DIDIER VINCENT, *Biologie des passions*

Modern medicine is profoundly dualist: It separates mental illnesses without organic cause from physical illness without mental cause. Patients unfortunate enough to fall into the institutional void created by this conception arouse only indifference. What doctor is capable of serious concern for the psychological troubles of a patient afflicted with asthma, an illness that is, to borrow a phrase from the lung specialist François-Bernard Michel, 100 percent organic and 100 percent psychological?[1] And what kind of attention is a psychiatrist prepared to give to the somatic disorders of his patients?

The vast and still poorly explored domain of the relationship between body and mind has long been left to philosophy and to the popular imagination. Philosophy has engendered a litany of "isms": from monism to dualism by way of mentalism, materialism, and interactionism. Mario Bunge, an insatiable philosopher of science, has enumerated no fewer than ten different conceptions that, in his view, suffer from critical epistemological deficiencies.[2]

Popular belief is not burdened with such subtleties, but it is profoundly marked by the idea that personality and temperament can affect health. Two centuries before Christ, the Greek physician Galen noted that depressed women run a greater risk of breast cancer than those of more sanguine temperament. Closer to our own time, at the end of the 1970s, the well-known journalist Norman Cousins provided a topic for medical journals when he claimed to have overcome ankylosing spondylitis, an articular complaint that principally affects the spine, through laughter and good humor. He called to his aid all the great comics—the Marx brothers, Laurel and Hardy, Charlie Chaplin, Tex Avery—and launched a regimen of intensive hilarity, simultaneously dosing himself heavily with vitamin C to stimulate his adrenals. To his doctors' amazement, the patient's symptoms subsided. When he recovered, Cousins wrote a best-seller exploring the curative power of optimism.[3] He was rewarded for these efforts by a professor's chair at the University of California, and until his death in 1991 spent most of his time delivering his message throughout the country.

Rejection can yield to acceptance. Fritz Zorn, a pseudonym adopted by the son of a middle-class family in Zurich, played illness and death against life. In a powerful autobiographical account[4] he defines the cancer that was killing him as a physical expression of his mental state: "All the tears I had neither wept nor wished to weep during the course of my life had massed in my neck and created my tumor because their true function—to be shed—had not been attained."

What is this power of spirit over flesh, this power that, depending on how it is used, either permits cure or provokes illness? And what are its mechanisms? The stakes are important. If such a power exists, everyone will calculate the advantages to be drawn from it. Everyone, at one point or another, has faked poor health in order to escape some unwelcome drudgery or, conversely, has dreamed of overcoming illness by force of will.

Some doctors have already tried to give substance to these popular beliefs. They call themselves psychosomaticians to demonstrate their desire to escape the dominant Cartesian dualism and to support the unity of mind and body, of psyche and soma. Products of the psychoanalytic school, they attribute somatization, that is, bodily illness, to contradictions and conflicts that the subject is unable to resolve in his mind. The therapist's task, therefore, is to discover what difficulties confront the patient and why his defense mechanisms are failing. In accord with psychoanalytic tradition, the deeper causes of these are sought in early childhood, in the child's relationship to his parents.*

For existential difficulties and unresolved conflict to affect the body, the language of the passions developed in the brain, the seat of the mind, must be comprehensible to bodily organs. Anyone who has ever felt violent emotion will understand this: the heart pounds, the face flushes or loses color, breathing is affected. Biologists studying the mechanisms by which emotion modifies bodily function chose the term *stress* to designate the biological storm that is unleashed by catastrophic events and conflicting passions.

In theory, it should have been possible, by combining psychosomatics and stress theory, to develop an understanding of how the brain communicates with the body and why dialogue between them can fail. But a synthesis has not been achieved: psychosomatic theory has scornfully rejected the mechanics of stress, and stress specialists have exhausted themselves attempting to trace hormones to the brain. Once again the patient has found himself rejected and dismissed: for one who is suffering, there can be no greater insult than to be told, "It's psychosomatic." Meanwhile, researchers who knew nothing of the dialectic of the relationship of body and mind perfected medications like the beta-agonists, which dilate the bronchial muscles, and the antihistamine antagonists of the H2 receptors. In the hands of general practitioners, these molecules have done more for the well-being of patients than has the entire body of discourse on the psychological origins of asthma or gastroduodenal ulcers.

Is psychosomatic medicine nothing but illusion? Should we now, after accumulated failures and disappointments, assume that its hour has passed? Modern medicine is increasingly oriented toward molecular biology: genomic analysis is used to identify those individuals who are more at risk than others for certain diseases. It

---

* The author has used male-gender pronouns throughout this book for ease of expression. Statements made in the book include all human beings, unless a specific individual is being discussed.

seems reasonable to hope that a genetic basis can be found for both cancer and depression. While psychosomaticians, lacking knowledge of an organic cause, still attribute essential hypertension to the inhibition of aggressive impulses, molecular biologists consider it the consequence of a genetic anomaly controlling the permeability of cell walls to sodium. The discovery of the cause of this anomaly can come none too soon: whole families of human beings as well as laboratory animals are afflicted by it.

The battle between the triumphant materialism of molecular biology and the nebulous illusions of psychosomatic theory is one the latter has already lost. Fixated on the overriding power of the mind, it is a discipline that has congealed within itself. Indulging in the pleasures of pseudo-philosophical discourse, psychosomatic theory fails to perceive the interaction of body and mind as an experimental proposition, whereas medical practice considers it a stillbirth. Can this be tolerated while the laughter of Norman Cousins still rings in our ears and the sad fate of Fritz Zorn still haunts us? No one with the slightest interest in humankind can afford to renounce the spiritual dimension of illness.

This presupposes, first of all, that we try to understand why some individuals, when faced with health problems, feel a need for psychological explanation. The ankylosing spondylitis that afflicted Norman Cousins is an illness that can undergo spontaneous remission. Either by coincidence or as a matter of cause and effect, at the moment of cure Norman Cousins laughed. Why did he conclude that his laughter had saved him? And if that *is* in fact what happened, it is important to know why. Fritz Zorn had incorporated within his being the immense anger (*Zorn* is the German word for that emotion) that sprang from a belated grasp of his illness's metaphoric nature. Again, how can this attitude be explained? An interest in questions of this kind necessitates inquiry into our belief systems and the ways in which they are put to the test by the uncertainties of illness.

Another basic question concerns the links between psyche and soma. By posing the problem in these terms, one already risks entrapment in dualism, for an individual is always simultaneously body and mind. Successful adaptation to the environment depends on a harmonious synergy between both aspects of a unique existential entity. An attack on one of these alone, without affecting the other, is therefore impossible—except through the illusion created by a perspective that emphasizes one aspect at the expense of the other.

"There are more things in heaven and earth, Horatio, than are dreamt of in your philosophy." And there are more ties between spirit and flesh than psychosomatic theory has ever imagined. But researchers are now beginning to explore this vast domain, which until the present time was left to philosophers and psychoanalysts. Scientific knowledge of the interaction between mental events and bodily functions has grown extensively during the last 20 years. Between psychology and biology there is no longer an unbroken void but a complex of new domains that are the subjects of active research. The disciplines involved bear compound names like psychoneuroendocrinology, psychobiology, and psychoneuroimmunology. The layman should not be discouraged by the complexity of these terms. They express an aim that had almost been abandoned: to escape the enclosed and stifling compartmentalization of disciplines that for far too long has inhibited contact between the biological sciences on the one hand and the social sciences on the other.

Considering human beings as unities is the trend at the cutting edge of the research we intend to review here, research that shows that modernity need not be incompatible with a return to humanism.

ABERRATIONS OF BODY AND MIND

One must not see reality as the self.

—PAUL ELUARD, *À toute épreuve*

The habit of attributing physical complaints to psychological causes is firmly rooted in popular common sense. The difficulties I experience digesting my evening meal are not necessarily due to the food or the cooking; they may well be the result of a fight with my wife over the best way to bring up our children. My neighbor's eczema is not unrelated to problems he has had at work since the new boss arrived. My sister, in the throes of a divorce following the departure of her husband, has just learned that the lump in her breast (which she never had time to deal with) is cancerous.

We believe so strongly in the pathogenic power of routine difficulties that we readily tell ourselves, "Everything will go better when I've had a little rest," and we unhesitatingly apply the same logic to the problems of others: "It's no surprise that he is sick; he leads a hellish life!" An actual bodily complaint isn't even necessary. If a medical examination of a relative or friend fails to reveal any recognized pathology, we are quick to deny his claims to actual physical suffering, dismissing the trouble as "all in the head" or "psychosomatic" (by which we mean that the trouble is physical but its origins are really in the mind). And in regard to an obviously disturbed person we tend to feel that everything would be all right if he would only show a little willpower.

Of course, when my son comes down with measles, I ascribe his illness to a virus picked up at school. But for other maladies one instinctively assumes some kind of psychological failure. This is true, for example, of complaints whose causes are not yet clearly understood, such as asthma and other allergic illnesses, autoimmune disorders (e.g., rheumatoid arthritis and thyroiditis), gastroduodenal ulcers, ulcerative colitis, essential hypertension, coronary complaints, diabetes, and various forms of cancer.

Popular common sense, often very wide of the mark, has not prevented many scientists from trying to illuminate the association between illness and psychological factors without waiting for objective studies proving that such an association exists. Thus, two schools of thought have gradually taken shape: one inspired by psychoanalysis and centered on the idea of psychosomatic illness; the other based on biology and centered on the idea of stress.

THE PSYCHOSOMATIC MOVEMENT

The psychosomatic movement was born in Austria and Germany in the wake of psychoanalysis and crossed the Atlantic with the heavy emigration just before World War II. For the first psychoanalysts a somatic symptom was just another conversion manifestation presented by a patient afflicted with hysterical neurosis. How Freud, in deciphering the history of an infantile neurosis, interpreted the state of chronic constipation suffered by his celebrated patient the Wolf Man is revealing: the constipation was seen as the result of unconscious suppressed homosexuality hysterically affecting the bowels.[1]

The actual founder of psychosomatic medicine was Georg Groddeck,[2] one of Freud's contemporaries. This maverick German psychoanalyst, who defined himself as a primitive psychoanalyst, was one of the first to claim that all human phenomena are expressed both psychically and physically. Organic illness has a meaning that the therapist must grasp in order to treat it accurately. This meaning is determined by the id, the God-Nature borrowed from Goethe, the life principle of which the psyche and the body are the expression. In the case of constipation the id is asserting that it wishes to retain for itself that which should be returned to the external world because the world is an unworthy recipient, the experience is pleasurable, or the donor is ashamed of the mediocrity of his gift. However, the notion that psychosomatic trouble might have a symbolic function was vehemently opposed by the two leaders of the psychosomatic movement in the United States— Franz Alexander, founder of the Chicago school of psychoanalysis,[3] and Flanders Dunbar, the author of a work on the emotions and physical change.[4] According to these authors, psychosomatic troubles are simply caused by states of chronic nervous tension produced by emotions that are inappropriate or inadequately expressed.

For Dunbar, somatic modifications occurring in conjunction with anger are not the same as those that accompany anguish. At the somatic level, therefore, each emotion has a specific signature of one kind or another; a concept that sheds some light on why personalities predisposed to ulcers differ from those predisposed to coronary illnesses or rheumatoid arthritis. On the basis of such correlations, according to the Dunbar school, it should be possible not only to predict what type of pathology a given individual might develop but also to alter the probability of that development by attempting to modify personality factors. So far, such a premise has not been notably successful.

For Alexander, psychosomatic specificity derives not from personality but from the type of conflict experienced by the patient. In skin complaints that involve itching, the important factor is the "impulse of hostility which a sense of guilt distracts from its original object, turning it against the subject himself."[5] Personalities that more easily than others repress their hostile impulses are predisposed to attacks of migraine. In the case of asthma, "the essential psychological factor is a conflict whose knot is an excessive and unresolved attachment to the mother." Alexander's approach is clearly multifactorial. Unresolved conflicts create conditions favorable to the development of psychosomatic difficulties, but illness is manifested only if two further conditions exist simultaneously: a facilitating condition, represented by somatic factors responsible for a constitutional or acquired susceptibility of the target organ; and a precipitating condition, for example, a sudden grief or disappointment.

Discussions on the pathogenesis of psychosomatic illnesses have played no part in the evolution of psychoanalytic theory. It is true that for the psychoanalyst, psychosomatic patients are deadly dull as subjects of analysis because as often as not they have very little to say. The concept of "operative thinking" was proposed in 1963 by the French psychoanalysts Marty, de M'Uzan, and David[6] to designate the poverty of imagination and symbolization that characterizes these patients. The mental activity of people suffering from psychosomatic troubles is oriented entirely toward the present and the concrete; most of their time is spent reexamining and reassessing their physical complaints. Not to be outdone, two American psychoanalysts, Nemiah and Sifneos,[7] coined a new term to designate the same phenomenon: *alexythymia*. Etymologically, alexythymia is an inability to read one's emotions (literally, alexia of the mind). The alexithymic patient is unable to verbalize his emotions or to sustain elaborated mental representations. The concept of operative thinking, or alexythymia, is a seductive one. It has the advantage of evoking the notion of a body language that is a substitute for the ability to symbolize and for a faltering imaginative power. Unfortunately, in both cases the approach has remained highly descriptive; the few attempts at an objective measurement of the degree of alexithymia or the operative nature of thought have never been properly validated. Operative thinking and alexithymia are therefore orphan concepts that have scarcely advanced our understanding of psychosomatic illness.

In purely medical terms it must be recognized that the apogee attained by psychosomatic medicine between the 1930s and 1950s has not affected our methods of preventing or treating psychosomatic complaints. The biomedical model, which focuses on the dysfunction of the target organ and does not take into account the possible role played by psychological factors, has been far more effective in developing new therapeutic techniques—and in certain cases obtaining cures—than have treatises on the psychogenesis of illness. This explains the gradual retrenchment of psychosomatic medicine to illnesses for which the possibilities of treatment—and, by the same token, hopes of cure—are very limited.

THE BIOLOGICAL APPROACH: THE CONCEPT OF STRESS

The biological approach to the role of psychological factors in illness dates to the beginning of this century, to the work of the American physiologist Walter Cannon and that of the pathologist Hans Selye.

By studying the reactions of cats frightened by dogs, Cannon showed that the somatic manifestations accompanying flight or attack are caused by the release into the blood of a hormone originating in the medulla, or central portion of the adrenal gland, situated above the kidney. This hormone, which was named epinephrine, is released from the adrenal medulla during nervous excitement. An injection of epinephrine given to a relaxed cat produces accelerated respiration and cardiac rhythm, a bristling of the hair, a rush of blood to the muscles and brain reducing visceral circulation, enlarging pupils, and increasing concentration of sugars in the blood. All these physiological changes characterize the frightened cat. For the first time it was possible to reproduce experimentally the visceral manifestations of emotion and to understand the physical effects of a mental event.[8]

Like Walter Cannon, Hans Selye tried to identify a hormone. In this case, however, it was a sex hormone prepared from bovine ovarian extract. To test whether or not it was active, Selye injected it into rats. To his great surprise, a majority of these animals died. When autopsied, they presented anomalies comparable to those Selye had already observed in his medical practice, in patients suffering from severe burns and in cases of suffocation and multiple fractures. Symptoms invariably present in any of these categories included gastrointestinal ulcers, atrophy of the thymus and the lymphatic ganglia, and hypertrophy of the adrenal glands.

Selye believed that these symptoms indicated an overload of an individual's defense capacities.

Confronted by psychological or physical stressors that threaten internal equilibrium, an organism launches a counterattack aimed at restoring the status quo. Because it does not depend on the character of the stressor, this reaction is nonspecific. It will produce identical manifestations in a mother who hears with brutal suddenness of her son's death in battle and in that same mother when she learns that the first report was false: that her son has survived and will return home. Both joy and pain were unexpected and therefore have the same visceral effects. The hormones responsible for the counterreaction are released by the adrenal cortex and are known as glucocorticoids because of their effects on the metabolism of sugars. The mechanisms for activating the nervous release of glucocorticoids subsequently became clear. Their synthesis and release are controlled by another hormone, ACTH, or adrenocorticotropic hormone, produced by the anterior portion of the pituitary. ACTH is itself regulated by another hormone: corticoliberine (CRF). CRF is synthesized in the hypothalamus and transported to the pituitary by a specialized vascular system, the portal stalk, which concentrates the transported hormones. A mental event, therefore, is translated into a visceral reaction by a flood of intermediary hormones.

The term *stress* emerges directly from the work of Cannon and Selye. Before them Claude Bernard, at the end of the nineteenth century, had shown that mammals and several other animal species were capable of maintaining a constant internal environment despite fluctuating exterior circumstances. This liberation from the constraints of a rhythmic life rigidly affected by external environmental factors is made possible in these species by the presence of mechanisms contributing to homeostasis: our internal temperature, despite important climatic fluctuations, is normally confined to a strictly limited range; similarly, the level of sugar in the blood is more or less constant despite irregular sugar intake. This regulation, however, continues only if environmental variation is moderate. In cases of extreme variation, other mechanisms begin to function. These initiate, on the one hand, stimulation of the sympathetic nervous system and the adrenal medulla, which supports the emergency reaction described by Cannon, and, on the other, activation of the adrenal cortex, which is responsible for the general adaptation syndrome described by Selye. Both of these reactions result from what physicists call stress, that is, from pressure applied to substance—or, in this instance, to homeostasis. When pressure becomes too great, the substance breaks. In the case of an organism, we find what Selye calls "diseases of adaptation"; these are the result of an overload of corticosteroids accompanying an excessively strong counterreaction. According to stress theory, an organism's resistance to attack is thereby compromised, either because the hormones participating in the adaptation are released in excessive quantities or for abnormally prolonged periods or because the capacity for synthesis of these hormones is diminished when the producing glands are exhausted.

The physiological studies conducted by Cannon and Selyes are important. They were the first to show clearly that an emotion (or, in the most general terms, a mental state) is a phenomenon that is not limited to the psychological sphere and that there are also repercussions on the body that involve organic modifications. This in turn made it possible to postulate that the physiological reactions accompanying emotion are intermediary mechanisms by which unresolved conflicts affect health. The psychosomatic movement had at last found its biological confirmation in a sequence of linear causality, summarized as follows:

psychological distress→ sustained neurohormonal reaction→ functional alterations in the target organ→ prepathologic structural alterations→ established pathology

Cannon and Selye had focused on the peripheral glands and the hormones they secrete, but it is clear that the brain is not simply an idle spectator. The neuroanatomist Paul MacLean has proposed a theory of the brain that includes and combines the facts of evolution and the concept of homeostasis.[9]

THE TRIUNE BRAIN

The mammalian brain is the product of an evolutionary process that developed over millions of years and resulted in a juxtaposition of three distinct cerebral layers, each with its own spatiotemporal organization.

The reptilian forebrain corresponds principally to the brain stem, the mesencephalon, the hypothalamus, and the basal ganglia. Equipped with a rudimentary cortex, this brain plays an essential role in the establishment of territory, in the search for shelter and food, in reproductive activity, and, more generally, in all of the basic activities necessary to the survival of both the species and the individual.

The paleomammalian brain corresponds to the development

of the primitive cortex and the formation of the limbic system. It enabled disengagement from the stereotypical behavior controlled by the reptilian brain, thus facilitating the acquisition of reactions suited to new circumstances. Further, it could elaborate an internal representation, a map of the immediate environment, with which the actual perception of that environment is compared.

The neomammalian brain results from the burgeoning neocortex that characterizes mammalian brains. It reaches its highest development in human beings and is responsible for cognitive functions.

In this grand geologic profile, the instincts (reptilian brain) and the emotions (paleomammalian brain) are controlled by the cortex, the seat of reason. According to this conception, psychosomatic illness is simply a banal account of defective brain functioning. Conflicts treated by the limbic system normally find expression in the neocortical area of the brain. If this is impossible, they register in the visceral sphere, through the links that connect the limbic system with areas of the reptilian brain involved in autonomous functions.

THE INHIBITION OF ACTION

Another way of conceptualizing control mechanisms of the individual's reaction to his environment is to imagine that behavior is the product of the interaction between two command systems, one that activates behavior and one that inhibits it. Each system corresponds to a complex of neuronal structures identifiable by the localization of cell bodies, the course taken by the constituent nerve fibers, and the type of mediator assuring transmission to interior parts of the system. The network of these systems traverses the brain and activates other structures that are as much the province of the reptilian brain as of the limbic brain or the neocortex. It is this vertical organization that makes possible the linkage between behavior and its organic concomitants.

The system for behavioral activation comprises two distinct subsystems: one that organizes reactions of flight and struggle and one that enables an active approach to reward and to the stimuli associated with it. The system inhibiting action supports the behavioral inhibition that occurs when a person is confronted by punishment or by the absence of anticipated reward. Prolonged hyperactivity by one of these systems can be a source of pathology. The English psychologist Jeffrey Gray attributes pathological anxiety to hyperactivity of the inhibitory system.[10] And Henri Laborit considers that chronic activation of the behavioral inhibition system induces psychosomatic disease.[11]

STRESS BECOMES TRITE

There are no strict parallels between the psychological explanations provided by the psychosomatic movement and the biological explanations proposed by theories of stress or inhibition of action. Nevertheless, it is tempting to combine these conceptions in a single physiopathologic model. This model assumes that the root of an illness can be found in the discrepancy between a subject's aspirations and the reality of overly intense reactive mechanisms[12] (Fig. 1.1).

While this model was being established, the nature of the phenomena for which it was supposed to account changed character. This change, however, occurred surreptitiously, as if it were already self-evident and therefore needed no discussion. It is true

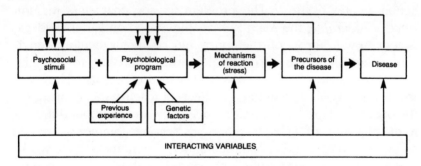

FIGURE 1.1.   The physiopathologic model of Kagan and Levi. A person confronts reality under the influence of motives that themselves depend on innate drives and previous experience. Frustration or conflict activates psychological and physiological stress reactions. The repeated activation of these mechanisms provokes functional changes at the level of the target organ. Eventually lesions may appear that indicate pathology. Many external factors (nutrition, standard of living, professional or leisure activities, etc.) accelerate or oppose this process. In addition, the chain of events is not strictly linear since these consequences can, in turn, function as causal factors.

that for each of us the notion of stress does not invariably evoke the catastrophic event imagined by Cannon and Selye. The term itself makes us think especially of the small problems of daily life that threaten our mental and physical well-being and are at the root of the unease or the distress affecting us, to a greater or lesser extent, at any time. Selye was the first to propose a theory of the stress of daily life that was directly inspired by the biology of organic responses to catastrophic events. If stress is inherent to life and cannot be entirely suppressed, we must try to master it, that is, transform into a good stress what might otherwise be a harmful one.[13] In this dialectic the harmful influence is "dystress," the good one "eustress." Eustress is, for example, what a mountain climber feels as he sets out for the pleasure of an arduous climb to the summit or what a tennis player feels as he prepares for a good match with a challenging opponent. Dystress is the stress our alpinist feels when his project is blocked by an impending blizzard and he sees his supplies dwindling, or our tennis player when he realizes that although he absolutely must win the match to keep his ranking, his opponent is, in fact, a far better player than he.

Laborit's conception is identical. Operation of the behavioral activation system corresponds to eustress whereas inhibition of action creates dystress. The problem for the characters in *Mon oncle d'Amérique,* the Alain Resnais film based on Laborit's ideas, is somehow to throw off the constraints of the sociocultural environment pushing them to self-inhibition rather than to struggle.

Those able to do the most can also do the least. The catastrophic scenarios describing the effects of reactive mechanisms on the organic sphere have therefore been extended without difficulty to the problems of daily life. Stress has become commonplace; it is a normal part of work, of commuting between home and the workplace, and even of family life, with parental authority challenged by restless children who are reacting to what they perceive as an excess of parental constraint. Popular magazines, with graduated scales of daily events drawn up by "stress experts," instruct us in how to measure the various stressors we encounter, and eminent specialists help us recognize signs of stress in ourselves and explain in detail the risks we face if we do not protect ourselves. And if we finally burn out despite all the warnings and whatever protective measures we may have taken—from jogging to group therapy to primal scream sessions—stress clinics are waiting to receive us, to recondition us, and to enable us to leave in better shape than ever.

THE LOGIC OF PSYCHOSOMATIC ILLNESS

It is difficult to perceive anything clearly through the hazy cloud that envelops notions of stress and psychosomatic illness. These ideas correspond to the world as we see it, and derive from all the attitudes engendered by our sociocultural environment. Rather than attempting to define the objects of pop psychology, it would be better to try and understand our need to create them as well as the nature of the realities they cover.

Medieval alchemists wished to extract "leadness" from lead in order to recover in the residual primary matter a new and more precious essence: "goldness." Some practitioners of our time claim the ability to detach an individual from his distress or his inhibiting tendencies and replace them with eustress or involvement in salutary activity. There is not much difference between these two attitudes; both are characteristic of the prepositivist stage of scientific knowledge. The world we perceive is composed of objects characterized by "attributes"; marble is cold, lead is heavy, the sky is blue, and patients have neurotic personalities or suffer from unresolved conflicts. Unable to discern the connections between these phenomena and other, more elementary, features, we discuss these immediate data as if they were fundamental.

Description is not explanation, despite the magic powers of speech. Research, however, has gone beyond this stage, even if that fact is not always reflected in practice. We are beginning to understand the subtle play of interaction not between psyche and soma but between the brain and the other organic systems that participate in adaptation. In the context of these interactions, what we call the influence of psychological factors on illness will no longer be seen as an isolated event but as the by-product of biological necessity, that is, of the participation of the whole organism in a struggle against pathogenic agents.

BETWEEN THE IMAGINARY AND THE REAL

Almost all of the individuals composing our species,
through the evolution of certainty and conscience, need a
coherent and, if possible, a motivated vision of the world.

—MICHAEL RIO, *Les jungles pensives*

Believing is what we humans do the best.

—MICHAEL S. GAZZANIGA, *The Social Brain*

MELODY AND SONG

The Imaginary

In a brilliant essay, "Illness as Metaphor,"[1] the American essayist and novelist Susan Sontag demonstrates with references from the world of arts and letters the degree to which our conception of illness is affected by the imagination. In the nineteenth century, before the identification of Koch's bacillus, tuberculosis was thought to be an emotional illness, an extension of spiritual consumption to the body. It affected artists and poets, persons of romantic sensibility. Consequently, people fell ill with tuberculosis in order to acquire the languid air so much in fashion at the time, an air that rendered them seductive and interesting. Today, leukemia has taken the place of tuberculosis, and those who lack the capacity to be in love with love die of it. Cancer, however, lacks the seductive power of these two maladies. Cancer attacks the body through hidden and unmentionable organs (the rectum, the uterus)

13

or makes desirable organs repulsive (the skin, the breast). Thus, a cancerous tumor is perceived as the curse that affects those who can no longer shoulder their responsibilities, those who abandon all their standards and lose all hope.

The metaphoric value of tuberculosis was lost to the popular imagination not when the bacillus was identified but, rather, after the discovery of anti-tuberculosis drugs. For the same reason, the idea of sin attached to AIDS (acquired immunodeficiency syndrome) has clear sailing ahead in the absence of effective treatment.

The medical profession itself is affected by such ideas. In a recent article on the mythology of psychosomatic medicine, Marc Bourgeois recalls that gynecologist-obstetricians have long claimed that spontaneous abortions have psychological causes.[2] These doctors have claimed that intrapsychic conflict between expulsive and relational tendencies, problematic parental (especially maternal) schemata, personality problems, and the actual physical and psychological difficulties of pregnancy provide adequate explanation for spontaneous abortions. During the 1970s proof of the importance of genetic factors in these cases was greeted by silence (perhaps a troubled one?) from psychosomaticians.

These considerations might lead one to suppose that the relationship between mind and body thought to be at the root of psychosomatic illness belongs exclusively to the domain of the symbolic and the imaginary. Such a conception, however, would be in error, as is demonstrated by the thousands of cases that link a proven psychological cause to the origin of an organic illness.

Or the Real

The following events occurred in 1977 in Seattle: A 28-year-old woman, born in the Philippines, went to see her doctor about a series of recurrent episodes of fever with joint pain. Clinical investigation and biological examination tended toward a diagnosis of disseminated lupus erythematosus, a serious autoimmune disorder that attacks a patient's joints and kidneys. A treatment based on strong doses of corticoids produced initial good results. But this improvement was short-lived, and subsequent examinations revealed an exacerbation of the biological signs of the illness and the beginnings of renal involvement. Increased doses of corticoids and initiation of immunosuppressant treatment were indicated. Rather than accept that solution, the patient, who was already suffering from important secondary effects due to the corticoids, decided to return to her native village. There she consulted the local sorcerer; he informed her that a rejected suitor had cast a hostile spell on her and that it was necessary to exorcise it. Three weeks later, on her return to the United States, the woman went to see her doctor. The doctor was no longer able to find any sign of the original illness. Furthermore, the young woman presented none of the deprivation symptoms usually present on abrupt cessation of corticoid treatment. Two years later, in excellent health, she gave birth to an infant, although lupus is normally aggravated by pregnancy.

This story is neither idle gossip nor a fairy tale. The doctor who treated this patient considered her case worthy of inclusion in the *Journal of the American Medical Association*.[3] At the end of his clinical description, the doctor considered the powers of the Philippine sorcerer, who had achieved a feat that modern medicine had not managed to do.

The influence of psychological factors on the evolution of illness is not simply anecdotal. Several statistical studies give this subject scientific validity. A team of English psychologists has noted a strong line between a patient's reaction to mastectomy and her chances of surviving breast cancer.[4] This study considered the cases of 41 women. On the basis of their answers to questions asked three months after their operations during interviews designed to reveal the manner in which each perceived her illness and her prospects for a successful outcome to treatment, the women were each assigned to one of the following four categories:

- Those who deny and say, "This isn't serious; my breast was removed simply as a precautionary measure . . ."
- Those who decide to become fully informed and to fight back
- Those who stoically accept their condition: "I know it's cancer, but what can one do? After all, one has to live life as best one can . . ."
- Those who feel totally desperate, and think constantly of imminent death, against which there is nothing to be done.

Five years later the women who denied their situation and those who decided to fight back were better off than those in the other two categories. The rate of metastases was 25 percent for the first group and 65 percent for the second; the mortality rates were 10 percent and 38 percent, respectively.

Both these examples suggest an underlying truth supporting popular common sense. The case of the woman afflicted with lupus and that of the woman with breast cancer seem difficult to refute. In both cases, it is tempting to go beyond coincidence and attribute a causal role to psychological factors in the development of illness.

Literary description captures and amplifies popular imagination; it mirrors our beliefs. Accounts of medical cases are clothed in the language of objectivity, but they are produced by individuals who share the beliefs, both negative and positive, of the sociocultural setting to which they belong. It seems wiser to address issues of more fundamental importance rather than argue about the legitimacy of one or the other source and engage in sectarian quarrels. First of all, why do we feel the need to turn to psychological explanations of illness? Might this be a form of representation of the world that is profoundly rooted in our biological organization? Should this indeed prove to be the case, one should be able to find the equivalent causal subjectivity in animals.

CAUSAL ATTRIBUTION: AN EFFECTIVE SNARE

The Pigeon: Consumer of Light

Let us take a pigeon that is fed at regular intervals no matter what it may be doing. If a colored disk is installed in the cage beside the feeding bowl and if the disk lights up just before the grain is put in the dish, the pigeon will associate the grain and the disk so closely that the two become a unity;[5] the bird establishes this link between two entirely unrelated events because the lighting of the disk occurs first; when the disk is lit after rather than before the grain is served, the pigeon does not make this connection.

Similarly, if an animal consumes an unfamiliar substance and then exhibits symptoms of indigestion, it will attribute its discomfort to the food in question. Human beings draw similar conclusions when discomfort follows the ingestion of something to which they are unaccustomed, for example, oysters.

Preference in Rats

In an ingenious experiment that consists of making available to some rats the possibility of a variety of associations between different sorts of stimuli—a sound signal or the sweet taste of a saccharin solution on the one hand and the pain of electric shock or gastrointestinal malaise on the other (Fig. 2.1)—the American psychologist John Garcia systematically demonstrated that rats impute malaise to saccharin and pain to sound. Pain is never attributed to saccharin, nor indigestion to sound.[6] This is how taste aversion develops in rats. Conversely, if the rats swallow a new substance just as they are recovering from indigestion, they develop a preference for that substance, as if it were responsible for the return of well-being (Fig. 2.2).

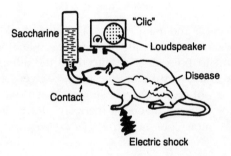

		CONSEQUENCES	
		Disease	Pain
Cues	Saccharine	Aversion	0
	"Clic"	0	Defensive reaction

FIGURE 2.1.   The manner in which the animal perceives causality in its immediate environment is biased by its sensoriperceptual equipment. Here a thirsty rat swallows a sweet liquid as it hears a sequence of clicks; the rhythm of these sounds is linked to the pace at which the animal licks. Simultaneously, the experimenter administers either painful electric shocks to the animal's feet or poison. The rat will refuse to drink the sweet liquid if it has been poisoned but will continue to sip normally if it was given electric shocks, except when it hears the clicking, which it now associates with electric shock (*adapted from Garcia et al., 1974*).

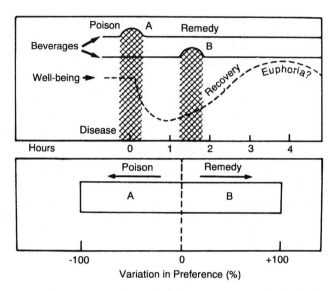

FIGURE 2.2.   Poisons and miracle cures. The same drink (milk or grape juice) is perceived as a poison or an antidote depending on the time it is ingested in relation to poisoning produced by the administration of a toxin. If the drink is ingested before the toxin is given, it is considered responsible for the poisoning and subsequently refused (A). But if its ingestion coincides with spontaneous recovery, the animal develops a preference for the miraculous liquid (B) (*adapted from Garcia et al., 1974*).

For species that are eclectic in their alimentary choices, like rats and human beings, some sort of selection mechanism is needed with which to identify both appetizing and toxic foods. This selective capacity operates through mechanisms that are both innate and acquired. Rejection of bitter tastes, often caused by the presence of toxic alkaloids, and a marked preference for the sugary tastes usually associated with glucides are both innate. Further, many animals are guided by the internal consequences of consuming food; therefore, they are careful to approach with moderation any food whose beneficial nature is still in doubt. The likelihood of survival in species that employ mechanisms of this sort is far greater than in those species that indiscriminately consume everything that comes their way. Likewise, an animal that learns to establish a causal link between events preceding an attack and the attack or its result, before it has been wounded, has a greater chance of surviving the repeated attacks of predators than an animal incapable of learning from previous experience.

The ability to make causal associations is predetermined by evolution. Even if associations of this kind sometimes result in error, the risk is less serious than it would be if the corresponding capacity were not part of the repertoire of a species. The inclination to form such associations is so strong that the process occurs even when basic information has been seriously degraded, as, for instance, when a long interval of time separates the "cause" from the effect.

In a more general way, acquisition of knowledge about the world around us begins with a series of elementary operations. With these the brain establishes links of temporal contiguity and contingency between events in the external or internal environment. This process produces an internal representation of the situation that serves as a guide for action. Depending on the consequences of the subject's behavior on the immediate environment, this internal representation of the external world is modified and may lead to fresh plans of action.[7]

Animal species differ in the degree of complexity of their internal representations, in their sensory modalities, in the relative importance of the roles played by experience and genetic heritage (instinct), and in the importance of the representation of the self in the motivation for action.

The data from animal experimentation show that perception and knowledge of the surrounding world are not always rational, and that they can form the basis for important biases. One must not assume that human beings escape this general rule. The work of psychologists confirms that we do not necessarily treat in an objective way information that is available to us.[8]

The Card Trick

Experimental subjects are given four cards, each with a number, even or odd, on one side and a letter, a consonant or vowel, on the other. The cards are laid flat on the table so that a vowel, a consonant, an odd and an even number can be seen. Subjects are then asked to test the following hypothesis by turning over the cards: Cards with vowels have even numbers on their reverse sides. To check this proposition most subjects will simply turn over the card with a vowel or an even number on the exposed side.

In other words, confirmation is favored over denial even though, from a logical point of view, the two operations are complementary. This tendency is strengthened by a basic predilection for a positive attitude.

Inner Conviction

At moments of uncertainty, affective judgments take precedence over reason, as the following experiment shows. Volunteers are shown slides, each of which bears the image of a characteristic octagonal object. The slides are shown several times, each time for a fraction of a second, which does not give subjects enough time to identify the object. In fact, when one of the slides already shown is presented a second time, along with a new slide, subjects are unable to recognize the one they have already seen. Nonetheless, they express preference for that slide, as if they had become familiar with it during its first projection.[9] Recognizing an object is a rational operation; expressing preference for the familiar is in the realm of affect.

Our sociocultural environment is composed of the familiar. When threatened, we reason on the basis of what is familiar, rather than on the basis of objective fact. The influence of reports in the media on the individual or collective risks to which we are exposed is telling here. If there has recently been a plane crash and I have to travel by air to go on my vacation, I shall be much more anxious than usual. According to a poll carried out in January 1989 on a representative sample of the French population concerning the principal risks facing France,[10] 39 percent of subjects, remembering Chernobyl, put nuclear accidents at the head of the list; 31 percent, thinking of the Basel incidents, mentioned chemical pollution; 22 percent, thinking of the damage in Afghanistan, chose earthquakes; and 16 percent, thinking of floods, chose the Nîmes catastrophe. On the personal level, dangers most feared ran from drugs to unemployment, AIDS, and industrial pollution. These answers do not reflect a realistic assessment of these dangers but, rather, the importance assigned by the media to each item and therefore the frequency with which we customarily think of it.

Initial belief in the importance of any given factor is so strong that it may be at the root of illusory correlation; we perceive correlations where there are none simply because they correspond to our preconceptions. This phenomenon is frequently observed in the projective tests of clinical psychology. Many psychologists try to detect possible mood or personality problems in their patients by having them draw a person. Exaggerated eyes are considered an indication of exaggerated suspicion, or paranoia, and an exaggerated mouth suggests excessive dependence on one's surroundings. Chapman and Chapman[11] gave this test to hospitalized patients; they then assigned to each drawing a psychological characteristic chosen purely at random from a list of six possibilities, including suspicion and dependency, and asked students to study both the drawings and the associated symptoms. Next, they questioned the students on any correlations they might have observed between particular features in the faces depicted in the drawings and well-defined psychological traits. Despite the purely random character of the samples given them and their lack of clinical experience, the students spontaneously recreated the associations that the projective tests were supposed to reflect. This bias can certainly be imputed to our tendency to associate suspicion with the scrutinizing aspect of another person's gaze and dependency with the entreaty mimicry that is especially marked in the area of the mouth. (We should also note in passing that these results have not prevented the continued use of projective tests in clinical psychology.)

IMPOSSIBLE OBJECTIVITY

All of the examples just analyzed demonstrate the facility with which we construct explanations even when, in reality, these are irrational. Primitive societies resort to three categories of explanation for illness: real objects ordinarily responsible for injuries (e.g., falling stones, an enemy arrow); the punishment of God (individual fault); spirits and witchcraft (fate or the fault of others).[12] These different levels of causality are combined to make a system of coherent explanation that not only permits comprehension of another's suffering but also explains why the suffering is visited on him, rather than on someone else, at that precise moment of his life. In western societies the explanation of illness is based on the following four predominant logical schemes: mechanical (a wound, injury, or functional alteration); degenerative (organic deterioration); invasive (germs); and disequilibrium (a disruption of the harmony between an individual and his surroundings).[13]

The logic of disequilibrium is very close to primitive explanations. Mystic entities—yin and yang, cold and hot—have been replaced by psychoanalytic and psychological jargon: conflicts, emotions, personality types, and moods.[14] Since the origin of these last factors is often social (one is more likely to be angry at others than at oneself), psychosocial factors are considered responsible for individual disequilibrium. Whenever the reasons for an illness are unclear, there is a considerable tendency to speak of psychosocial factors as the cause of individual disequilibrium. Illnesses in which the intervention of such factors is postulated are most likely to have an unknown or insecurely established etiology, and the possibilities of therapeutic intervention are limited or nonexistent. In the face of such uncertainty the model of linear causality (in which one event becomes the cause of a subsequent event simply by preceding it) become preponderant. The spectacular character of the postulated cause is enough to make it credible, especially if the possibility of such intervention is supported by the surrounding culture. From the moment the belief is established, it maintains itself by selective attention paid to other cases that reinforce the notion of intervention by psychic variables. Belief contradicts the critical sense.

The young woman stricken with lupus erythematosus was completely cured after a sorcerer in her native country exorcised her. Her doctor was astounded. He did not believe in sorcery and imagined that some extraordinary mental process had led to rapid cure. Isn't it astonishing that he never asked whether the young woman who had returned was in fact the same young woman who had left? We sometimes have difficulty distinguishing between Asiatic faces; if the young woman's family had kept the invalid at home and had given her hard-to-obtain visa to a sister or a cousin, who would have known the difference? Why didn't the doctor think of this possibility? Why do we associate illness and state of mind in the case of women stricken with breast cancer when no causal significance is attached to behavioral changes observed just before the onset of the fever and skin eruptions that characterize illnesses like German measles or chicken pox?

Although the analysis we have made in no way prejudges the truth of the examined causal relationship, it must now be clear that on an individual level positive or negative beliefs in the effects of psychological factors on illness are highly unlikely to be rational. As Paul Watzlawik stresses, what we think we know is often only a partial construction based on our perceptions and what we call reality is a simple interpretation maintained by and through communication.[15] The invention of a pretended reality that becomes a true reality for us is all the more likely in the case of psychosomatic illness, where we find ourselves in a world of uncertainty. This reality becomes analogous to the mythic construction whose three functions have been catalogued by Claude Lévi-Strauss: labeling, explanation, and justification.[16]

THE SCIENTIFIC APPROACH

The systematic study of the role of psychosocial factors in illness began outside the field of medicine, with the work of sociologists at the end of the nineteenth and the beginning of the twentieth century, and became a part of it in the middle of the century, thanks to the methodological developments in epidemiology, the medical discipline that attempts to define the causes of illness.

The Input of Sociology: Anomie

The French sociologist Émile Durkheim is credited with the first objective effort to attribute immoral individual acts to social causes. The inequalities created by the division of labor in industrial societies produced the appearance of class conflict. Traditional values declined to the point where dominant sociocultural models and the rules by which society had functioned up to that point were rejected. These were replaced by a state of anomie (literally, an absence of law) that favored the emergence of deviant attitudes manifested by violence directed at the self (suicide) or others (delinquency): "Suicide diversifies in reverse proportion to the integration of religious, domestic, and political society."[17]

Durkheim's work is remarkable for its time because it proposes to "consider social facts as things" and to identify the laws that govern them by using comparative history, ethnology, and statistical analysis. The concept of anomie derives from the study of suicide as a social fact and as a phenomenon that was found to correlate, through the use of statistical techniques, with social condition, religion, and lifestyle. Durkheim did not limit himself to the analysis of statistics, but tried to understand them as well. The variation in suicide rates as a function of the factors considered indicates that this phenomenon is inversely proportional to the integration of an individual with his social setting. As we shall see at the end of this chapter, epidemiologists have recently revived this concept of social isolation after a long eclipse.

Introduced by Durkheim, the concept of anomie was taken up by R. K. Merton and the American school of sociology. For Merton,[18] every society engenders a system of dominant values, which in turn produce the ideal to be pursued by each member of the society. In American society between the 1930s and the 1960s that ideal was the one of the self-made man, the man who begins with nothing and achieves power and fortune by strength of character and will. In an ideal society this model is theoretically accessible to everyone. But in reality equality of opportunity scarcely exists; there is a discrepancy between individual aspirations dictated by the dominant sociocultural model and what is in fact possible. And the greater the gap, the greater the incidence of deviant behavior like drug abuse and alcoholism, suicide, delinquency, violence, vandalism, and fraud.

Merton's approach is based on an analysis of deviant behavior. He tries to understand why the incidence of deviant behavior varies as a function of the social structure and how this behavior can assume different forms within the dominant social context. In what might be considered one of the first objective attempts to link pathology to behavioral factors, Merton proposed classifying individuals in five broad categories according to how they adapt to the dominant sociocultural norms (Table 2.1). These different categories do not correspond to personality traits but to behaviors adopted in various well-defined circumstances.

The Epidemiological Approach

Although the idea of anomie has served primarily to link social conditions and deviant behavior,[19] an analogous idea inspired epidemiological research into the possible links between illness and sociocultural factors. These studies have assumed various forms, from a comparison of the frequency of illnesses like essential hypertension in various cultures to the study of pathology in socioeconomic groups exposed to particular conditions (e.g., telephone operators at major urban switchboards during the 1950s or airline traffic controllers). Taking advantage of the temporary groupings of heterogeneous populations in relatively homogeneous settings, like men in military service in the navy or undergraduates residing

TABLE 2.1

BEHAVIORAL CLASSIFICATIONS OF INDIVIDUALS, ACCORDING
TO DEGREE OF CONFORMITY WITH SOCIOCULTURAL NORMS

	DOMINANT IDEAL[1]	RULES OF CONDUCT[1]
conformity	+	+
innovation	+	−
resignation[2]	−	−
marginality	−	−
rebellion	±	±

(*Adapted from Merton, 1949*)
[1] + = acceptance; − = rejection; ± = rejection of dominant values and acceptance of substitute values.
[2] Merton uses the term *ritualism,* which has a religious connotation in French.

at a university, researchers attempted to demonstrate a relationship between unexpected stressful events in the months just preceding entrance into the new situation and either objective pathology (the frequency or gravity of afflictions noted by members of the medical corps) or subjective pathology (sensations of discomfort and unease reported by subjects during the course of an interview). There were other systematic inquiries as well on the influence of personality or mood on health.

These studies were highly disparate with respect to the epidemiological techniques, investigative methods, and even basic conceptions employed. Without a minimum acquaintance with these methodological and conceptual aspects, one can neither discuss the significance of these studies nor comprehend the often important differences between their results.

Various Types of Research

To identify the objective causes of illness, the epidemiologist examines in systematic fashion the differences between a group of subjects affected by a given disease and a control group free of symptoms. His working hypothesis is that the explanation for the illness can normally be found among the demonstrable differences between the two groups. It is important to understand that this explanation is only relative and has only statistical value. In this way it was established that an overly high blood cholesterol level, high blood pressure, and heavy smoking increase the risk of coronary disease. A person with all three risk factors is six times more likely than others to have an infarct. That does not mean that all persons who have all three risk factors are going to develop coronary disease. At the ten-year follow-up this illness actually was found in only 14 percent of those at grave risk.[20] This proves once again that organic pathology does not necessarily follow causal mechanical schemas. If the driver of a car checks neither his battery nor his spark plugs and forgets to change his oil, his car will surely break down.

One can divide epidemiological research into three broad categories depending on when researchers attempt to detect the risk factors in connection with the onset of an illness. First, there is retrospective inquiry. This is the most frequently encountered and the least reliable; by looking backward one attempts to determine which of the differences perceived between subjects who are ill and those who are not might actually explain the illness. But if psychic factors are considered, researchers encounter a biased attitude, since knowing that one is gravely ill affects one's perception of the past. To correct errors deriving from this source, researchers attempt to compare the group of patients affected with the illness under study to a group suffering from some other complaint or to a group of individuals for whom diagnosis of the first illness is not yet established. The problem in this last case is that most of the time patients already have presentiments of the definitive diagnosis. For example, in a group of 67 women consulting a doctor because of suspected breast cancer, biopsy confirmed the patients' expectation in three-quarters of the cases.[21] In such cases, depression, denial, loss of hope, or feelings of helplessness are more likely to reflect a reaction to the anticipated positive diagnosis than to constitute premorbid elements.

The second type of research is a prospective, forward-looking inquiry: during a given length of time a precise population is followed to determine its pathological future. Pursuit of such research is difficult, however, because of the length of time and size sample required, especially if the pathology under study is uncommon. The Western Collaborative Group Study undertaken in California beginning in 1960 is an example of this kind. The study pursued some three thousand male subjects, initially in good health, for 8½ years to determine the correlation between coronary risk and be-havior type.[22]

The third type of inquiry is retro-prospective and is a compro-mise between the two preceding groups in that it combines infor-mation known before diagnosis with information whose acquisition began once the diagnosis was made. The difficulty here is that one must draw on highly fragmentary data that are available only for certain heterogeneous socioeconomic categories. For ex-ample, in the case of illness with a psychosomatic component, the usual reference is the Minnesota Multiphasic Personality Inven-tory.[23]

From Personality to Behavior

The confusion dominating studies of relationships between psy-chological factors and illness is not entirely due to the diversity of current epidemiological approaches. The broad heterogeneity of measures employed in the attempt to understand the psychological influence on illness and the multiplicity of theoretical hypotheses supporting the choice of those measures play an equally important part.

Many studies have tried to measure the effects of depression on cancer. Results have been contradictory. According to the study by English psychologists already cited,[4] resignation and despair increase the risk that breast cancer will metastasize. Conversely, a prospective study by Derogatis and his colleagues[24] shows that in metastatic patients mortality during the year in which psychologi-cal testing was undertaken was less frequent in depressed subjects than in those who reacted to their circumstances more positively. In the first study, two observers evaluated subjects' depressive state during a structured interview; in the second, depression was scored from written answers to two psychological questionnaires. The difference between these two investigative methods may well ex-plain their contradictory results. Depressed women certainly refuse to recognize themselves as such when they answer written ques-tions.[25] In other words, the pertinent psychological variable is nei-ther anxiety nor depression but the type of defense or coping strategy adopted by the patient. The difficulty is that these strate-gies are not necessarily any easier to quantify than degrees of depression.

This explains why many experimenters, rather than continue to explore a subject's personality or mood, prefer to turn to the number and weight of the stressful circumstances with which the patient is confronted. In the first place, the concept that has had the most success is undoubtedly that of Type A behavior. This involves a complex of reactions first described by two cardiologists, Friedman and Rosenman.[26] These include pronounced competitiveness and aggressiveness, impatience, and a rapidity of speech and gesture. Type B individuals are calmer and more patient, show little or no aggressivity, and are generally far more relaxed. The characteristics of Type A individuals do not represent a personality trait: they express themselves in characteristic fashion at moments of provocation. This particular mode of reaction can be measured in various ways. The most reliable, however, is a structured interview conducted by a trained interviewer whose object is to provoke signs of impatience and aggression.[27] Type A behavior is associated with a risk of coronary disease that is, on average, at least twice as great as the risk associated with Type B behavior. The predictive value of this concept is, at present, considered doubtful, but it has proven quite useful in studies on the influence of psychological factors in coronary disease. This concept has made it possible to broach the question of intermediary physiological mechanisms by unifying methods of approach and reaching beyond simple description.

The success encountered by the construct of Type A behavior has led many writers to propose replacing the characterization of personality factors that are difficult to grasp with more objective behavioral standards. Essential hypertension, for example, has long been associated with a personality profile characterized by suppressed aggressivity, but, once again, available data are extremely contradictory.[28] Rather than continue working with psychological questionnaires of doubtful reliability, researchers at present are trying to characterize the behavior of patients in well-defined situations.[29] They might also study socioeconomic groups exposed to the risk of essential hypertension (e.g., bus drivers) and analyze work conditions in a specific way.

Quantifying Stress

The easiest way to know whether or not stress is contributing to an illness is to compare the state of health of people who are stressed and those who are not. But what should we categorize as stress, and how should we measure it? In 1967 Holmes and Rahe made one of the first serious efforts in this regard.[30] They asked a representative sample of adults in Seattle to determine the relative importance of various events in their professional or family life in terms of the effort required to adapt to changes provoked by those events. The life event serving as a point of reference was marriage, which was given a score of 50. Events considered more stressful than marriage were given higher scores, with 100 being the highest possible score. The death of a spouse was scored as 100; divorce, 73; imprisonment, 63. Less important events received scores under 50: getting laid off from one's job, 47; troubles with the boss, 23; and departure of children from the family home, 29.

This type of scale for life events is used in both psychiatry and somatic medicine. In a psychiatric study, morbidity that could be imputed to stressful events ran at about 32 percent, with figures for women somewhat higher, reaching 41 percent.[31] These events were neither more frequent nor more serious than those faced by normal subjects, but they had greater impact and a more important affective reaction.[32] In the case of somatic illness, several studies show that a high score on the Holmes and Rahe scale corresponds in general to a more serious morbidity, a morbidity measured by a wide variety of indicators—from an increase in the number of sick days in a student population[33] to an increase in the risk of myocardial infarct.[34] Although this tendency was confirmed by simultaneous retrospective and prospective studies, there is still a possibility of bias in both cases. A person who is already ill might be more tempted than someone in good health to remember all the difficulties he has suffered in the past. And without necessarily being hypochondriac, patients in prospective studies are more likely to complain of the existential difficulties facing them than are people who do not easily see a doctor.

This is why epidemiologists have seen fit to circumscribe their field of research and are more interested in following the pathological development of patients confronting a specific stressful event, such as the death or illness of someone close to them. It has been established, for instance, that in men aged 55 or older the risk of death increases by 40 to 50 percent in the months immediately following the death of the spouse.[35]

Counting on Others

In the face of adversity it is important to be able to count on others. Several studies indicate the importance of support from one's surroundings when one must resist stress. For example, one study found that the incidence of depression in a female population exposed to stressful events was 40 percent for those women who were isolated, as opposed to 4 percent for those who had someone to confide in.[36] Further, in a prospective study of 2,754 adults of both sexes done by a group of epidemiologists in Michigan over a period of 9 to 12 years starting in 1967, it was observed that mortality rates for people who were surrounded by companions were significantly lower than for people living alone.[37] Several studies in the United States and in Scandinavia point in the same direction.[38] As a general rule, the mortality rate for people with social contacts is almost half that for people living alone. The advantage persists when other factors, like arterial pressure or nicotine abuse, are neutralized by appropriate statistical techniques. The beneficial effect of social support is even clearer in the case of men than in the case of women. The reasons for this are not known.

Any detailed analysis of the effects of social support will encounter several methodological difficulties. Normally, one is content with very global measures: family status, number of friends and frequency of contact with them, membership in associations, religious practice. But these are not always enough; more information is required about the need for social contacts and the ways in which it is satisfied, which brings us back to the problem of psychological questionnaires. Furthermore, one cannot always isolate social support from the other factors with which it is associated. The need for social contacts affects the demand for care, and illness itself modifies social relations; for instance, among women with breast cancer those with the least favorable diagnosis suffer most severely from a lack of support.[39]

THE PROBLEM OF CHRONIC DISTURBANCE

An epidemiologist is sometimes compared to a detective. After exhaustive inquiry into minute details he identifies the guilty party (or parties), whom he delivers to the authorities, and order is restored. However, when psychosocial factors are at issue, things are not quite so simple. An epidemiologist can neither reform society nor modify the personalities of patients as easily as he can neutralize the effects of the classic pathogenic agents of a toxic or microbial nature.

This is not to say that epidemiologists are uninterested in social reform. Thus, the authors of a recent article[38] argue that the absence of social support has an influence on the etiology of illness that is comparable to the influence of nicotine addiction; they advocate publicity campaigns with slogans like "Don't live all alone; don't abandon your health." In many parts of the world, after all, the authorities require cigarette packages to carry the warning "Smoking may be dangerous to your health."

The temptation to act on psychosocial factors may not always be justified. In a classic epidemiological study it is possible to measure the symptomatology of illness and the possible risk factors independently. Thus, one can be reasonably certain that a demonstrated relationship between these two categories of variables is based on something real. And this is a necessary condition for the efficacy of means used to modify risk factors. Thus, if nicotine addiction aggravates cardiovascular and respiratory disorders, one might hope to reduce the frequency of these complaints by reducing consumption of cigarettes. If, on the other hand, the association between tobacco and these illnesses is due simply to the fact that nicotine dependency is a behavioral disorder that affects patients suffering from cardiovascular and respiratory illnesses, the effects of modifying that association would be of no great consequence. This last example is, of course, extreme; nonetheless, the distinction is not always so obvious. When considering the pathology of ill health, it is very easy to confound cause and effect. The subjective experience of the illness, the frequency of nonspecific symptoms reported by those who are not feeling well—these are factors profoundly affected by depression. During the epidemic of Asian flu that developed on the east coast of the United States in the winter of 1957–1958, people suffering from anxiety and depression exhibited subjective symptomatologies far more intense than those of normal people and took longer to recover from an actual attack. However, the objective signs of illness—antibodies against the virus, fever, the severity of flu-like symptoms—were identical for both groups.[40] These data show that depressed individuals attach greater importance to illness than normal people do. They complain more often and demand more attention. But it would be a mistake to conclude that depression aggravates the flu!

In regard to chronic illness, another difficulty arises from the fact that a patient is often seriously affected well before diagnosis by a licensed medical practitioner. The patient's reactions, his behavior toward others, and his perception of the world around him have already been affected by his illness when a doctor first sees him. When the supposed causes and observed effects point to the same conclusion, it is scarcely surprising that a positive relationship between the two is noted. The same difficulty occurs in prospective studies when the same sets of assessments are made at different times. It is, in fact, known that in chronic illnesses a patient's pathological condition at any given moment will heavily affect the condition in which he will be at the end of any given duration of time: initial observation explains—in the statistical sense of the word—some 30 to 40 percent of the variability in the measures that are repeated 1 year after the first consultation. This is high in comparison to life events and social support, which only explain a small proportion (1 to 3 percent) of this same variability.[41]

Thus, when one claims to prove a relationship between psychological factors and illness, it is highly probable that one has been taken in by the pathology of a protean ill health that expresses itself on two levels, the mental and the organic. When one studies the incidence of illness by beginning with patients' subjective experience of their own state of health, one realizes that a quarter of the population suffers from more or less chronic health problems.[41] This is a heterogeneous group made up of at least four subsets.

- Persons suffering from depressive tendencies, whose reactions to the normal difficulties of daily life are exaggerated and who are dissatisfied with their circumstances and often hostile; somatic complaints in this subgroup are particularly pronounced
- Persons on the borderline of psychopathology, who have chronic, fluctuating anxieties that normally are not treated
- Persons suffering from handicaps or serious medical problems
- Persons profoundly destabilized by a long succession of family and socioeconomic problems

These data, collected in the United States, may seem exaggerated. But the important point is the close correlation between depressive tendencies and somatic complaints. A French study from the Centre de Recherches, d'Étude et de Documentation en Économie de la Santé,[42] based on objective factors (e.g., medical prescriptions), shows that depression associated with neurasthenia and nervous fatigue affects three French citizens in every hundred, with a notably higher incidence among women (4.5 percent as compared to 1.6 percent for men). These rates double with age for both sexes, the threshold of aging coming earlier for women (somewhere between ages 40 and 50) than for men (between ages 50 and 60). And, as in the American studies, one notes a strict correlation between a depressive condition and many organic illnesses: depressed men have, on average, some six illnesses (including depression) between the ages of 20 and 79, which is twice the normal rate. The same phenomenon can be observed in women. And the demand for care, whatever the illness, is distinctly higher among depressed individuals than among those who are not depressed.

An examination of the difficulties encountered when studying the influence on illness of psychological factors readily suggests why some writers maintain with confidence that psychological factors play an essential part, a claim supported by many statistical studies, and that in dealing with illness these factors must be taken into account. Others, however, are more cautious; for them, psychological factors may play some causative role but one that is not important enough to merit any particular attention in any therapeutic scheme. Whatever importance may be accorded to them, psychological factors at the very least merit inclusion in the category of "soft" sources of illness (as opposed to the "hard" sources represented by identified pathogenic agents). The most precise study on the influence of these "soft" sources fluctuates between two perspectives: one, inspired by psychology, attributes a determining role to personality; the other, a more materialistic approach, attaches greater importance to behavior and to existential events.

What is certain is that attributing everything to psychological factors makes no sense. This is particularly evident when one considers patients with chronic disturbances and must confront a strict coincidence of mental and somatic distress. To make use of this source of distress to explain the other is analogous to that vain inquiry about whether it is the chicken or the egg that comes first.

Rather than attempt to apprehend a pseudo reality that obstinately defies analysis, it makes more sense to study the mechanisms by which an individual resists stress from the surrounding environment and to try and understand why these mechanisms sometimes do not work.

THE LABYRINTH OF STRESS

At the end of his novel *Breakfast of Champions,*[1] Kurt Vonnegut, Jr., puts in a personal appearance, entering the account to give the principal character, Kilgore Trout, his freedom. Vonnegut appears in a construction company supply yard, where he can observe Trout without being seen, and is suddenly attacked by Kazak, a fierce Doberman attached to the establishment's security force whose existence the author had forgotten:

> I saw Kazak out of the corner of my right eye. . . . My eyes told my mind about him.
>
> My mind sent a message to my hypothalamus, told it to release the hormone CRF into the short vessels connecting my hypothalamus and my pituitary gland.

The CRF inspired my pituitary gland to dump the hormone ACTH into my bloodstream. My pituitary had been making and storing ACTH for just such an occasion. . . .

And some of the ACTH in my bloodstream reached the outer shell of my adrenal gland, which had been making and storing glucocorticoids for emergencies. My adrenal gland added the glucocorticoids to my bloodstream. They went all over my body, changing glycogen into glucose. Glucose was muscle food. It would help me fight like a wildcat or run like a deer. . . .

My adrenal gland gave me a shot of adrenalin, too. I turned purple as my blood pressure skyrocketed. The adrenalin made my heart go like a burglar alarm. It also stood my hair on end. It also caused coagulants to pour into my bloodstream, so, in case I was wounded, my vital juices wouldn't drain away. . . .

But my body took one defensive measure . . . without precedent in medical history. . . . I also retracted my testicles into my abdominal cavity, pulled them into my fuselage like the landing gear of an airplane.

Thus fortified, the author clears the barrier in one powerful leap, while the dog flings itself against the railings and falls back half stunned.

The reaction Vonnegut describes, its mechanisms and effects on the body, is part of the standard defense process employed by the organism at times of danger. With a few minor variations, this could be a biologist's description of the changes that occur in an individual subjected to stress. The catecholamines (epinephrine and norepinephrine) permit the cardiovascular adjustments necessary for action and supply the corresponding energy from the glycogen stored in the liver. The glucocorticoids amplify and prolong the action of the catecholamines through the complementary supply of energy that the conversion of fats and proteins into sugar makes possible. The allusion to testicles being drawn into the abdominal cavity paraphrases the inhibition of reproductive function thought to occur simultaneously: the struggle against attack inhibits all functions that do not directly contribute to the outcome.

Stress specialists have studied the kinds of reactions to various stressors in great detail. At first, matters seemed relatively simple; the organic changes consequent to stress were thought to derive entirely from the action of two hormones, epinephrine and cortisol. As it became clear that other hormones were involved, the situation grew more complicated. Furthermore, although the process had been thought to be linear, proceeding from perception of the stressful situation to the release of hormones, it became evident that stress hormones themselves modify both the perception of the stressor and the reaction to it. The presumed direct route linking the hypothalamus to the adrenal was replaced by a labyrinthine passage with branches and returns to the starting point.

Biological complexity is not random. What is at stake in the stress reaction is individual survival and, consequently, species survival as well. It is hard to understand how biologists were able to accept the proposition that this urgent biological necessity depends on a single mode of reaction set in motion in semiautomatic fashion in organisms that are endowed with the capacity to adopt, in order to defend themselves, a variety of strategies by which to confront an environment characterized by an extreme diversity of stressors.

THE MECHANISMS OF STRESS

The adrenal cortex releases glucocorticoids in response to stimulus from pituitary ACTH, itself controlled by corticotropin releasing factor (CRF), which originates in the hypothalamus.

This elegant linear schema strongly suggests the rigid hierarchy of the armed forces or of a traditionally structured industrial enterprise. There is, however, a troubling detail. A great deal of time was spent attempting to identify the leader, or initiator, of these events, the "brains" of the enterprise. And there has been a plethora of candidates. For a long time the extraction and purification of hormones from the hypothalamus proved fruitless because these efforts only revealed factors already known for other functions, such as vasopressin, the hormone that regulates water reabsorption by the kidney. CRF remained elusive.

The Illusion of Hierarchy

In 1981 Willy Vale and his team at the Salk Institute in California finally managed to identify CRF, establish its chemical structure, and demonstrate that the action of the synthetic peptide and the native hormone are identical.[2] Further, this research indicated that the corticotropic cells of the pituitary that secrete ACTH are not regulated by a single agent but by several (Fig. 3.1). There are, accordingly, several independent pathways for activation of the stress reaction at the level of that vital center, the pituitary. The

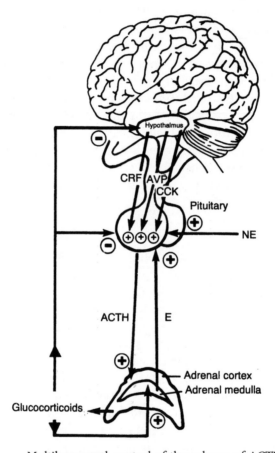

FIGURE 3.1.   Multihormonal control of the release of ACTH. Secretion of ACTH by the anterior pituitary gland is stimulated by hypothalamic peptides, principally corticotropin releasing factor (CRF) and secondarily vasopressin (AVP) and cholecystokinin (CCK); and by hormones of peripheral origin, epinephrine (E) and norepinephrine (NE). ACTH stimulates the adrenal cortex to synthesize glucocorticoids, which inhibit release and synthesis of new ACTH by the pituitary and of new corticotropin releasing factor by the hypothalamus. Glucocorticoids similarly facilitate the synthesis of catecholamines by the adrenal medulla (*adapted from Axelrod & Reisine, 1984*).

release of ACTH, activated by falling levels of glucose in the blood, is blocked by the administration of propranolol, a beta blocker. However, this treatment has no effect on the elevation of the blood level of ACTH that is observed in animals subjected to painful electric shocks.[3]

The nerve cells that synthesize CRF are situated in the paraventricular nucleus of the hypothalamus. Multiple afferent nerves converge on this structure. At least two kinds of stress were known to exist well before the discovery of CRF: systemic stress and neurotropic stress. Exposure to ether (a systemic stress) provokes a stress reaction even when the hypothalamus is totally disconnected from the rest of the brain. However, this is not the case for neurotropic stress such as forced immobility or painful electric shocks. More recently, neuroanatomical research[4] has revealed three major groups of inputs at the level of the paraventricular nucleus (Fig. 3.2):

- Visceral inputs that instruct the hypothalamus on conditions within the body (variations in blood volume and activity by the vagus nerve, which innervates the viscera, and by the glossopharyngeal nerve, which innervates the oropharynx);
- Inputs from the limbic system that transmit information about the external world;
- Intrahypothalamic inputs that play an important part in the

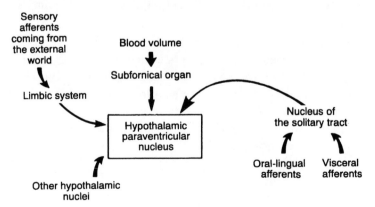

FIGURE 3.2.   Convergence of sensory information from external and internal sources on the CRF neurons of the hypothalamic paraventricular nucleus. The neurotransmitters involved in these neural pathways are unknown (*adapted from Swanson, 1987*).

coordination of behavioral and vegetative responses to internal stimuli and stimuli from the environment.

In a neuronal circuit, transmission of information from one nerve cell to another occurs through the release of chemical substances, the neurotransmitters. As some neurotransmitters are inhibitory and others excitatory, it was naturally assumed that a mechanism of this kind was responsible for regulating the release of CRF. A series of experiments was done to demonstrate the importance of the acetylcholine (excitement) and norepinephrine (inhibition) pair. The results of these tests were highly contradictory, and it must be conceded that the way the CRF receiving nerves of the paraventricular nucleus are regulated and precisely which neurotransmitters are involved are not yet clearly understood.

At the other end of the sequence, the mode of functioning of the adrenal gland seems, a priori, simpler. The organ in question is composed of two embryologically distinct parts: the medulla, of neural origin, and the cortex. The medulla contains chromaffin cells that produce catecholamines, epinephrine and norepinephrine, cells that are in fact neurons specialized in the release of transmitters into the circulatory system. This release always depends on nerve activity, transmitted, when circumstances require it, by the splanchnic nerve that innervates the adrenal. Meanwhile, coexistence with the adrenal cortex, in which glucocorticoids are abundantly secreted, has brought about a major change in the nature of the transmitters produced by the chromaffin cells. A new enzyme has in fact appeared, under the control of glucocorticoids: phenylethanolamine N-methyltransferase, which converts norepinephrine into epinephrine. The stimulation of the splanchnic nerve is responsible, therefore, for releasing into the blood a mix of catecholamines in which epinephrine predominates. Norepinephrine and epinephrine have different physiological properties: the primary effects of epinephrine are cardiac and metabolic whereas those of norepinephrine are vascular. Species in which the chromaffin cells are not fused with the adrenal cortex to form a single gland equivalent to the adrenal do not present this specialization.

The adrenal cortex is entirely responsible for the synthesis and release of glucocorticoids. The orders come from the pituitary by way of ACTH. It seems that there is also a second route of transmission, neuronal rather than hormonal, at the level of the adrenal cortex, but the exact nature of this second system and how it operates are not well understood.

From the Bottom to the Top

Communication between the hypothalamus, the pituitary, and the adrenal cortex does not occur in one direction only. The glucocorticoids do not simply carry out orders; they also provide feedback to both the pituitary and the hypothalamus to inform these hierarchically superior organs that their orders have been transmitted and the consequent tasks performed and that it is time to end the state of red alert in which the organism has been placed. This information does not require a specialized signal. The hypothalamic and pituitary cells react directly to the level of glucocorticoids in the bloodstream; an increase results in a rapid decline of ACTH secretion. The release of glucocorticoids following stress is not, therefore, generally prolonged for more than 1 or 2 hours. But higher nervous centers do not always follow these directions, especially when the information they already have suggests that the danger is still present. In this case, the system becomes less responsive to the feedback provided by the glucocorticoids, so much so that blood concentrations of glucocorticoids remain chronically elevated. This situation is typical of certain kinds of depression accompanied by disturbances in hypothalamic and pituitary regulation and also in cases of adrenal hypersecretion (during prolonged exposure to cold, for example, or in the event of malnutrition). The best way to demonstrate this is to administer a synthetic corticoid like dexamethasone. This treatment usually produces a rapid decline in circulating levels of ACTH and, therefore, in the quantities of glucocorticoids secreted by the adrenal cortex. In cases of chronic hyperactivity of the pituitary-adrenal system, this feedback mechanism loses its efficiency and dexamethasone is no longer effective: cortisol is said to escape suppression by dexamethasone.

Another way of deactivating the system is to cut the communication between the hypothalamus and the pituitary. Biochemists have identified several ways in which a cell on the receiving end blocks messages. The number of receptors of the hormone involved may decrease, they may lose their sensitivity, or they may fail to transmit information to the next actor of the chain. This last mechanism is used by pituitary corticotropic cells. When one of the activating channels is stimulated excessively, a decoupling occurs between the receptor and the second messenger, the intermediary that normally transmits information to the intracellular structures responsible for the release of ACTH. This decoupling is specific: other channels of transmission are not affected.

Until recently it was thought that regulation of the stress response depended exclusively on what was occurring in the corticotropic system. Recent experiments on rats by Sapolsky and his collaborators[5] demonstrate that in these cases, too, complexity is the rule. In addition to the feedback mechanisms at the level of the pituitary and the hypothalamus, the glucocorticoids released in response to stress act on the hippocampus, a nervous structure of the limbic system. The neurons of the hippocampus contain receptors for glucocorticoids. When these neurons are destroyed by an experimental lesion or in the normal course of aging, the pituitary-adrenal response is prolonged. Reversible modifications can also appear at the level of these neurons, as, for example, on occasions of repeated stress. In these circumstances a transitory reduction in the number of glucocorticoid receptors in the hippocampus can be observed, as well as simultaneous increase in the duration of the stress response. The plasticity of this regulatory system and its role in cerebral functioning are impressive: rats handled frequently between birth and three weeks of age have a greater density of hippocampal receptors for glucocorticoids than do control animals. Although consequently reared in conditions identical to those of the control group, these animals, two years later, are far more resistant to neuronal degeneration in the hippocampus during the course of aging, as well as to the deleterious consequences of this process on cognitive functions.

From these data one can readily see how inadequate a hierarchical, linear mode of organization is to describe what transpires between perception of a stressor and the organic reaction to it. The basic machinery of stress can respond variously to different stressors, and the multiplicity of the regulatory response is an important asset in a system's capacity to resist disorder.

THE STRESS REACTION: HELPFUL OR HARMFUL?

One of the major problems confronting students of stress is determining whether or not a particular reaction to stress is helpful or harmful. This problem was poorly formulated at the outset. Instead of taking a lead from Cannon, who had shown in the very beginning the necessary connection between the organic reaction and the behavior of flight or fight in response to sudden danger, Selye wanted to interpret bodily reactions without considering the psyche. And by this approach he sowed the seeds of a confusion that is still widely present.

The first element of Selye's theory is that stress is accompanied by a release of corticoids and by organic lesions (thymic atrophy and gastroduodenal ulcers) that are apparently due to an excess of corticoids. The second element is that adrenal insufficiency (exhaustion from excessively intense or prolonged secretion) leads to decreased resistance to stressors, a characteristic that can be corrected only by exogenous administration of corticoids. Selye's conclusion was that we should learn to spare our adrenals and avoid releasing too many corticoids in response to the pressures of daily life. The implication of his theory is that psychosomatic illnesses such as rheumatoid arthritis, collagen disease, and allergic reactions are due to an excess of corticoids. For good measure these are lumped together and rebaptized diseases of adaptation.

Selye spent many years trying to provide experimental support for this last proposition by administering powerful doses of corticoids to animals that had undergone a unilateral ablation of the kidney followed by a high sodium diet. The organic lesions presented by these animals were in fact similar to those that appear in diseases of adaptation. However, the discovery of the anti-inflammatory properties of corticoids at the beginning of the 1950s and the demonstration of their beneficial effects in some of the diseases of adaptation studied by Selye (in particular, rheumatoid arthritis) dealt his theories a fatal blow.

The second source of confusion lies in the medical uses of corticoids. There are now synthetic analogues whose action is largely superior to that of the natural hormones. When these medications are used to combat inflammation or allergy, we know that attention must be paid to their secondary effects, which can include suppression of the immune system, growth retardation, and gastroduodenal ulcers. It is therefore tempting to attribute, by analogy, troubles of the kind observed in cases of acute or chronic stress to hypersecretion of endogenous corticoids. However, it seems highly unlikely that blood concentrations of these, even in circumstances of prolonged or repeated stress, could reach levels as high as those attained in the course of medical treatment.

The corticoids that intervene in a stress reaction are glucocorticoids, whose principal function is to promote neoglucogenesis, the production of sugar from proteins and lipids. This contribution to energy metabolism is important for organisms taking defensive action again immediate danger. Epinephrine, in effect, draws on immediately available supplies of hepatic glycogen whereas glucocorticoids facilitate the use of accumulated reserves. In addition to this stimulative action, glucocorticoids play the part of watchdog or moderator of organic reactions, inhibiting the synthesis and release of various cellular mediators, such as insulin, which is involved in the metabolism of sugars; inflammatory mediators like the prostaglandins and interleukin-1; and immune mediators like the lymphokines. These various mediators represent the first line of defense in an organism's reaction to stress. Each of them, however, is also a double-edged sword, since prolonged secretion risks organic damage. The inhibiting action of the corticoids, therefore, limits such overproduction.[6] For this mechanism to function in timely fashion the corticotropic axis should not be activated by the attack itself but should be secondary to the initiation of the process of defense (Fig. 3.3).

GLUCOCORTICOIDS ALERT THE BRAIN TO DANGER . . .

The role of glucocorticoids in stress reactions is not only supervisory. They also regulate the psychic processes activated at moments of stress. We have already seen that glucocorticoids exercise a feedback effect on certain areas of the brain, such as the hippo-

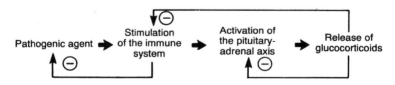

FIGURE 3.3.   Limitation, by corticoids, of the possible overreaction of the organism's immune system in response to a microbial attack.

campus, to limit the extent of the hormonal response to stress. The hippocampus is a brain structure that plays an important part in memory. Experiments on laboratory animals have shown that the release of glucocorticoids during stress reactions influences retention processes.

One of the most spectacular results in this domain was obtained by psychologist Alan Leshner in Washington, D.C.[7] He gave adrenalectomized male mice palliative injections of glucocorticoids so that these hormones were maintained at a constant level irrespective of the degree of stimulation. When the mice were confronted by a highly aggressive opponent, they conceded defeat and accepted submission far less readily than normal mice. Conversely, normal mice resorted far more rapidly to a posture of submission, putting an end to attacks by their adversary, if immediately before the first encounter they were given an injection of ACTH or corticosterone, the dominant glucocorticoid for this species (Fig. 3.4).

Everything, therefore, suggests that the hormonal response to stress is perceived by the brain as a signal that the experience of defeat is important on a biological level and should not be forgotten. This in itself is fundamental to understanding the relationship between memory and emotion. It is not possible to memorize every detail of every event during the course of a day. Therefore, the brain needs a selective capacity to distinguish between the important and the trivial. This sorting process classifies events according to their potential impact on an individual's survival or on his physical or emotional integrity. These conditions correspond exactly to stress situations. The hormones released by the adrenal cortex during a stress reaction inform the brain that the event in question merits recollection.[8]

Since we have objective methods with which to study the action of adrenocortical hormones on the brain, efforts to understand the mechanisms involved have become exceedingly valuable. Two types of receptor exist at the periphery: Type I receptors, abundantly present in the kidneys, bind with the same affinity glucocorticoids and mineralocorticoids, the corticoadrenal hormones that control hydro-mineral metabolism, while Type II receptors have a stronger affinity for the glucocorticoids. The specificity of the signal for Type I receptors derives from the fact that the glucocorticoids are not released into the bloodstream as

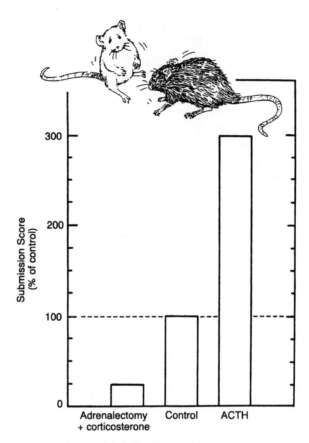

FIGURE 3.4.   Influence of glucocorticoids on submissive behavior in mice confronted by an aggressive adversary. In subsequent confrontations, treated mice react to attack by adopting (more or less rapidly) a submissive posture, which stops the attacks. The submission score measures the rapidity with which the submission posture appears. Adrenalectomized mice, whose circulating corticosterone is maintained at a constant level by exogenous infusions of synthetic hormone, achieve lower scores than control mice; conversely, stimulation of the adrenal cortex by ACTH injected after the first encounter facilitates adoption of submissive behavior (*adapted from Leshner, 1981*).

free agents: they are bound to a large protein that inhibits their binding to receptors. The affinity of Type II receptors is sufficiently high to capture the few glucocorticoids left in free circulation.

Inside the brain the situation is different[9]: the glucocorticoids are unbound. Type I receptors in the hippocampus and the septum are, consequently, almost entirely saturated by corticosterone. At this level, regulation of action by corticosterone depends on the number of receptors present, while the amount of glucocorticoids actually reaching receptors is not very important. It is in this way that the extent of the hormonal response is regulated in the hippocampus.

The affinity for corticosterone of Type II receptors, which are widely distributed throughout the brain, is relatively weak. Because of this weak affinity they are not saturated by baseline levels and can respond to the phasic variation in concentration that occurs during a stress reaction. They are responsible for the behavioral effects described earlier, as well as for the feedback effect of glucocorticoids on the release of ACTH at the pituitary level.

Glucocorticoids are normally turned into inert derivatives by enzymatic transformation. Some of these derivatives might affect the nervous system. Metabolites capable of interfering with the action of gamma-aminobutyric acid, an inhibiting neurotransmitter of the brain, have been described. Whether these metabolites are present in sufficient quantity to be effective is, however, still not known.

. . . OTHER HORMONES DO, TOO

In addition to classic hormonal properties, the possibility of nerve activity leading to behavioral and cognitive change exists in hormones other than the glucocorticoids. Epinephrine has comparable behavioral effects.[8] It facilitates learning when administered in weak doses, but larger doses have disruptive effects. Since epinephrine cannot penetrate the blood-brain barrier separating the brain from the rest of the body, its action is necessarily indirect. It may perhaps function through a metabolic intermediary, as comparable effects are obtained by glucose injections.

Work by David de Wied and his group at the Rudolf Magnus Institute of Pharmacology at Utrecht, in Holland, has shown that ACTH also has behavioral effects in animals. In these experiments, rats were taught to jump onto a platform in order to avoid electric shocks. As the shock was removed, this learned behavior was gradually forgotten. But this was not the case after injections of ACTH: treated animals continued to jump onto the platform as if they still feared the shocks. These effects were thought to reflect a transitory increase in intensity of motivation. The behavioral action of ACTH is not coded by the same part of the molecule as hormonal activity, since fragments of ACTH that have no effect on the adrenal cortex continue to modify behavior.[10]

The behavioral tests used by pharmaceutical laboratories to prove the psychotropic activity of medications indicate that peptides derived from ACTH have some weak antidepressive action, but this effect is insufficient for any clinical application to be drawn from it.

The experience gained from the study of ACTH has not proved fruitless: When CRF was discovered, neurobiologists immediately tested this peptide for its effects on the nervous system. These possibilities were investigated by a combination of techniques: neuroanatomic techniques were used to establish the cartography of CRF in areas of the brain other than the hypothalamus; pharmacological techniques were used to study the physiological and behavioral effects of CRF and of the synthetic peptides that block them when these molecules are injected directly into the brain.

CRF is localized in the hypothalamus at the level of the median eminence, which corresponds to the area in which the CRF neurons of the paraventricular nucleus come to an end. CRF is also present in the cerebral cortex, in various structures of the limbic system, in the brain stem, and in the spinal cord. This relatively diffuse distribution suggests that CRF might function as a coordinator of the physiological and behavioral reactions to stress. In fact, intracerebral administration of CRF, besides activating the pituitary-adrenal axis, stimulates the sympathetic nervous system, the consequences of which are hyperglycemia, increased consumption of oxygen, accelerated heartbeat, and elevated arterial pressure.[11]

Animals that have received CRF in the brain also exhibit exaggerated reactions to their surroundings: locomotor activity is intensified when animals are placed in a familiar cage but slackens in a new environment. Aggressive behavior is facilitated, as is, more generally, all the behaviors motivated by fear or anxiety.[12] In fact, anxiolytic medications like Valium or Librium block some of the behavioral effects of the intracerebral administration of CRF. Likewise, intracerebral injection of a CRF antagonist peptide has a calming effect shown in some tests to be comparable to that of anxiolytic medication. This treatment overcomes, for example, the inhibition toward taking food presented by animals, even starving animals, that have been forcefully restrained for one hour or more.[13] (Fig. 3.5).

These physiological and behavioral effects are joined by neuroendocrine effects similar to the negative consequences of stress on hormonal systems that are not directly involved in the stress response. The administration of CRF inhibits the secretion of growth hormone and interferes with hypothalamo-pituitary mechanisms regulating the release of sex hormones. Conversely, in studies with rats the administration of an antagonist of CRF normalizes secretion of the luteotropic hormone, a pituitary hormone regulating secretion of sex hormones, when this function has been disturbed by electric shock.[14]

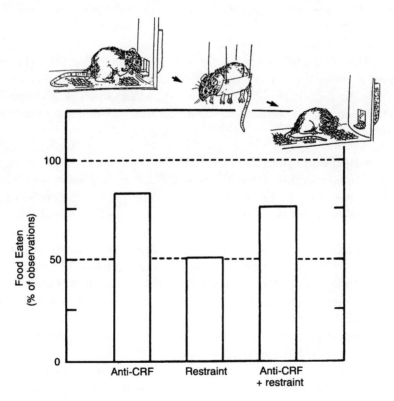

FIGURE 3.5.   The intracerebral administration of an antagonist of CRF (anti-CRF) blocks the decrease in food consumption induced by immobilization (restraint stress) without affecting spontaneous consumption of food (*adapted from Krahn et al., 1986*).

THE EXTENDED FAMILY OF STRESS HORMONES

Stress hormones belong to an extended family in the Italian sense—with many brothers and sisters and a multitude of first and second cousins. Sometimes the kinship is real and sometimes it is a matter of circumstance—or, more precisely, of location. Endorphins, or endogenous morphines, are the most talked-about members of this group.

Morphine is the active component of opium. Apart from its sedative action, nothing predisposes this alkaloid to play any role in stress. It is known primarily for its analgesic and antidiarrheal properties (paregoric elixir) and its antitussive properties.

The history of endorphins begins in the 1970s with the discovery of specific receptors in the brain for morphine and for substances capable of binding selectively and with a very strong affinity to those receptors.

The term *endogenous morphine* is deceptive because it suggests a single molecule whose effects are similar to those of morphine. In fact, it designates three large categories of molecules whose origin, anatomical distribution, and mechanisms of action are very different:[15]

- Beta-endorphin derives from the fragmentation of proopiomelanocortin (POMC), a peptide of much greater size. This precursor, or pro-hormone, is synthesized in the corticotropic cells of the anterior pituitary and produces both ACTH and β-melanotropine, a melanotropic hormone. POMC can also be found in the neurons at the base of the hypothalamus, in the arcuate nucleus, and in the nucleus of the tractus solitarius, a brain stem structure that plays an important part in visceral function. Branches of these neurons innervate the limbic system and many areas of the brain stem. Beta-endorphin can itself be divided into active fragments like γ-endorphin and α-endorphin.
- Peptides derived from pro-enkephalin: the small peptides, the enkephalins (leu- and met-enkephalin, depending on the nature of the terminal amino acid), and various other peptides of more important dimensions. Like β-endorphin, these peptides have been localized simultaneously in the brain and in an endocrine gland. This time, the endocrine gland is the adrenal medulla; the enkephalins are present in

the same infra-cellular formations as those that already contain the catecholamines. The kinship, therefore, is spatial. In the brain, the distribution of enkephalins is far more diffuse than that of β-endorphin; the enkephalins are contained in short neurons that form local circuits, as well as in the spinal cord.

- Peptides deriving from prodynorphin; this is a heterogeneous group principally composed of dynorphin and the neo-endorphins. These peptides are present in the pituitary and, like the enkephalins, can also be found in various brain structures and in the spinal cord. In these latter cases, the relationship to stress hormones is quite distant.

As if this diversity of structure and anatomic localization of endorphins were not enough, various types of receptors for these peptides have also been identified; between the mus, kappas, deltas, and sigmas, pharmacologists have their hands full!

The excitement of discovering endorphins created its share of fantasy. Wild hypotheses were launched, and judging from articles written at the time, specialists saw themselves already engaged in curing schizophrenia, autism, intractable pain, and so on. A connection with stress was inevitable when the following were taken into account:

- The simultaneous coexistence of stress hormones and endorphins in the adrenal medulla and in the pituitary
- The appearance of an analgesia, a transitory diminution of sensibility to pain, on exposure to various stressors, this form of analgesia based in certain cases on the release of endorphins

FEAR REDUCES PAIN

Researchers were thrilled when they realized that exposing rats to painful electric shocks or immobilizing them (restraint stress) produced an analgesic effect similar to that of morphine. They had proof, at last, that endogenous morphines exist in the brain, proof that opened the way to studying the uses to which these morphines are put. It would be difficult to find a simpler experimental schema. Anyone can expose rats to easily quantifiable stress—electric shocks, for example, regulated in both intensity and duration; or rotation at a well-determined speed for a specific length of time. And anyone can estimate the sensitivity to pain exhibited by these animals by measuring the reflex interval in retracting the tail when a beam of infrared light is concentrated on it. The latency of this reflex is normally about three or four seconds. After stress, however, the interval grows longer and becomes something closer to ten seconds.

How to produce irrefutable proof that analgesia is caused by the release of endogenous morphines?[16] If this is a true causal sequence, it should be disrupted by the preliminary administration of a chemical substance, like naloxone or naltrexone, that blocks morphine receptors. Another criterion is what the experts call "cross-tolerance." Repeated administration of morphine rapidly creates tolerance, that is, a reduction in the analgesic effect of this substance. If the analgesia produced by stress is due to the release of endorphins, animals that have experienced repeated stress should also "tolerate" morphine. These two criteria have been used to distinguish so-called "opioid" analgesia from so-called "non-opioid." Only the first is produced by endorphins. Thus, administering a continuous electric shock for three minutes produces a non-opioid analgesia whereas intermittent electric shocks (every few seconds for some 20 minutes) produces opioid analgesia (Fig. 3.6). The region of the body given electric shock also affects the nature of the analgesia: opioid analgesia appears as a consequence of electric shocks administered to the front paws whereas non-opioid analgesia follows electric shocks administered to the hind paws.[17]

The origin of the endogenous morphines that produce opioid analgesia is not known. Beta-endorphin of pituitary origin and enkephalins from the adrenal medulla play a part since some forms of opioid analgesia disappear after surgical removal of the pituitary or the adrenal medulla. This effect is not constant, however; furthermore, the same glandular extirpation can affect certain kinds of non-opioid analgesia. Because of this, analgesia can be differentiated into two categories: hormonal analgesia and neural (or nonhormonal) analgesia, a classification that is superimposed on the preceding one but without becoming confused with it.

Action Takes Precedence over Tending Wounds

With four kinds of stress-induced analgesia to consider—opioid, non-opioid, hormonal, nonhormonal—researchers have had their

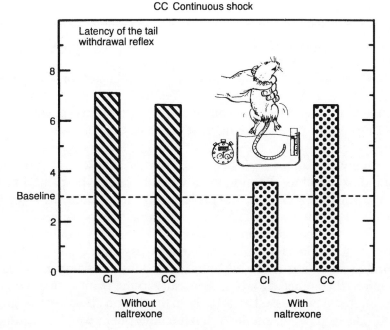

FIGURE 3.6.   Latency of the tail-withdrawal reflex. Rats are subjected to intermittent electric shock (CI) or continuous shock (CC). The interval of time before retracting the tail from heat is measured before the test begins (baseline) and after it. Pretreatment by naltrexone, an antagonist of opiate receptors, blocks the analgesia induced by intermittent shock. However, analgesia as a consequence of continuous shock is not affected (*adapted from Terman et al., 1984*).

hands full. Accordingly, they have devoted considerable time to describing the consequences of various experimental stressors used in the laboratory, and in trying to understand the neural mechanisms that are activated. The question that is at least as important as these was not seriously considered until 1980 (and then only by a small number of researchers), namely, What are the possible functions of stress-induced analgesia? A priori, a reduction of sensitivity to pain should translate into a more effective focusing of organic resources on the means of confronting the threatening circumstance. An animal attacked and wounded by a predator may find that the only possibility of safety resides in flight, not in any contemplation of its wounds. Conversely, once the immediate danger has passed, it will be able to treat its wounds at its leisure. This highly teleological point of view was formally stated by two American psychologists, Robert Bolles and Michael Fanselow, who suggested that pain should be considered not simply as sensation but, rather, as a genuine motivational system for confronting fear[18] (Fig. 3.7).

Categorizing it as a motivational system, the authors designate a central state that simultaneously organizes both perception and action. A frightened animal concentrates its attention on everything that represents potential danger; at the same time, it is prepared to flee, to attack, or to remain frozen in place, depending on the proximity of danger and the probability of attack. A creature in pain devotes all its attention to its wounds, keeps the painful part of the body immobilized, and protects it from contact with objects. Involved as they are with totally incompatible perceptions and actions, fear and pain can not coexist. Thus, when a diluted solution of formalin is injected into a rat's paw, producing a keen burning sensation followed by a more diffuse inflammatory discomfort, the animal avoids any pressure to the painful area, keeps the injured paw pressed to its body so that it won't bear any weight, and licks its paw repeatedly. But if the rat is put into a cage bearing the scent of another stressed rat, this pain-motivated behavior vanishes and is replaced by attempts at flight, then increased vigilance, and, very quickly, a posture of frozen immobility in a corner. How-

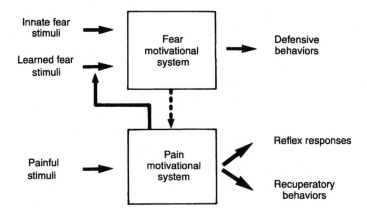

FIGURE 3.7.   Interactions between defensive behavior and behavior motivated by pain (recuperative behavior). Facilitating influences are represented by solid lines, inhibiting influences by dotted lines (*adapted from Bolles and Fanselow, 1980*).

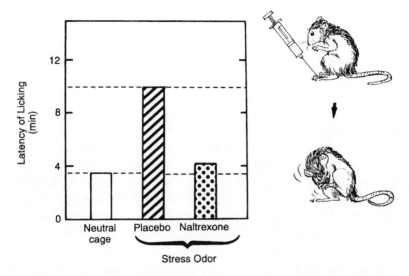

FIGURE 3.8.   Fear inhibits behavioral responses to pain. Rats that had
received an injection of diluted formalin in the paw were placed either in
a neutral cage or in a cage imbued with the odor of another rat that had
been exposed to electric shocks (stress odor). In the latter instance there
was a noticeable increase in the rats' latency of licking the paw. This
phenomenon is due to the release of endogenous opioids, since it is
blocked by previous injection of naltrexone (*adapted from Fanselow,
1985*).

ever, if the rat is put back into its home cage, it rapidly resumes
attention to the injured paw. There seems to be a genuine functional antagonism between fear and pain[19] (Fig. 3.8).

Panic and Withdrawal into Oneself

Given the diversity of defense reactions when an organism is faced
with danger and the many kinds of endogenous analgesia, one can
postulate a preferential association between certain kinds of analgesia and the strategy adopted when confronting danger. According to Rodgers and Randall, who studied the analgesia developed
by mice faced with highly aggressive opponents, the kind of analgesia observed depends on the subject's capacity for action and,
in particular, on its distance from the danger. When an organism is
exposed to a relatively diffuse danger, in the face of which there
are several possible responses, a non-opioid analgesia is mani-

fested. But in animals confronting a danger that cannot be mastered, the analgesia that occurs is typically opioid.[20] In these cases the activation of endogenous opioid systems accompanies a change in defense strategy, which is manifested by a greater facilitation of immobilization reactions (freezing) and of the subject's withdrawal into itself and by a reduced attention to external stimuli. Indeed, a mouse put into the cage of an aggressive mouse exhibits a non-opioid analgesia from the moment of the first attacks. Conversely, the adoption of a submissive posture toward the opponent is accompanied by an opioid analgesia. Meanwhile, the aggressor mouse develops a hyperalgesia. The theory of Rodgers and Randall complements that of Fanselow and Bolles: moderate fear is accompanied by non-opioid analgesia whereas, conversely, opioid analgesia is characteristic of panic.

This concept of the part played by endogenous opioid systems sheds light on some facts that were previously difficult to interpret. For instance, β-endorphin and the enkephalins have amnesiac effects in animals. If one administers these peptides before conditioning or immediately afterward to rats that receive an electric shock upon entering the dark part of a cage with two compartments, one observes in these animals a decreased retention of the experience. Conversely, learning is facilitated by the administration of naloxone, a morphine-receptor blocker.[21] The tests used for measuring memory require an active behavioral response from the animal, that is, flight from a danger zone or approach to a part of the cage associated with reward. If activation of the endogenous opioid systems has the effect of changing the priority of adaptive strategies by increasing the probability of "freezing" behavior and reducing the capacity for processing incoming information from the environment, one can readily understand that an animal's performance, as a result, might be disturbed. Conversely, elimination of these behaviors in situations requiring sustained attention to the environment can only facilitate the acquisition and processing of information.

It is tempting to extrapolate from these findings and assign to a conditional hyperactivity of the endogenous opioid systems a causal role in pathologies that are characterized by a deteriorating interaction with the social or physical surroundings. Hypotheses of this kind were formulated to explain infant autism[22] as well as some forms of depression and even psychotic states. But since treatments diminishing the activity of endogenous opioid systems were shown not to be very effective (recent data show weak activity for opiate antagonists), these hopes have been disappointed.

SOCIAL STRESS: A MYTH

When the idea of stress was still simple it was used not only to describe what was happening but also to explain why things were happening in one way rather than another. We are still living with that simple conception, even though it is outmoded and often unproductive. Accordingly, if an individual is dominated by others in his social group and this situation affects his physiology, the outcome is considered a consequence of the social stress to which he is subjected.

According to stress theory, the activation of defense mechanisms is accompanied by an inhibition of all functions that do not directly contribute to the struggle against the stressor. This inhibition applies to growth and reproductive functions and is, in Selye's view, a purely endocrinologic mechanism. The mobilization of hormones with catabolic action necessarily opposes the simultaneous production of hormones with anabolic action. It seems probable that there are inhibitory interactions between these hormonal systems involved in the stress response and other hormonal systems, at the level of either the target cells for these hormonal systems or the hypothalamic-pituitary complex.

Overpopulation, Stress, and Infertility

The notion of social stress was eagerly embraced by ecologists interested in the varying densities of animal populations. These densities generally fluctuate around a stable level that does not represent the maximum reproductive capacity of the species. The regulatory factors easiest to identify are environmental: available food resources, climatic variations, predators, and pathogenic agents. These factors alone, however, do not adequately explain variations in population density. It is not unusual, in fact, to observe a brutal reduction in numbers after a period of population growth without being able to identify any discernible limiting environmental factor. For some species this phenomenon is cyclical and relatively independent of environmental variation. The explanation most frequently advanced is that increased population density means an increased incidence of aggressive interaction and activation of neuroendocrine stress mechanisms, resulting in decreased fertility and increased susceptibility to illness.[23]

The experimental facts that support this hypothesis were drawn from populations of rodents able to multiply freely in an enclosed space, with food and water freely available. As the number of individuals per surface unit increased, hyperactivity of the pituitary-adrenal axis was observed. This relationship between density and adrenocortical activity was first demonstrated by a study of the variation in size of the adrenal, then by studies of the levels of circulating glucocorticoids and studies of the adrenal's *in vitro* capacity to respond to stimulation by ACTH. For example, there is a positive relationship between the density of population and adrenocortical activity, with thresholds varying according to species; mice, a territorial species, react to far weaker densities than do rats, which are gregarious[24] (Fig. 3.9).

Enhanced pituitary-adrenal activity means stress, with its consequent sequence of unfavorable effects on general health and reproductive capacity. The idea of some kind of "densostat" regulating population density through stress mechanisms is attractive to many biologists. Even though it provides a scientific basis for genetic theories that postulate selection at the individual, rather than group, level (with those individuals most sensitive to stress

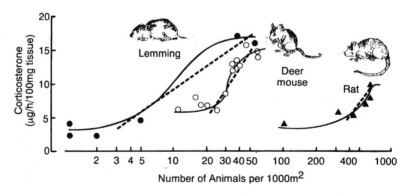

FIGURE 3.9.   Secretion activity of the adrenal cortex in response to population density in wild populations of lemmings (left-hand curve), deer mice (middle curve), and rats (right-hand curve). Estimates of densities are based on trapping. Thresholds of reaction to increased density are lower in territorial species than in gregarious species (*adapted from Andrews, 1979*).

preferentially eliminated), the validity of this notion is open to question. Mortalities in overpopulated rodent colonies studied in the laboratory are due for the most part to profound behavioral disturbance rather than to the hormonal consequences of stress. The disappearance of maternal behavior is noted, for instance, together with an increased incidence of cannibalism and infanticide,[25] but reduced fertility is rare. The factors intervening most frequently for regulating population density are territoriality and emigration.

Reproductive rates and the ways in which these are regulated constitute the standard by which sociobiologists differentiate between the so-called "opportunistic" and "competitive" species. The former have an elevated potential for growth and a high proportion of individuals reaching their maximum reproductive capacity; populations of the latter remain below their reproductive capacity and ordinarily maintain a steady level of density.[26] The first group is highly dependent on available resources. When these are abundant, opportunistic populations increase rapidly; when supplies are short, they migrate to more favorable surroundings—or disappear. Competitive species, lacking the power to adjust population size as rapidly as the evolution of resources permits, must draw all they can from the environment in which they are evolving. These species, therefore, have recourse to forms of more or less elaborate social structures that are based on territoriality and patterns of dominance and submission. Most species of mammals and birds belong to this second category. By contrast, rodents, on the whole, are intermediate and, depending on the species and on conditions, belong to one or the other of these two categories.

Extrinsic Modulation of Sexual Activity

When the growth capacity of a population depends on available resources, mammals with long gestation periods are faced with a difficult problem. A herbivore that gives birth during the winter, when pastures scarcely grow, would hardly favor the survival of progeny. Waiting for spring, therefore, is highly desirable. Since gestation requires several months, reproductive action must be taken in the autumn. External factors usually effective in regulating the rhythm of sexual activity are photoperiod, temperature, and, for certain plant-eating species with short reproductive cycles, the phyto-estrogen content of food. As female sexual activity is particularly affected by these factors, males, always ready for action, find themselves in some sort of waiting situation, at the disposal of their female partners.

Social factors are added to this extrinsic modulation of sexual activity in order to refine it and make it more efficient. Individuals most affected by environmental circumstances transmit relevant information to others through social signals, thereby synchronizing the sexual activities of the entire group. Social influences can affect the timing of puberty, the onset of estrus in populations with either seasonal or permanent sexual activity, and the revival of sexual activity after parturition.[27] In each of these cases, members of the same or the opposite sex can exercise either facilitating or inhibiting influences on sexual activity. Therefore, those effects of social stress on reproduction that are considered negative represent only a particular instance of a biological phenomenon that is far more general and whose mechanisms are not necessarily much affected by stress.

Those Excluded from Reproduction

The important concept of reproductive exclusion can be illustrated by using as an example the social inhibition of the sexual cycle as observed in females of various primate, rodent, canine, and herbivorous species. These populations are all ordinarily territorial, and density is regulated by migration. Social structures are based on cooperation between members of the group for raising the young and exploiting available resources. These structures may be organized around a family group composed of a monogamous couple and its descendants or a harem in which a single dominant male lives with a group of several females (sometimes including other males as well). Reproduction in these harem groups is usually limited to a single couple, while other members of the group exhibit varying degrees of reproductive inhibition.

Tamarins and marmosets present the most typical examples. Among these American monkeys of the Callithridae, a single family in each group is sexually active while the others are excluded from the reproductive cycle. However, if one of these females is removed from the group, she will rapidly exhibit sexual cycles and, if exposed to males, will prove normally fertile[28] (Fig. 3.10).

In terms of neuroendocrine function, noncyclical females present a reduction in basic secretion of the pituitary luteotropin,

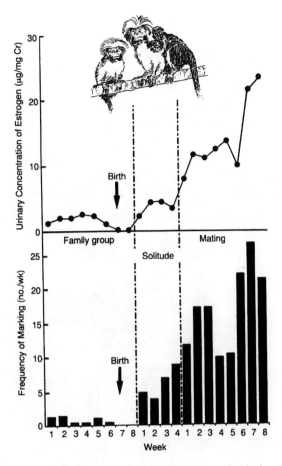

FIGURE 3.10.   The influence of social status on the behavior and ovarian activity of a female tamarin monkey. When the female lives within a
family group, her ovarian activity, measured by urinary concentration of
estrus derivatives (calculated in micrograms by milligram of urinary discharge), remains weak and acyclic. Marking behavior remains unobtru-
sive: the female usually signals her hormonal status by rubbing her ano-
genital glands against objects in her vicinity. This inhibition of sexual
activity becomes even more marked when the mother of the female under
study has given birth to twins. If the animal is isolated, hormonal activity
and marking behavior increase. Pairing with a male produces cycles and
a major rise in the frequency of marking (*adapted from Savage et al.,
1988*).

or luteinizing hormone (LH), and a diminished response of this hormone to stimulation of hypothalamic origin. At the same time sensitivity of the hypothalamus to the feedback action of estrogens is reduced so that ovulation cannot occur. Isolation produces a rapid rise in levels of LH, and the cycle returns to normal[29] (Fig. 3.11). The dominant female is under no pressure to display aggressive postures toward other females; her odor, in itself, constitutes the necessary message.

This basic schema has several variations. In both the tamarin and the marmoset the mechanism responsible for the inhibiting influence of the dominant female on the synthesis and release by

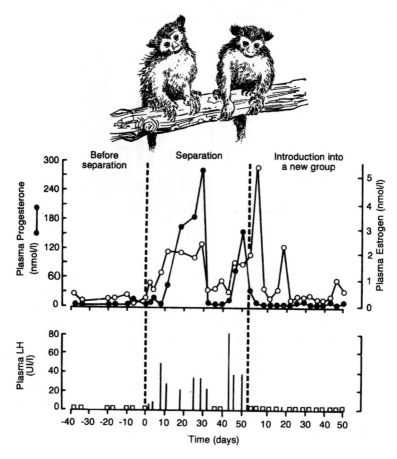

FIGURE 3.11.   Blood concentrations of progesterone, estrogen, and luteotropin (LH) in a female marmoset monkey as a function of her social status (*adapted from Abbott et al., 1988*).

the hypothalamus of LH in other females is not known. In a microcebus belonging to the lemur family[30] and in the talapoin,[31] a small cercopithecus, a rise in prolactin levels is the causative factor. In fact, administration of medication inhibiting the release of prolactin reinstitutes cyclicity in acyclic females while the inverse procedure, administering medication that augments the concentration of circulating prolactin, blocks ovulation in normally cyclic females. As for social factors in lemurs, tamarins, and marmosets, olfactory stimulation alone is enough to retard ovulation. However, in talapoins, attacks perpetrated against the subordinate female are responsible for the inhibition of sexuality.

Similar phenomena can be observed among males. In some species, rivalry between males is such that simple perception of the dominant male is often enough in a number of cases to diminish testicular activity. An extreme case can be found in the tupaiia, a primitive Indonesian monkey. When a submissive male is put into a cage with a dominant male, the former dies within a few days even when it is protected from attack by wire netting or bars.[32] However, one should not conclude that dominant males invariably present higher levels of circulating testosterone than do their submissive counterparts. In cases of this kind many variations are possible, and very often the possibility of sexual interaction is regulated by behavior rather than by neuroendocrine mechanisms. Among talapoins, for example, testosterone levels of submissive males are lower than those of dominant males. Administration of testosterone can artificially raise circulating levels of male sex hormone among the submissive individuals to levels comparable to those in the dominant male. However, sexual initiatives toward females by these formerly submissive individuals still fail because there is a corresponding increase in attacks from the dominant male.[33]

For the human species the existence of similar influences can scarcely be treated as pure speculation. Some studies have suggested a possible modulation of the sexual cycle by odors, as in the synchronized menstrual periods of dormitory students observed by Martha McClintock in 1971 or, more recently, the regulatory influence on the female cycle of axillary male odor.[34] More precisely, in regard to the possibility of stress affecting reproductive capability, it is well known that women in programs of intense physical training present irregular menstrual cycles and sometimes even amenorrhea. Since physical exercise is accompanied by a release of endorphins and enkephalins, some writers consider these to be responsible for the irregularities observed. Administration of opioid peptides suppresses release of FSH and LH, the two pituitary hormones that control ovarian function. These effects are blocked by the administration of naloxone, an antagonist of opiate receptors. However, direct proof implicating endorphins in menstrual cycle disturbances observed in female athletes has yet to be produced.

THE MULTIDIMENSIONAL NATURE OF
THE STRESS REACTION

Given the complexity of stress reactions, it is tempting to reach for easy solutions, focusing on this or that mediator as the one likely to provide complete information. This is what happened with adrenal hormones, then ACTH. Now, the last vestiges of euphoria about endorphins are yielding to the all-encompassing power of that grand regulator, CRF (corticotropin releasing factor).

Stress is omnipresent and is held responsible for every kind of misfortune. There can be no doubt that, some day, when *the* mediator has been identified, *the* antagonist will in due course be discovered as well and that to it will be ascribed all the nefarious consequences of stress. Whoever makes these announcements will enjoy a wild success. But researchers are not magicians.

During the course of this critical exploration of stress mechanisms, we have seen that the hypothesis of an express track for stress that serves to channel the effects of various stressors on the body is false. The multiplicity of means by which an organism can confront stress is impressive. A single system like the pituitary-adrenal axis contains a wide range of mediators capable of playing a critical part in an adaptive reaction. In this chapter I have chosen to limit the description of reactive mechanisms to those operating in this axis and to endogenous opioids. The fact that I have not discussed other hormones involved, particularly the catecholamines, should give some idea of the distance still to be covered before everything is explained.

The unitary concept of stress relies on the major idea of nonspecificity. For Selye, this nonspecificity is written into the solution itself. Regardless of what actually disturbs homeostasis, the problem is the same: to return to equilibrium. Biologists who have succeeded Selye have not thrown any doubts on nonspecificity but have attributed it to emotions aroused by a provocative situation.[35] If an animal is suddenly exposed to intense cold or heat, it responds in both cases by increased blood concentrations of cortisol because both cases involve a situation that is entirely unexpected. The adrenal response of an animal gradually exposed to temperature change varies according to circumstance: cortisol diminishes with increasing heat and increases with growing cold. Similarly, the pituitary-adrenal axis is activated in circumstances of food deprivation only when the subject experiences disappointment and frustration, that is, when he had been expecting food and then did not receive it. On the other hand, if he is given food with the same organoleptic qualities as its usual diet but deprive of all the nutritive content, cortisol levels do not change.

As long as the stress reaction is considered in terms of variations in blood cortisol, the idea of a unique reaction reflecting a subject's degree of emotional engagement seems to be well founded.[36] But as soon as other hormones are taken into account, hormones whose secretion is directly or indirectly modified by stress, the situation is seen to be far more complicated, and it becomes necessary to postulate the existence of several modes of reaction.

This multiplicity of mechanisms is no matter of chance. The link between elementary behavioral strategies and hormonal activation is a close one. Adaptation to stress activates various mechanisms that organize behavior and make the corresponding physiological adjustment possible. The mechanism activated when an organism cannot avoid stress is different from the one that intervenes when there is a possibility of foresight and preparation for action. One cannot, therefore, explain the physiological and hormonal changes in an organism without considering the various kinds of behavioral reactions, or coping strategies, adopted by that organism when faced with the stressful circumstance. And it is only at this point that the psychic and the physiological can be reconciled, factors that biologists of stress have for too long kept separate.

Four

CONFRONTATION

Well-regulated environments rarely produce biological, physiological and behavioral disturbances. Disorders of that kind tend to appear when control of the immediate surroundings becomes impossible. And from that circumstance a complete pathology develops.

—HENRI LABOURIT, *La vie antérieure*

Early in the 1960s American military physicians launched what they considered to be the study of the century on stress.[1] Their object was to make a systematic determination of the usefulness of various psychological and physiological indicators of stress and to use that information to identify soldiers who would best adapt to the difficult circumstances of combat. The researchers readily conceded that some of the tests might be dangerous; in fact, the emphasis on danger was so strong that had a statement of intent been submitted to an ethics committee, the study would probably not have been approved! Soldiers were divided into several groups. One group was sent up in an airplane. When the plane was over the ocean, mechanical problems were announced, including the probability that these might lead to a crash. A second group was sent into an isolated and deserted region to follow the battalion to which they belonged; they were informed by radio that they would shortly be confronted by a forest fire, a cloud of toxic gas, or erroneously directed artillery fire. Furthermore, they were given to understand that in none of these cases was there any possibility of a timely departure from the threatened area! Despite an abundance of radio communications, artillery fire, and smoke bombs and despite the realistic character of the situations to which the soldiers were exposed, the experiment produced no hard evidence; no connection between responses to psychological questionnaires and behavior in the grave circumstances to which the respondents were exposed could be demonstrated. Furthermore, urinary excretion of adrenal hormones was so variable from one individual to another that there was no point in searching for constants in their behavioral responses.

At that time the dominant concept in behavioral studies was still the stimulus–response schema, that is, the notion that an organism's response to a given stimulus derives from the character of that stimulus, just as the trajectory of a football reflects the force and direction of a player's kick. But an organism is not a football. Or, more precisely, an organism's behavior is like that of a football that leaves its starting point sometimes in one direction, sometimes in another, perhaps even remaining in place, in response to a series of strictly identical kicks. The organism is not simply reacting, it is acting as a function of its own imperatives.

Stress specialists were slow to grasp the necessity of distinguishing between action and reaction. The situation was not clarified until research finally concentrated on the diversity of methods by which any individual confronts stress. If, for instance, my neighbor is given to making a loud, disturbing noise after 10 P.M., I might ask him straight out to moderate his practices. But if I know that he's very touchy—and, furthermore, that he's far stronger than I—I certainly wouldn't want to be involved in an argument that might go badly for me. Therefore, as I curse my neighbor, I may also decide simply to ignore him. I may, for example, take a walk outdoors, watch television, or read a hair-raising detective story with plugs in my ears. Each of these options corresponds to what is called a coping strategy, that is, a process that an individual interposes between stress and himself in order to reduce the effects of that stress on his own being. The term *coping* is used to describe the ways in which individuals attempt to confront and surmount problems as they present themselves.[2]

Studies of coping strategies correspond to a fundamental change in our conception of stress. We no longer try to describe stress reactions by the challenges to which an individual is exposed but, rather, by the ways in which he copes with them. As we shall see in this chapter, such an attitude opens up new and important questions involving the origin of diversity in coping strategies as well as the best way of measuring the effectiveness of such strategies.

COPING

For psychologists, coping corresponds to efforts undertaken to resolve problems aroused by external or internal demands confronting an organism, problems that a subject perceives as potentially threatening.[3] In this definition several terms are important:

- The term *effort* indicates that the adaptation in question is not a passive one; it is not like the process that occurs, for example, when I arrive for a skiing holiday in the mountains and find that I need a few days to grow used to the rarefied oxygen content of the air. In the case we are considering here, the individual must exert himself to make the adaptation. This does not mean that the effort has to be conscious or voluntary. It must, however, be an effort, for the same results cannot be achieved by the automatisms already providing responses to the demands of daily life.
- The term *resolve* must be understood in a transactional sense. The point is not always a physical disappearance of the problem; it may, to some degree, be a matter of mastery and tolerance and learning to live with it. If I find that my state of health requires a stay in the hospital and a serious operation sometime soon, I will simply have to accept those facts in one form or another.
- The term *demand* is borrowed from the terminology of stress and designates any factor soliciting in an exaggerated manner an organism's adaptive capacities. This factor can be of external origin, that is, from the socioeconomic, familial, or physical environment, or of internal origin, that is, from an

illness or the perception of a symptom associated with an illness.
- The term *perceive* indicates the importance of cognitive processes with regard to coping. A subject's perception of seriousness in a given circumstance is more relevant than the actual importance of the event.

Coping efforts can be directed toward either the problem itself or the emotion the problem engenders. In the first instance, one attempts to modify the course of events that constitute a difficulty in order to control them or, alternatively, to tolerate them more readily. In the second instance, an individual gives primary emphasis to preserving his emotional balance.

One can also distinguish between an action strategy and a defense strategy. The former consists of doing something in order to surmount the difficulty with which one is confronted, either directly, that is, by alerting the course of events (I've just had a fight with my boss, so I quit my job), or indirectly, by allowing the emotion engendered by perception of a problem to dissipate on confrontation with something else. (For example, after the argument with my boss I go home in a rage. My daughter meets me in tears; she has just broken her doll and begs me to repair it. I try, but fail. My daughter's sobs increase, and instead of trying to soothe her I hit her.)

Defense strategies designate purely intrapsychic processes of reinterpreting a situation, such as minimalization or denial (e.g., a woman with a lump in her breast arrives at the hospital for a biopsy declaring, "This is a routine exam; there's no question of cancer"), repression ("I don't want to hear any more about it until the results of the test are in"), rationalization ("Biopsy is a necessary and valuable diagnostic tool"), or distraction ("If I go to see a film to get my mind off my troubles, the sun will still come up tomorrow").

Defense mechanisms have long been a subject of interest, beginning with Freudian psychoanalysts. Subsequently, psychologists have attempted to systematize the study of this subject by a variety of means, including films with controlled emotional content and self-administered questionnaires. A classic example of this approach is provided by a study of reactions to a film containing scenes of mutilation.[4] Subjects were shown a film depicting ritual incisions of the penis and scrotum performed on aboriginal adolescents during rites of passage to adult status. There were three possible sound tracks to accompany the images: one insisted on the painful and barbarous character of such practices, the second made no allusion to pain but emphasized the ritual character of the ceremonies and their social significance, and the third described in minute detail the operative techniques employed and the skill of the practitioner, given the primitive character of the implements (which were made of sharpened stone). Although the visual images in each case were identical, the second and third commentaries produced in subjects viewing the film fewer negative reactions than did the first, the difference being all the more marked in that subjects spontaneously tended—as the sound tracks that did not emphasize pain suggested they would—to draw back from the film.

The diversity of coping strategies makes a study of them both fascinating and difficult. The problems raised by a description and classification of these strategies are enormous. We are highly flexible in our selection of strategies. As if that weren't enough, we are not even capable of correctly describing a strategy we have used in the past to confront a specific event; furthermore, we rarely resort ·to the strategy we have fantasized using in a particular situation when that imaginary situation becomes a reality. Emphasis on a description of coping strategies has led psychologists to behave like the first botanists, who spent their time making lists of plant varieties. Of course, it is important to know what the various possible defense mechanisms are—especially if one's object is to help a patient organize his perceptions and defenses so that he can make a better adjustment to his environment—but taking into account the inexhaustible range of *a posteriori* justifications for human behavior, it makes more sense to begin with objective indicators of the impact of stress on an organism. The stakes are high because, as psychologists have noted in a recent review of this subject:[5]

> In summary, despite the enthusiasm and interest that have been shown for the construct of coping, we have just barely begun to scratch the surface. There is debate about how coping strategies should be conceptualized, and little progress has been made in developing objective, reliable, and valid ways of capturing the coping process. Although it is widely assumed that choice of coping strategies can ameliorate the impact of stressful experiences, there is surprisingly little sound, empir-

ical research bearing on this assumption. Hopefully, subsequent research will augment current knowledge about the determinants of particular coping strategies and the conditions under which they are likely to be effective. It would also be desirable to enhance our understanding of how coping strategies are acquired or how maladaptive strategies can be changed.

AROUSAL

Direct questioning of a subject does not always provide an adequate basis for judging the effectiveness of the strategies he adopts in response to immediate problems. He may in fact try to put the best face on things by pretending to master the difficulties that confront him even when this is not the case. Conversely, if he is a pessimist, he will tend to take a negative view of the situation and dwell on his problems even when circumstances have in fact improved.

With an objective standard for calculating the impact of circumstances on an organism, the problem of incongruance between thought and reality collapses. Rather than attempting to measure degrees of perceived tension, anxiety, frustration, or anger, psychologists have posited a common dimension for the various emotional states that incite an individual to action. This dimension is called *activation.* If one admits that such a dimension exists and if techniques for measuring it are available, matters become very much easier. If, for instance, an individual engaged in a well-defined response to a particular stress demonstrates weaker activation than that observed in the absence of such a response, then, by definition, the strategy adopted by that individual is effective. Furthermore, the effectiveness of various coping strategies can be quantified by using the reduction of activation as a standard.

Psychologists did not embark on this strategy as a totally new enterprise: activation, in fact, has a long history behind it. The concept expresses the notion that all behavior has two components, one deriving specifically from its object and another that is nonspecific and that corresponds to its dynamic. The relationship between activation and performance provided one of the earliest contributions to this idea and was demonstrated by Yerkes and Dodson:[6] In any psychological test requiring an effort of sustained attention, performance is good when the subject is alert and in full possession of his capabilities. Conversely, when a subject is sleepy or tired, or agitated, performance is mediocre. There is, in consequence, a curvilinear relationship between activation and performance whereby optimum performance is achieved at a moderate level of activation, a level that varies according to the demands of the task at hand.

Activation is also found in the concepts of impulse and motivation. It is the force with which motivated behavior is expressed, irrespective of what causes the motivation. A rat placed in an exercise wheel runs more swiftly if he is simultaneously starving and exposed to signals associated with the distribution of food, or of water if he is thirsty, or if he receives a small number of moderate electric shocks. If different combinations of internal conditions and external stimuli can produce identical results (in this case turning the exercise wheel), it is because they have in common an activating component that modulates the intensity of the behavior independent of its nature. It was therefore logical that Clark L. Hull, one of the foremost theoreticians of learning, should postulate that behavior at any given moment can be described as the tendency to engage in the activity corresponding to the current drive multiplied by the sum of the forces pushing the subject to action.[7] The current trend is to equate motivation with a particular state of mind that is produced by the interaction between environmental stimuli and the inner condition of the subject and that simultaneously directs both perception and action.[8] In this model, activation is subsequent to the formation of a motivational state and determines the intensity of the subject's excitement and reactivity.

This conception brings us very close to the physiological idea of activation formulated by neurophysiologists working on states of waking and sleep. For them, activation is the passage from a condition of sleep, defined electroencephalographically, to one of active cortical alertness.[9] By extension, level of activation corresponds to a condition of brain activity as registered on a continuum between sleep and maximum arousal. This formulation has the advantage of transcending pure abstraction, since it permits the linking of activation with a nervous substratum, in this instance, the mesencephalic reticular formation, a web of tangled nerve fibers and a scattering of nerve cell bodies too dispersed to constitute nuclei. This reticulated formation receives information from various sensory systems. It is also sensitive to alterations in the physicochemical composition of the internal environment, and it transmits that information to the thalamus and the cortex (ascending activating reticular system) and to neurons of the spinal cord involved in motor function (descending activating reticular system). Thus, the reticular formation is well positioned for the simultanous modification of arousal, perception, and motor function in a nonspecific fashion in response to information from both external and internal environments.

Activation and stress are not entirely disjunctive notions; activation might be considered the psychological equivalent of a stress reaction. Similarly, bidirectional relations between the brain and the rest of the body, long neglected by stress theory, are finally integrated: stress hormones simultaneously depend on activation and are responsible for it.

Herein lies an old story, familiar to those whose area of expertise is the emotions. Thirty years ago two opposing theories attempted to explain the relationship between the somatic components of emotion and their subjective aspects. For two psychologists—an Englishman, James, and a Scandinavian, Lange—somatic manifestations provoked emotion; that is, a person feels frightened because he can feel his heart beating in his chest. Conversely, Cannon denied peripheral manifestations any causal role, arguing that when a person perceives a threat, he is afraid and his fear is expressed by an increased heart rate.

In the fifties and sixties two American social psychologists, Schachter and Singer, suggested that emotion might in fact be produced by an interaction of two components, a nonspecific arousal caused by activation of the sympathetic nervous system and a perception resulting from the fact that one attributes the cause of the arousal to this or that component of the circumstance that provoked it.

This suggestion was the product of an experiment that went roughly as follows: Subjects were told that the effects on vision of a new medication would be tested. They did not know that the medicine being used was epinephrine, which has no effect on vision. Subjects were then divided into two groups. One group received a subcutaneous injection of epinephrine, the other a placebo. Some subjects, before injection, were told of certain secondary effects; others were left in ignorance. Each subject, however, regardless of preparation, sat in the waiting room, anticipating an eye examination, in the company of a confederate, a member of the research team who passed himself off as another experimental subject. The confederate was given a precise role to play, exhibiting either anger or euphoria. The object of the charade was to test the emotion felt by the subject. The results were as follows: Subjects injected with epinephrine permitted themselves to feel their partner's pretended emotion more readily if they had not been informed about the secondary effects of the product. Epinephrine, therefore, induces an undifferentiated activation, which becomes emotion only in a favorable context, if one does not know the reasons for the arousal[10] (Table 4.1).

This type of result is entirely comparable to the behavioral effects one observes in animals after the administration of stress hormones (cf. Chap. 3). The Schachter–Singer theory enjoyed great success and became part of the classic psychological theory of the emotions. It is unfortunate that the results were not nearly as clear as expected: the other subjects of the experiment, those who were given only placebos, reacted in almost identical fashion to those

TABLE 4.1

EFFECTS OF ADMINISTRATION OF EPINEPHRINE ON THE EMOTIONS

Epinephrine was injected into volunteers placed in different emotional situations; some subjects were told of the secondary effects on the treatment (information), others were not (no information). For each column, scores carrying a different index (^{a} or ^{b}) are significantly different. Each group comprised 22 to 26 subjects, except that the groups who saw the film contained 40 subjects.

TREATMENT	EUPHORIA*	IRRITATION**	REACTION TO A FILM COMEDY**
epinephrine + information	0.98^a	-0.18^a	—
epinephrine without information	1.78^b	2.28^b	17.8^a
placebo	1.61^b	0.79^b	14.3^a

(*Adapted from Schacter and Singer, 1962*)
*Score based on self-evaluation.
**Score given by an observer.

treated with epinephrine. None of this, however, is in any way surprising. The belief that the role of mediator of emotional activation can be attributed to any single agent is naive in view of the multiplicity of alarm systems, from release of CRF in the brain to increased metabolism of brain neurotransmitters through the secretion of catecholamines.

In sum, the notion of activation is unarguably attractive, but it risks being as approximate as the notion of stress. This, however, is no reason for wholesale rejection; the idea can be a helpful guide if one is careful not to overuse it. A pragmatic approach would be to say that the difficulties confronting a subject provoke an activation whose intensity, in turn, can be measured by various autonomous or hormonal indicators of the stress reaction. The effectiveness of a particular coping strategy can then be objectified by the variations in these indicators. In the end, it does not matter if the chosen measure is indeed an indicator of activation or if activation does in fact exist. The point is to have an objective and quantifiable index for measuring the impact of a situation on an organism. And in this way, the importance of control and foresight in reaction to stress can be effectively demonstrated.

TO CONTROL OR TO SUBMIT

When I play tennis with an opponent whose skills are more or less equal to mine, and I can place shots where I intend them to go, I feel far more satisfaction than I do when I, dominated by a superior opponent, must focus all my attention on countering his moves and can never manage to seize the initiative. Controlling a situation seems, a priori, to be preferable to simply accepting it.

In order to objectively study the importance of the control factor in stress reactions, Jay Weiss at Rockefeller University in New York compared the reactions of rats able to end a course of painful electric shocks by a specific behavioral response to those of rats electrically connected to the others but whose behavior had no effect on the presence of shocks. Control rats kept in the same experimental unit were never given shocks (Fig. 4.1). After several hours of testing, all the rats were sacrificed and their stomachs examined for potential ulcerous lesions. Despite an identical number of shocks, the rats that were able to end the shocks showed

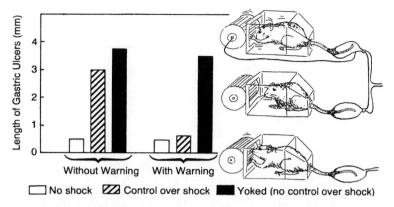

Length of Gastric Ulcers (mm)

Without Warning   With Warning

☐ No shock   ▨ Control over shock   ■ Yoked (no control over shock)

FIGURE 4.1.   Influence of control over electric shock on the severity of gastric ulcers induced in rats by that shock. Rats able to terminate shocks or delay their appearance by turning the wheel (control) formed fewer ulcers than animals receiving the same number of shocks but without any ability to influence them (0 control). Incidence of ulcers observed in the first group approximated that of the control group (no shock) only when the uncertainty of the situation was removed by a sound signal immediately after an appropriate response was made (*adapted from Weiss, 1972*).

fewer initial gastric ulcers than the rats that were connected to them but without the possibility of control.[11]

Results obtained from rat studies by Weiss ran counter to those reported a few years earlier by John Brady in research on monkeys at the Research Institute of Walter Reed Army Hospital, Washington, D.C. Monkeys able to control electric shocks by operating a lever were more likely to have ulcers than those receiving the shocks passively[12] (Fig. 4.2). In Brady's tests it was thought that the first group realized that their efforts affected a comrade as well as themselves, a comrade for whom they had some sort of responsibility. However, this highly paternalistic vision of relations between a "boss" and a dependent was biased: For economic reasons, Brady has used as his active animals monkeys that had already learned how to avoid shock by moving a lever; the passive animals were those that had not learned that lesson. By using the same method of division, Weiss obtained with rats the same results as Brady with monkeys. It is therefore at least plausible that Brady's "manager" monkeys developed ulcers not because they felt overwhelmed by the weight of their responsibilities but because they were more sensitive to electric shock.

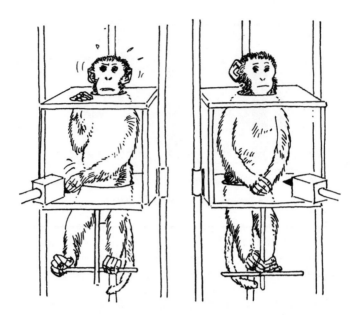

FIGURE 4.2.   Influence of "responsibilities" in ulcerogenesis in monkeys. The monkey stopping the shocks does this not only for himself but for a partner he has responsibility for. After three or four weeks, the "responsible" monkey has more gastric ulcers than does his partner (*adapted from Brady, 1958*). However, the results of this experiment were biased: Monkeys assigned the passive role were those that had not learned how to control the shocks.

In subsequent research, efforts were made to measure with some precision the impact of controllability on stress hormones.[13] Activity of the pituitary-adrenal axis, as measured by circulating levels of glucocorticoids, is generally weaker in animals that have control over the experimental stimulus than in animals without such control. For example, rhesus monkeys trained to stop a violent noise by pressing a lever showed lower blood levels of cortisol than did monkeys exposed to the same noise but without the power to intervene.

Differences are not always so obvious. In many experiments, blood levels of cortisol are the same in both the animals that have control and those that do not. According to some authors, this similarity derives from the fact that the beneficial effects of control cannot be deduced from the intensity of the pituitary-adrenal response but only from its temporal dynamics, that is, from a measure of the time it takes for circulating concentrations of hormones to revert to normal levels. However, this hypothesis was not confirmed in several systematic studies on the time course of changes in the blood level of corticosterone after exposure to shock. In rats placed in experimental conditions duplicating those used by Weiss, blood levels of corticosterone at the conclusion of the experiment and the kinetics of return to base values were identical in animals with and without controllability.

These discrepant results can be explained by the fact that the beneficial effects of controllability are not evident as long as a subject has not mastered the situation, since the effort to do so can itself induce high levels of activation. Because the task is difficult, mastering the situation can take time, during which subjects that are assumed to control will not be different from subjects that cannot control.

Inability to control external events also affects sensitivity to pain. Testing at various points during a first session of exposure to uncontrollable electric shock indicates that analgesia is initially non-opioid and subsequently opioid. Opioid analgesia seems to occur only when the uncontrollable nature of events is apparent. In fact, transition between the two forms of analgesia, opioid and non-opioid, can be observed in animals exposed to uncontrollable electric shocks but not in those receiving controllable shocks. Furthermore, a second exposure to a small number of shocks is enough to restore opioid analgesia in animals that had previously received uncontrollable shocks whereas this response does not occur in animals that previously received controllable shocks.

Similarly, food-deprived rats struggling to obtain food by pressing a lever develop a lesser degree of analgesia than those receiving food irrespective of effort.

In sum, available experimental data indicate that the possibility of influencing the course of events has positive consequences, provided that the effort required to exercise this control is not too great.

CONTROL AND MASTERY OF THE SELF

The ability to control the immediate environment can be instantly beneficial by reducing the consequences of adverse events. There are also some long-term gains in that subjects exercising control will master future difficulties more readily. Thus, rats raised in circumstances permitting them to control access to food, water, and visual stimulation are, consequently, less disturbed by a move to a new environment[14] (Fig. 4.3). A similar experiment was performed using rhesus monkeys, aged six weeks to six months, that were kept in a group cage requiring the manipulation of levers for access to food, water, and special delicacies. When separated from their fellows to be tested individually in a chamber furnished with objects that were more or less frightening, these monkeys dis-

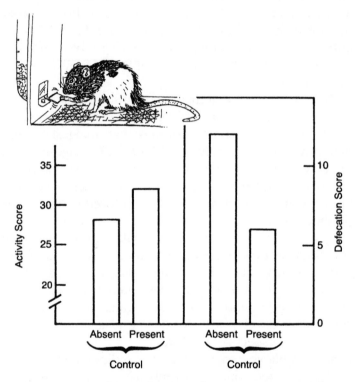

FIGURE 4.3.   Control over the immediate environment reduces emotional disturbance. Rats were kept for two months in collective cages furnished with levers for obtaining food and water and regulating light both in their home cages (control present) and in those of yoked animals (control absent). At the end of this period the animals were individually tested in a new environment; locomotor activity and defecation were studied as indicators of emotionality. Animals with previous experience of controllability (control animals) manifested greater inquisitiveness and defecated less frequently than those without such experience, suggesting that the experienced animals were less afraid of their new circumstances (*adapted from Joffe et al., 1973*).

played fewer signs of disturbance than did animals that lacked a similar past experience.[15]

Several tests on nursing animals produce comparable results:[16] Young animals possessing the possibility of control over their environment learn more readily, explore more extensively, and seem less easily disturbed.

In old age loss of control is poorly tolerated.[17] As a general rule, old people who are moved into a retirement home during renovation of their familiar quarters manifest a rapid deterioration of physical and mental health; this occurs despite an objective improvement in hygiene and standard of living. It should be noted as well that placement in an institution is accompanied by a diminished capacity for initiative in dealing with everyday concerns. Intervention experiments in retirement homes confirm the role of the controllability factor in the deterioration of an elderly person's state of health. A typical study organized two groups of elderly people; the members of one group could choose their daily activities and participated in the administration of the home whereas those in the second group were subjected to conditions of daily life in the same establishment but without consultation. Members of the first group exhibited far greater physical and mental alertness than those in the passive situation. The general health of the first group was better as well; during the period of observation their mortality was half that of the control group.

LEARNED HELPLESSNESS

At the end of the 1960s two American psychologists, Seligman and Maier, found themselves confronted by an entirely unexpected phenomenon while studying the effects of fear on avoidance behavior toward electric shocks. Dogs that had received inescapable electric shock before a conditioning experiment subsequently proved to be entirely incapable of learning and seemed paralyzed when confronting the shocks (Fig. 4.4).[18]

Called *learned helplessness*,[18a] this phenomenon was produced neither by adaptation nor by a tolerance to the shocks received, since increasing the intensity of the shocks did not affect the deficit displayed by the shocked animals. Conversely, animals that had learned to avoid shock before being subjected to the inescapable shocks were not affected. Further, no deficits in learning were

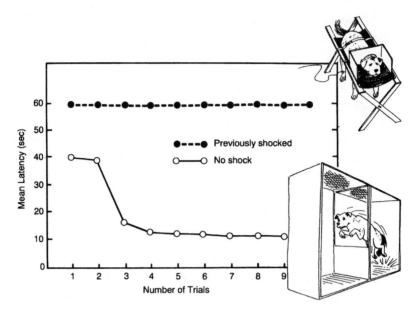

FIGURE 4.4.   The phenomenon of learned helplessness. Dogs immobilized in a harness and subjected to uncontrollable electric shocks were
then placed in a two-section cage in which they might learn to avoid
further shocks by jumping over the barrier. They could not learn to do
this, although controls who had not experienced previous shocks quickly
mastered the task (*adapted from Maier et al., 1969*).

shown by animals that were able to end shocks during the session
of initial stress by activating a mobile plate above them with a
movement of the head.

   This accidental observation was the origin of an extremely in-
fluential but also very controversial theory of human depression. According to Seligman,[19] events occurring independent of behavior
ineluctably induce in a subject a sense of his own inability to affect
what happens to him. This experience simultaneously removes any
inclination to action, since action will make no difference in any
case. The sense of helplessness produces a profound depression
that affects every aspect of psychology—cognition, motivation, and
emotion.

   Of course, there is a great difference between an animal exposed to uncontrollable electric shocks and a depressed human
being,[20] as the results of subsequent experiments on laboratory
animals demonstrated. To extend observations and to test Seligman's theories more systematically, dogs were replaced by rats,

which are easier to handle and have quieter reactions to pain. But to produce signs of a deficit, very strong shock was necessary; that is, it was necessary to use particularly stressful conditions and to then place the animals in situations that were very difficult to master.[21] Furthermore, it was readily apparent that the stressed animals did not present any cognitive deficits, since they were still capable of learning simple tasks; instead, they suffered from a deficit in initiating a response and displayed exaggerated reactions to shock.[22] Rats forced to swim in icy water and then required on the following day to learn to avoid electric shock by jumping from one side to the other of a two-compartment cage were observed to present a deficit in comparison to unstressed animals. However, during their forced swims they had obviously been unable to learn that the shocks were uncontrollable. Furthermore, this deficit was a function of the motor requirements of the task, since they readily learned how to poke their noses into a hole when that maneuver would spare them shock.[23]

With human beings, Seligman's predictions were also quite disappointing. Subjects exposed to an insoluble problem were not at all handicapped with regard to subsequent problems except when these were identical to the first problem or when subjects were inclined to attribute any failure to themselves[24] (Table 4.2). In psychological jargon, learned helplessness is internal (a subject sees his difficulties as deriving more from himself than from external circumstances), unstable (he can only confront his problems in certain circumstances rather than undertake a sustained effort toward them), and specific (his difficulties are limited to a type of problem rather than encompassing the range of problems encountered). Depressed subjects, on the other hand, are thought to blame themselves for whatever happens to them and to attribute this blame in a stable and generalized manner.[20]

WHEN THE BRAIN NO LONGER FOLLOWS

Rather than use the term *learned helplessness,* especially in regard to animals, it makes more sense to use a term like *interference,* which is more neutral with regard to the mechanisms in question.

Physiologists have tried to explain the phenomenon of interference in terms of changes in the metabolism of brain neurotransmitters that result from exposure to uncontrollable electric shocks.

TABLE 4.2

CONSEQUENCES OF EXPOSURE TO AN INSOLUBLE PROBLEM IN HUMAN SUBJECTS

In a first experiment, volunteers were confronted by a noise that they could—or could not—stop by pressing a button correctly. In a second experiment done consequently, subjects had to discover how to stop another noise (similar task) or how to solve a series of anagrams (different task). A deficit appeared only in the first case and only in subjects initially exposed to an insoluble problem.

INITIAL EXPERIENCE	SIMILAR TASK*	DIFFERENT TASK**
controllable sound	4.7	9.2
uncontrollable sound	12.5	8.3
observation (no sound)	4.6	11.6

(*Adapted from Tiggeman and Winefield, 1978*).
*Number of attempts to achieve the criterion (3 successive responses of escape).
**Number of anagrams solved.

Stress is understood to augment the synthesis and release of norepinephrine in various brain areas like the brain stem, the hypothalamus, the hippocampus, and the cortex. When a subject is unable to modify the stressor, the increase in the rate of use of norepinephrine exceeds the capacities of synthesis so that concentrations of this neurotransmitter fall rapidly. Conversely, when stress is controllable, the rate of utilization is moderate and concentrations of norepinephrine remain stable[25] (Fig. 4.5).

The consequences on the metabolism of other neurotransmitters when a subject is unable to control the situation are less well understood. The phenomenon of interference is associated with a diminished release in the hippocampus of gamma-aminobutyric acid, an inhibiting amino acid, and with a diminished release of serotonin in the septum. These alterations are corrected by administration of *imipramine*, an antidepressive medication that also reduces behavioral deficits.[26]

Rather than killing the animals at the end of the experiment and quantifying the various neurotransmitters and metabolites

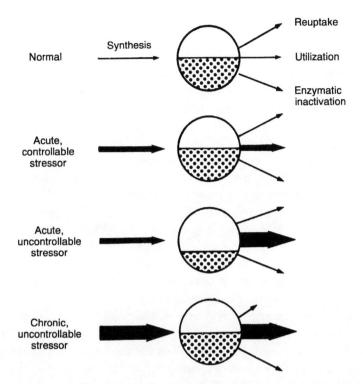

FIGURE 4.5. Neurochemical consequences of controllable or noncontrollable stress. Levels of brain neurotransmitters are usually kept at a constant level that is maintained by a balance between the rate of synthesis and the rate of utilization, enzymatic degradation, and recapture by neurons. In cases of marked stress, utilization increases. This increase remains moderate and is balanced by increased synthesis when the stress is controllable. Conversely, when stess cannot be controlled, the increase in the rate of utilization exceeds the capacities of synthesis and brain concentration of the neurotransmitter falls. In cases of chronic stress, compensation is obtained by a supplementary increase of synthesis and a reduction of recapture (*adapted from Anisman and Zacharko, 1982*).

present in the brain, one can assess the effects of stress on brain function by measuring degrees of behavioral modification produced by drugs that act on precise *neuronal* targets. These indirect techniques are often more sensitive than neurochemistry. They have been used particularly to evaluate the effects of uncontrollable electric shocks on the metabolism of dopamine in the brain. This neurotransmitter plays an important part in the regulation of brain functions. The drug of choice for studying the activity of central dopaminergic systems is amphetamine, a well-known psy-chostimulant that stimulates the release of dopamine from presynaptic nerve endings. Behavioral modifications vary according to dose. With a weak dose the stimulation of motor activity is particularly apparent; stronger doses produce broadly stereotypical behavior. In rodents, this essentially means constant sniffing and mastication for the entire duration of the drug's effect. In rats exposed to three sessions of electric shock that can be controlled by moving from one compartment to another in a two-compartment chamber with an electrified grid floor, stereotypical behavior provoked by the injection of a fixed dose of amphetamine the day after the final conditioning session is less marked than that presented by animals unable to control the shocks, but does not exceed the intensities reached in animals not exposed to shocks[27] (Fig. 4.6). These results indicate that central dopaminergic systems are more heavily tapped in cases of uncontrollable stress than they are in cases where stress can be controlled.

Anisman's group in Toronto and Weiss's in New York have both advanced the notion that changes in the metabolism of brain norepinephrine might be responsible for the reduced motor capabilities in animals exposed to uncontrollable electric shocks. On the basis of this idea, Jay Weiss has recently developed a theory

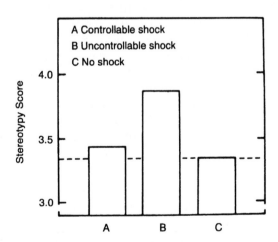

FIGURE 4.6.   Exposure to uncontrollable electric shocks sensitizes the dopaminergic systems. This sensitization is indicated by the intensity of stereotypical behaviors induced by administration of amphetamine to rats that had been exposed the previous day to uncontrollable electric shocks (*adapted from MacLennan and Maier, 1983*).

assigning a key role to the noradrenergic neurons of the locus coeruleus, a nucleus of the brain stem that projects toward the forebrain and the hypothalamus and that contains the principal noradrenergic neurons of the brain.[28] Activity in these neurons is normally regulated by a mechanism of negative feedback in which norepinephrine released into the synaptic cleft acts on the presynaptic alpha-adrenergic receptors to reduce the speed of release. In cases of uncontrollable stress this mechanism is rendered inoperative by increased postsynaptic use of norepinephrine and a sharp decline in concentrations of that transmitter. The absence of any further brake on the activation of neurons in the locus coeruleus and the rapid depletion of norepinephrine stocks that ensues in consequence produce deep behavioral depression (Fig. 4.7).

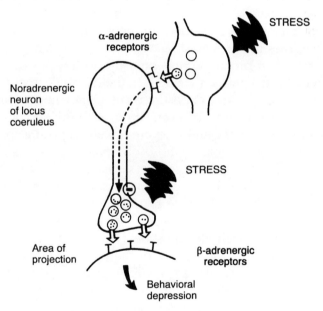

FIGURE 4.7.   Neurochemical mechanisms of behavioral inhibition caused by exposure to uncontrollable electric shocks. The noradrenergic neurons of the locus coeruleus are normally inhibited by the effects of norepinephrine on alpha-2 noradrenergic presynaptic receptors. Under the influence of stress, levels of norepinephrine fall, their inhibiting action is no longer operating, and neurons continue to be activated. Increased presynaptic inhibition, therefore, is translated by an accelerated decline in norepinephrine levels and an increased postsynaptic release of norepinephrine, which encourages behavioral inhibition by acting on beta-adrenergic receptors (*adapted from Weiss and Goodman-Simson, 1984*).

This elegant construction, supported by various pharmacological, behavioral, and electrophysiological data, unfortunately resembles rather too closely a laundry line hanging in a void. On *how* these modifications are produced and on the mechanisms that ensure an articulation between the neurochemical changes and behavior, this scheme remains silent. Furthermore, it is well understood that at the level of a structure like the locus coeruleus, neuronal activity is affected not by one neurotransmitter only but by a balance among several systems of transmitters. Any scheme attributing all the symptoms observed in animals subjected to electric shock to one neurotransmitter is, therefore, illusory. In response to this criticism other models have been proposed that emphasize an interaction among several neurotransmitters.[29]

In terms of brain function, the most important element in cases of uncontrollable stress is not the impact on this or that neurotransmitter but the onset of neuronal sensitization. This term designates the increased reactivity of neurochemical systems while stress is in progress. First exposure to inescapable electric shock provokes significant changes in the metabolism of the neurotransmitters only if that exposure is sufficiently intense and prolonged. But exposure to even a small number of shocks subsequent to a sufficiently severe initial exposure produces modifications comparable to those observed on the initial occasion. Increases of this kind in the sensitivity of neurochemical systems are not observed when shocks can be controlled. Sensitization is such that a complete reaction is launched not only by a small number of reminder shocks but also by simple exposure to cues associated with electric shock. The phenomenon of sensitization is certainly responsible for the performance deficits apparent in shocked animals. It is interesting to note—although this result has not been systematically tested—that these deficits vanish when the air in the cage is scented with an odor other than that breathed by the animals during the course of uncontrollable shocks.[30]

The psychogenic analgesia of the opioid type that is provoked by the administration of uncontrollable electric shock is also affected by sensitization since it reappears after a small number of shocks. But it has no causal role in the phenomenon of interference, since drug treatments that block or reduce it have no systematic effects on the performance deficits that characterize animals exposed to uncontrollable shock.

LOSS OF OBJECT AND LOSS OF CONTROL

Since the earliest days of psychoanalysis, practitioners have stressed the importance to future emotional development of the ties linking a child to its mother or to a substitute object.[31] Separation provokes a reaction that evolves in two phases: a period of agitation marked by cries, tears, hyperactivity, and profound physiological activation; and a withdrawal phase in which the child withdraws into itself, manifesting general depressive behavior and indifference to its surroundings. From time to time efforts have been made to establish a parallel between loss of an object and loss of control.[32] In these schemes, attempts to reestablish contact with the mother constitute a means of maintaining control whereas withdrawal into the self indicates helplessness. This conception is not necessarily highly heuristic. A scheme that categorizes attachment as a form of emotional dependence in effect sees the physiological and behavioral changes that occur when attachment is broken as simple correlates of an emotional reaction. There is no denying the fact that emotions exist and play a powerful part in the construction and maintenance of attachments, as attested by the work of innumerable psychologists.[33] However, excessive emphasis on emotional factors risks obscuring the important effects of other factors.

Recent studies show that the object of attachment produces a whole range of regulatory effects on the physiology and behavior of a child. In the case of squirrel monkeys raised in a social group, deprivation of the mother provokes severe behavioral disturbance and elevated blood levels of cortisol. When the mother disappears, other females in the group assume an interest in the orphan, which is quickly adopted. Contact with the adoptive mother quiets the orphan's agitation but alterations in the infant's physiology continue; the elevated blood level of cortisol that the orphan continues to present disappears only after contact with the real mother is resumed[34] (Fig. 4.8). In monkeys prematurely separated from their mothers and raised with a substitute object—a blanket, for example—the behavioral agitation and increased blood level of cortisol following removal of the attachment object can be returned to normal by furnishing a second substitute that is equivalent and similar to the first: a new blanket or a blanket that has been used by a relative. In this case the attachment is much less specific.

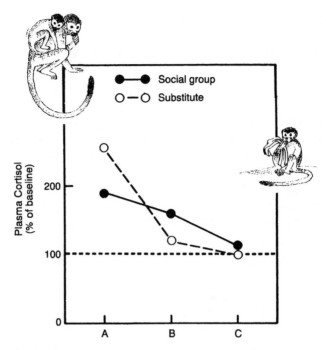

FIGURE 4.8.   Hormonal responses to separation in squirrel monkeys. When the infant is removed from the social group and placed in a separate cage, it manifests a marked elevation of blood levels of cortisol (A). Removal of the mother produces the same consequences, even when the infant is adopted by other females in the group (B). Reintroduction of the mother immediately normalizes hormonal activity (C). Conversely, hormonal response occurs in young monkeys raised by substitutes when the young one is moved to a new cage (A) without the substitute, but there is no response to either removal of the substitute (B) or introduction of a new substitute (C) into the nursery cage (*adapted from Levine, 1980*).

According to the American psychiatrist Myron Hofer, attachment includes biological regulators that are "hidden," that is, not apparent to superficial investigation.[35] Psychoanalysts speak of "organizers," a fundamental concept in which the mother regulates the infant's physiology and this regulation organizes maturation of the child's physiological capacities. The mother and child form a symbiotic union endowed with its own homeostasis. At an individual level, various aspects of the child's physiology are organized by stimuli from the mother: activity of the autonomic nervous system, for example, is conditioned by the amount of milk ingested, the cycle of sleep and waking by the rhythm of feeding times, growth by tactile stimulation, thermoregulation by contact, and sensorimotor development by the vestibular stimulation of being carried in adult arms.

The presence of these regulatory stimuli has important consequences for the child. Rhesus monkeys separated from their mothers and raised alone in cages containing a rocking horse play with this object at regular intervals. In consequence, these animals do not present the abnormal swinging and stereotyping behaviors that are generally observed in solitary animals raised without this toy. Furthermore, when they are tested as adults these monkeys adapt far more readily to new environments and integrate more easily with social groups.[36] Rats subjected to forced immobilization are far more likely than others to develop gastric ulcers if they were weaned precociously.[37] This is not the hyperemotional response initially claimed but, rather, a latent disturbance of thermoregulative capacity.[38]

In their search for explanations as to why infants use objects as replacements—or complements—to stimuli furnished by the mother, psychoanalysts have projected a great deal into the infant unconscious, projections involving both the transitional object described by Winnicott and the precursor-objects and sensation-objects described by Gaddini and Tustin.[39] A transitional object is the baby's own creation whereas a precursor-object is furnished by the mother or forms part of the baby's own body. A transitional object is thought to derive from the intermediate space between the baby's illusion of being a single unit with its mother and its recognition of its own identity. In psychoanalytic terms, a transitional object represents simultaneously both baby and mother, and attaching meaning to this object is the infant's first genuinely creative act. In biological terms, objects of this kind have passive sensory qualities (structure, odor) and active ones (derived from manipulation) and are far more important for their regulation of the child's physiological and emotional processes than for their symbolic value.

Attachment is equally strong in adolescence and childhood. When the attachment is to another person, the relationship is interactive and the couple can be considered a symbiotic unit.[40] With physical objects, the functions of the sensation-object and the transitional object used in childhood still apply. The relationship that builds up during long voyages between a solitary sailor and his boat provides a ready example of the concept of the selfobject. The sailor becomes attentive to the movements and to the very life of his boat, as if the vessel were a well-loved and living friend. He is even reproached by some of his friends for loving his boat more than he loves his wife.

Each of these transactions includes rhythmic factors. Indeed, most of our behaviors and physiological activities are rhythmic; eating, sleeping, body temperature, hormonal secretion, urinary elimination of potassium and calcium—all of these vary throughout the day with a predictable periodicity. Rhythms are regulated by two internal clocks: one controlling the sleep/wake cycle and the other, central temperature and pituitary-adrenal activity. The oscillators regulating these clocks are located in the suprachiasmatic nuclei, a specialized structure of the hypothalamus. These oscillators keep somewhat imperfect time because, left to themselves, their periodicity is circadian, that is, regulated by a 24-hour clock, but with time lags that can be as long as ten minutes. The oscillators are normally synchronized by the alteration of daylight and darkness. Maturation of circadian rhythms occurs during the postnatal period; the rhythmic structure of the infant's activities derive in great measure from the mother. These social influences on rhythm are also found in adults; a shared life synchronizes the rhythms of partners. The part played by social influences is particularly clear when rhythms are de-synchronized; during jet lag produced by transoceanic travel, adaptation to a new timetable is greatly facilitated by social contacts. Subjects enjoying such contacts adapt relatively easily while those who are isolated adapt far more slowly, When separation means the loss of a synchronizer, an individual must acquire new habits. The perceived extent of difficulty in doing so seems to be in direct proportion to the degree of dependence on the other person.

DEPRESSION: A PSYCHOSOMATIC ILLNESS?

Every student of learned helplessness and separation distress has wondered whether these phenomena harbor possible mechanisms for the expression of nervous depression.

Characteristically, a depressed patient exhibits no interest and no pleasure in his daily activities.[41] He feels sad, desperate, powerless, and incompetent. All of his psychomotor activities have slowed down. He feels incapable of concentrating or of making a decision. He is infused with a profound sense of guilt and often claims that he wishes to end his life. This condition affects at least one in every ten people during the course of a lifetime, with a greater frequency in women than in men.

The link between depression and separation distress derives at least in part from a group of common casual factors, whether the issue is one of anaclitic depression, as observed by Spitz in institutionalized infants, or, in the case of adults, of depression as a consequence of grief. A symptomatic description of the apathetic phase or of the detachment despair that follows the initial distress accompanying the breaking of close ties puts greater emphasis on the anxiety and the abnormal behaviors of an autistic kind than on depression *per se*.

The analogy with learned helplessness has been extended even further. It is based on psychological data (the similarity of symptoms),[19] as well as on biological findings (the effects of uncontrollable stress on the metabolism of brain neurotransmitters and the action of antidepressive medication on the same targets).[25,29,30] Nevertheless, the analogy remains highly superficial. We still don't know the exact role of the various neurotransmitters in the behavioral disturbances observed in animals exposed to uncontrollable electric shock nor the precise nature of the neurochemical changes that accompany depressive problems. It is now thought that reduced activity of the central noradrenergic systems is characteristic of depressed patients, although until recently specialists made diametrically opposite claims with great conviction.

After so many years of fruitless effort, one might very well ask whether or not we are on the right track and whether psychological and neurochemical explanations of depression might perhaps be mistaken. In support of such inquiry it should be emphasized that none of the neurochemical theories of depression takes true account of the important sequence of somatic disorders that accompany that affliction. There is, in particular, a profound disturbance of biological rhythms in the form of a de-synchronization between the wake/sleep rhythm and the rhythms of central temperature and pituitary-adrenal activity. Such a phenomenon is sufficient to explain the sleep disturbances that characterize depression, especially insomnia of the predawn hours and changes in appetite and in libido. Moreover, depression is well known to be cyclic; in particular, there is a seasonal depressive syndrome, with remission in summer and fresh attacks in winter, that can be treated by exposure to intense artificial light at the end of the afternoon.

The vegetative disorders that accompany psychic problems are generally thought to be secondary. One might, however, consider the problem inversely and ascribe depression to *chronobiology* rather than to the psyche. A disturbance of circadian rhythms caused by a shift in time zone, circumstances at work, or experiments in living without schedules and customary synchronizers has effects on the psyche that are similar to those observed in cases of depression, although of lesser intensity. These include difficulties in concentration, general lassitude, and reduced motivation as well as sleep disorders. One can readily imagine, therefore, that in some individuals the functioning of coupling mechanisms between the internal clocks might be weakened because of genetic predisposition or developmental problems. A modification of the corresponding neuronal transmissions (i.e., the neurochemical consequences of exposure to uncontrollable stress) or the disappearance of one of the synchronizers (i.e., loss of object) could reveal a latent problem that might amplify the impact of these events on the individual's psyche.

BEHAVIOR IN SITUATIONS OF CONFLICT

How can emotions be regulated when one cannot control the circumstances that produce them? For drivers who are often caught in traffic jams and who lose their tempers easily, a gadget has appeared that is enjoying some popularity. This is a plastic device that can be attached to the dashboard. By pressing a button, the driver releases a cacophonous discharge that suggests a series of exploding grenades or a round of machine gun fire and is accompanied by little flashes of light. This gadget, according to its inventor, allows an irascible driver frustrated by sluggish traffic to discharge his anger against those impeding his progress without inflicting any real harm on anyone. Aggression is quite commonly linked to frustration and is seen as a means of releasing tension. According to the American psychologists Dollard and Miller, "aggressive behavior always presupposes the existence of frustration. Equally, frustration always leads to some form of aggression."[42] However, studies of behavior provoked by frustration, in both animals and human beings, demonstrate the exaggerated nature of this declaration. Aggressive behavior is only one of several possible modalities of response to frustration. Furthermore, when a frustrated individual manifests aggressive conduct, this conduct is not induced but is simply facilitated by the frustration.[43]

In experiments on the relationship between frustration and aggression, frustration is usually provoked by stopping the distribution of food to animals expecting to be fed as a reward for undertaking a particular behavior. The intensity and frequency of aggressive action by animals in this situation can be measured in different ways, according to the species involved and the aims of the test. No limits are imposed on the ingenuity of the experimenters. Aggressive behavior in the pigeon, for example—a preferred species, along with the rat, for experimental psychologists—can be measured by the frequency and intensity of pecks a bird directs at its mirrored image (Fig. 4.9); the pigeon sees the reflection and,

FIGURE 4.9.   Method of studying aggression provoked by frustration in pigeons. When it can no longer obtain grain, a pigeon will begin to peck the mirror at the back of the cage. Movements are imprinted on the mirror, enabling researchers to quantify the intensity of this behavior.

not realizing it is his own, begins to peck it. The difficulty is that he never manages to touch any part of the "other" bird except its beak. Another, more effective, technique involves putting a second pigeon behind a protective screen so that the animal under attack is not harmed. In the case of monkeys, the force of bites on a length of tubing is measured. With human subjects, experimenters measure the frequency and force of pressure applied to a push button or the blows directed against a nonfunctioning vending machine.

In each of these situations, omission of the anticipated reward provokes a more or less intense manifestation of aggression; however, in all cases, aggressive conduct occurs only when the situation includes a certain probability of spontaneous manifestation of such conduct, independent of any frustration. In chickens exposed as couples to grain that they can see but not reach, attacks are by the dominant bird only. In piglets suddenly deprived of food, aggressive conduct occurs only if the animals belong to different social groups and have already displayed spontaneous tendencies of aggression toward each other; conversely, piglets from the same social group confronting deprivation remain calm[43] (Fig. 4.10). With human subjects, the kicks or punches directed at a malfunctioning machine can be interpreted in the same way; shaking up the machine is sometimes enough to get it started, and if such conduct has proved effective in the past, the chances of repeating it on a similar occasion are high.

The energizing effects on behavior produced by frustration have been known since the classic experiments of two American psychologists, Amsel and Roussel, who measured the speed required for rats to negotiate a straight passageway leading to an enclosure containing food.[44] The apparatus used by Amsel included two successive passageways with an exit chamber at one end, an entrance chamber at the other end, and an intermediate chamber between the two passages. During the course of preliminary trials, the rats were trained to explore the entire apparatus. The intermediate chamber contained food only every other visit (partial incentive), and the final compartment contained food every time (constant incentive). Under these conditions, the speed with which the rats ran through the second passageway was greater when the intermediate chamber did not contain food than when it

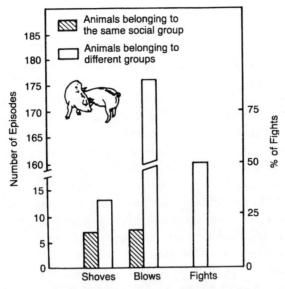

FIGURE 4.10.   Frustration does not provoke aggression but does facilitate its appearance. When two pigs are placed in the same cage, each of them having learned to activate a switch for a reward of food, there are few manifestations of aggression if the pigs belong to the same social group. But if, conversely, they come from two different groups, a considerable increase in shoving and kicking and even a real fight can be observed. The animals confront each other in a shoulder-to-shoulder posture, each trying to bite the other in the region of the head and shoulders (*adapted from Arnone and Dantzer, 1980*).

did. It seemed that the frustration provoked by the absence of food in the intermediate chamber induced the animal to run through the second passageway with greater vigor.

The preceding phenomena were not simply laboratory curiosities. Ethologists[45] have long been fascinated by the striking actions undertaken by wild animals confronting situations of conflict. A blackbird threatened by an intruding bird prepares to attack but suddenly stops to furiously peck at leaves scattered on the ground or to preen its feathers. Such reactions are not uncommon in animals oscillating between attack and flight.

Within the widely diversified range of conflict behaviors there are several categories which can be distinguished by their modes of expression:

- Redirected activities: behavior appropriate to one of two or more conflicting drives is displayed but is directed toward an object other than the one that initially provoked the conflict (e.g., a blackbird's pecking at the leaves on the ground or an employee's anger discharged at a member of his family instead of at the boss with whom he argued at work)
- Displacement activities: behavior that seems to belong to a repertory different from that of the competing drives (e.g., a sudden grooming of feathers that interrupts a bird's preparations for attack or head scratching by a person who finds she can't say precisely what she means)
- Intention movements: gestures that are normally displayed when the animal is provoked are begun but not completed, remaining frozen at an intermediate stage
- Ambivalent behavior: behavior that combines the motor elements of opposite activities
- Sexual inversion
- Regression to activities characteristic of the juvenile phase
- Freezing

Under perfectly controlled laboratory conditions, one can study the mechanisms of conflict behavior and the significance of various redirected and displacement activities. Exposure of food-deprived animals to an intermittent distribution of food constitutes one highly effective and practical way of conducting such a study. Food is offered every minute on the minute but in minuscule quantities, a situation designed to produce intense frustration and tension, particularly in the very hungry. If the animals are given something to do while they wait, for example, drinking or chewing on a piece of wood or a length of chain, this available behavior becomes compulsive. Thus, a rat with access to water can drink an amount equal to a third or a half of its own weight in the course of a few hours (Fig. 4.11). This conduct is called "adjunctive" to indicate that it occurs as an adjunct to the normally motivated behavior incited by the circumstances.[46]

One can also demonstrate adjunctive behavior in human beings in situations that produce periods of anticipation alternating with brief periods of activity. Games and problem solving are typical situations for the occurrence of adjunctive activities. Behavior most frequently observed includes addictive smoking, compulsive

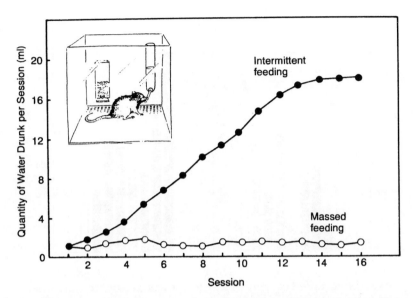

FIGURE 4.11   Development of psychogenic polydipsia in rats. Exposure to intermittent distribution of food (a pellet every minute) produces an inordinate consumption of water. This pattern disappears if the animals are given the same quantity of food in a single serving at the start of the session (massed food).

hand motions (e.g., tearing paper and fiddling with the scraps), drinking, and eating[47] (Fig. 4.12).

SENSATION SUBSTITUTES FOR AFFECT

Situations of conflict in which displacement activities or redirected behavior occurs provoke marked physiological arousal, which can be quantified by various behavioral or physiological indicators. For example, Killeen, an American psychologist, has shown that the development over time of locomotor activity in pigeons exposed to intermittent feeding conforms to the theoretical model of cumulative arousal engendered by the situation[48] (Fig. 4.13).

Behaviorists find the idea of cumulative arousal attractive; they often use it to explain the onset of motivated behavior. An internal need (in this instance, hunger) involves a state of tension that slowly increases until it is strong enough to trigger an appropriate

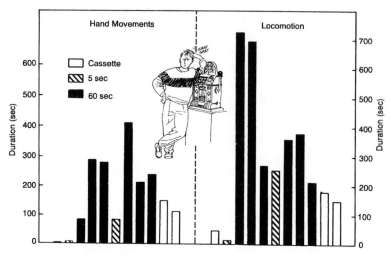

FIGURE 4.12.   Examples of adjunctive activities in a subject obliged to
listen to a prerecorded cassette or able to earn money by working a penny
machine that is functional every 5 or every 60 seconds. The subject must
remain standing during the 30-minute test. When the machine's interval is
60 seconds, the frequency of hand movements (drumming with the fingers, scratching, tearing paper, rubbing the face, passing the fingers
through the hair) and locomotor activity is far greater than when the
interval is 5 seconds or when the task is listening to the cassette (*adapted
from Wallace et al., 1975*).

response (seeking and finding food). Such a response satisfies the
initial need and relieves tension, after which everything returns to
normal until the next time. The physical analogue of this situation
is the hydraulic model of motivation proposed by Lorenz[49] (Fig.
4.14).

This conception is simplistic in that it disregards both the complexity and the diversity of motivated behavior. Nonetheless, it
strongly colors ideas about the finality of action strategies. Traditional ethologists have posited that an individual in a situation of
conflict, unable to perform the actions toward which he is motivated, must find a palliative in order to liberate, if only to some
extent, his pent-up motivational energy. Similarly, the Norwegian
psychologist Holger Ursin claims that behaviors provoked by a
threatening situation are effective if they result in a reduction of the
arousal produced by the situation.[50]

In the case of displacement activities, the dissipation of accumulated energy by an alternative activity is not the only possible

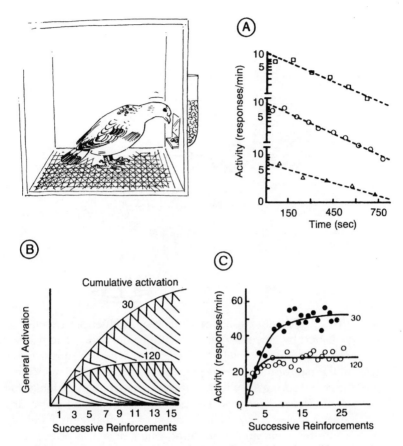

FIGURE 4.13.   General accumulation of arousal induced by intermittent distribution of food to starving pigeons. Starved pigeons are placed individually in a cage designed to register motor activity; a small amount of grain is given at the beginning of their time in the cage. Figure A shows a reduction of activity by three pigeons over a period of time that follows distribution of grain. When grain is offered every 30 seconds, there is no time for the arousal induced by the presentation of food to dissipate. Such arousal therefore must accumulate from one moment to the next, following the theoretical model illustrated in B. The phenomenon is less marked when the interval is 120 seconds. Figure C shows results obtained during the experiment and their conformity to the theoretical model shown in figure B (*adapted from Kileen, 1975*).

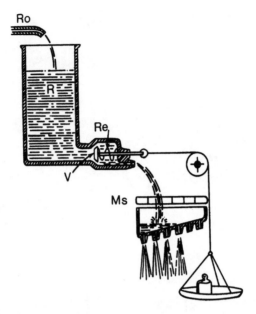

FIGURE 4.14.   Hydraulic model of motivation. Influenced by internal stimuli represented by faucet Ro, reservoir R fills gradually. The water it contains represents energy available for action. When the pressure of releasers on the pan of the scales is great enough to counterbalance the power of the coiled spring Re, which corresponds to the central inhibition of behavior, the sluice, V, opens. The gushing water has an energizing effect on behavior selected by a combination of internal stimuli and objects present in the environment and functioning as a selection mechanism Ms (*adapted from Lorenz, 1950*).

mechanism. An English ethologist, David McFarland, has shown that one activity might replace another through the use of two basic mechanisms: competition and disinhibition.[51] The example of a driver on a highway, torn between wanting to make the fastest possible time on a tank of gas and the necessity of stopping from time to time in order to empty his bladder illustrates the idea; since driving is normally given priority, the optimal strategy would be to use stops for gas as opportunities for emptying the bladder as well. This disinhibition, however, might be replaced by competition if the driver's bladder—or that of any passenger—is not amenable to such precise control. In that case, refueling the car every time the bladder is relieved might not be a practical option. In either case, the alternation between the two opposing behaviors can be described by the fluctuation of their causal factors.

Using McFarland's model for how time might be divided between activities, one can readily see how exaggerated activities can occur in circumstances of frustration or conflict. Such activity is not called on to dispel the tensions produced by frustration; producing sensations that permit the individual to direct his attention away from the provocative circumstance is enough. The intensity of this activity should reflect its effectiveness in producing distracting sensations.

A similar idea was proposed by the American psychologist John Staddon to explain the diversity of behavior observed in the interval between food deliveries in circumstances of intermittent supply.[52] The diverse behaviors can be grouped into three broad categories (Fig. 4.15):

- Interim activities, which correspond to the adjunctive activities already described and which occur just after food distribution, at the moment when the probability of further food is the weakest
- Terminal activities, which occur most frequently at the end of the interval, when the probability of food delivery is increasing
- Facultative activities, which occur roughly at the midpoint of the interval, when the probability is low that behavior from either of the other two categories will occur

In animals with simultaneous access to a feeding trough, a water bucket, and an exercise wheel, drinking immediately after food delivery is an example of interim activity, running in the wheel is a facultative activity, and exploring the contents of the feeding trough is a terminal activity whose frequency increases as the time for resupply of food draws near. In Staddon's opinion, each activity corresponds to the animal's "mood." When the animal is drinking or running on the wheel, it disregards stimuli associated with food; however, when the interval between instances of food delivery draws to an end, such stimuli become a unique preoccupation.

If the substitution of sensations for affect has some consequence in situations of conflict, one should be able to detect physiological or hormonal effects, provided the sensory stimuli are not

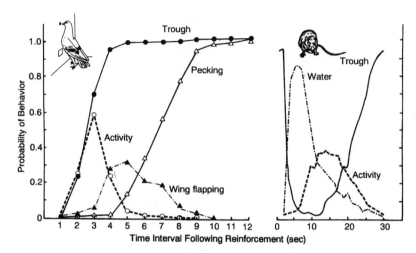

FIGURE 4.15.   Division of time between various competing activities. The left-hand schema shows as a function of time the evolution of the probable manifestation of various activities in a pigeon exposed to deliveries of grain at intervals of 12 seconds. Immediately following receipt of food, the pigeon begins to move restlessly and to flap its wings. As the interval draws to a close, these activities yield to a series of pecks at the feeding trough. When a rat receives a pellet of food every 30 seconds, the animal licks the tube leading to the water bottle immediately after swallowing the food. Then, if there is still time, the rat makes a tour of the cage—and will even run in an exercise wheel if one is provided—before returning to further investigate the feeding trough at the end of the interval (*adapted from Staddon, 1977*).

in themselves overly arousing. Many experimental results support this view. Pairs of rats, for example, that are given electric shock and are engaged in displaying aggressive behavior toward each other present a weaker pituitary-adrenal activation than rats exposed to shock in solitude[53] (Fig. 4.16). Likewise, hungry rats that drink excessive quantities of water when fed only intermittent and inadequate portions of food present reduced blood level of corticosterone at the end of the experimental session whereas in those animals exposed to the same conditions but without the opportunity to drink, the level rises.[54]

Only a few studies have been done on the functional consequences of displacement activities in humans, but the available findings are extremely interesting. For example, many people jiggle their legs when they sit down, a move whose frequency in-

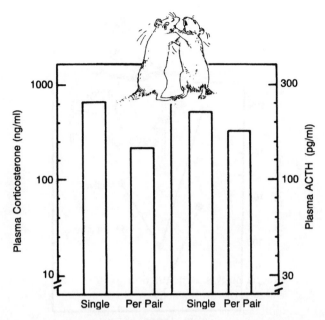

FIGURE 4.16.   Influence of displacement activities on physiological arousal. Rats shocked in pairs engage in aggressive behavior and respond to electric shock with a smaller increase in circulating concentrations of ACTH and corticosterone than do rats that are individually shocked.

creases as the subject's disquiet grows. One of my colleagues frequently manifests this tic; he is also very afraid of flying. I once sat beside him during a plane trip, and our row of seats shook from the vehemence of his movements during takeoff and landing!

Under more rigorously controlled conditions Soussignan and Koch have shown that frequency of leg swinging by primary school children, six or seven years old, increases when the teacher obliges them to sit still for lessons in arithmetic, reading, or writing. These movements are accompanied by reduced cardiac rhythm, although one would normally expect a heightened cardiac rhythm because of the muscular activity[55] (Fig. 4.17).

Another example of displacement activity is provided by babies sucking a pacifier. (The term itself indicates the calming influence this accessory has on infant behavior). A Swedish biologist, Kirsty Uvnas-Moberg, has shown that the use of a pacifier has far from negligible effects on the infant's circulating levels of gastrointestinal hormones; somatostatin increases while insulin and gastrin diminish. This hormonal profile reflects the predominance

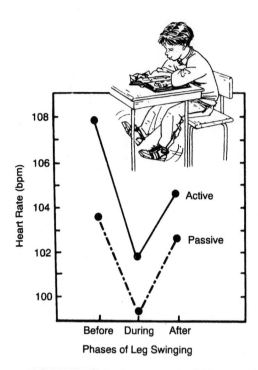

FIGURE 4.17.   Influence of displacement activities on physiology. Stereotypical leg swinging in children is accompanied by diminished cardiac rhythm, whether or not the children participate actively (active) or passively (passive) in scholastic activities (*adapted from Soussignan and Koch, 1985*).

of the parasympathetic nervous system over the sympathetic, makes possible better gastrointestinal assimilation of nutriments, and favors the growth and maturation of the digestive tract.[56]

According to these findings, engagement in an activity that yields sensations or fresh perceptions permits arousal engendered by conflict situations to be reduced, even if the activity deployed has no effect on the provocative circumstance itself. Precisely what mechanisms are used is not yet known; perhaps the physiological system participating in the activation is inhibited, or perhaps there is competition in information processing by the brain, especially if sensation prevails over affect. Despite these inadequacies, one can understand why some activities occur more readily than others, and one can also identify the risks of pathological deviation. In an environment in which intrinsic stimulation is relatively scarce, the best way to create sensation for oneself is to engage in activities that stimulate bodily sensory receptors. In view of the sensory importance of the oral sphere, it is scarcely surprising that a major proportion of displacement behavior is devoted to chewing, licking, and sucking. The incidence of such activity is higher in the young than in mature animals. In human subjects one would expect to frequently encounter activities that involve the hands. Other productive activities are swinging, which stimulates the vestibular apparatus, and locomotion, which stimulates the proprioceptive afferences that innervate joints and muscles.

The risks attached to such regulatory processes are far from negligible. If a subject has access to artificial means of creating sensation, he will be tempted to use them and will succumb all the more readily if he is encouraged to do so by the social environment. Here we encounter one aspect of drug addiction. The other risk—to which we shall return in the next chapter—is the development of habits, or tics.

TO CONTROL AND TO ANTICIPATE

In daily life one must anticipate events in order to have any kind of control. Finding oneself at the beginning of a weekend with an empty refrigerator is an exceedingly unpleasant experience; so is reaching the end of the month without enough money to pay the gas and electricity bills!

Experiments in the importance of prediction in stress reactions compare the behavior and physiological reactions of animals subjected to painful electric shocks that are delivered at regular intervals, or preceded by a warning signal, with those of animals receiving shocks that are similar but delivered at random or in the absence of a warning signal.

Animals able to make a choice between a situation in which shocks are predictable and one in which they are not spend more time in the first situation than in the second. It seems that foresight is preferable to uncertainty. Psychologists have made considerable efforts to explain this phenomenon, with theories involving security,[57] the reduction of uncertainty,[58] or preparation for action.[59] Each of these theories explains an aspect of foresight; this one deals with all these aspects simultaneously.

Unlike behavioral data, which ascribe a net advantage to foreseeable events, physiological results are a great deal more confused. Exposure of laboratory animals to electric shock delivered without warnings or predictable patterns may, depending on circumstance, be accompanied by circulating glucocorticoids at levels that are elevated, reduced, or unchanged in relation to levels in animals exposed to the predictable condition. And the same can be said of weight loss or the incidence of gastric ulcers.

These results are not necessarily contradictory. Physiological arousal depends not only on the manner in which a subject experiences the events (foreseeable or not foreseeable) to which it is exposed but also on the efforts made to deal with the situation when events are predictable.[60] Confronting an event is less difficult than maintaining an alert posture toward an equally dreaded situation in full knowledge of when the ax will fall. It's another version of the tale of the Gauls who were afraid of only one thing: that the sky would fall on their heads. Since any occurrence of that event is highly uncertain, it does not constitute enough of a threat to interfere with a wholehearted devotion to normal life. The story would be quite different if it were known with certainty that the sky would fall at the next full moon.

At an individual level, the effects of foresight on an organism are not solely a function of the available information. Another important factor is the tendency to seek (or, on the contrary, to refuse) information: some people try to amass as much knowledge as they can about what lies ahead, while others systematically refuse information, preferring not to know and perceiving knowledge as a profound handicap.

A visit to the dentist provides an ideal example of this kind of distinction. Some patients wish to know every detail of what the dentist is doing, with a running commentary on how matters are progressing, while others limit themselves to opening their mouths, hoping they can shut them again as soon as possible.

Some psychologists think that a subject's capacity for distraction is the important factor. That a lack of capacity in this regard is a disadvantage is indicated in a study of women undergoing colposcopy (visual examination of the cervix) and cytologic examination of the cervical smears, a standard examination to check for cancer of the cervix[61] (Fig. 4.18). Before examination the women were divided into two groups, classified according to whether sub-

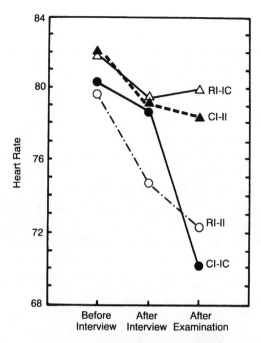

FIGURE 4.18.   Influence of defense strategy and of information received on physiological arousal measured at different stages of a medical examination. Before the examination patients are divided into two groups: those refusing information (RI) and those who want to know what will be done to them (CI). Reaction to the examination is registered by heart rate measured before and immediately after the pretest information session and again after the examination itself. The information supplied gave a detailed description of how the test would proceed (complete information, IC) or was confined to the general principles on which the examination was based (incomplete information, II). Women refusing information were able to relax only when they did not know what lay in store for them (group RI-II). Conversely, women who wanted information about what would be done were adversely affected when this information was withheld (group CI-II) (*adapted from Miller, 1980*).

jects were likely to ask for information or preferred to think of other things. Some patients in each group were given a step-by-step explanation of the examination to be performed, while others received a deliberately trivial questionnaire. It was noted that patients who had sought the most information were the least relaxed during the examination and the most depressed before, during, and after it. Precise information on diagnostic methods and on how the examination would proceed diminished the reactions of these patients but intensified those of patients in the second group.

Beyond the individual dimension, this work demonstrates that the arousal produced by difficulties encountered is not uniform over the course of time. For individuals who use available information to better confront a situation, arousal is more important before than during or after confrontation. Variations of this kind are apparent in animals as well as human beings. Rats subjected to a daily regimen of compulsory swimming in cold water will, after a few sessions, manifest increased blood levels of glucocorticoids as soon as they enter the room where tests are held. Conversely, these levels fall at the end of the test[62] (Fig. 4.19). These hormonal variations suggest that when an event is entirely predictable, animals are capable of using available cues to prepare themselves for confrontation and to relax their tension when the challenge has passed.

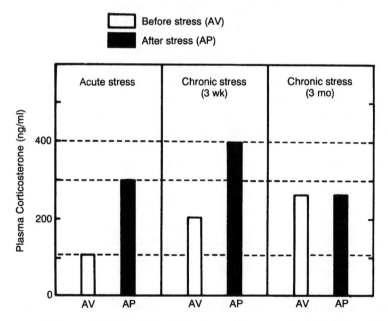

FIGURE 4.19.   Effects of prediction on pituitary-adrenal activity. Rats exposed to temperatures of -20°C five days a week for three months manifest elevated blood levels of corticosterone in anticipation of stress and, compared to variations noted three weeks before experiment began, reduced response at the end of the session (*adapted from Burchfield et al., 1980*).

TOLERANCE

Rats leading an otherwise monotonous life in their home cage recognize that the arrival of a lab assistant in a white smock and transfer to a room with particular smells and sounds mean a series of unpleasant experiences of limited duration. Given the aptitude of animals to anticipate events on the basis of available information, this is not in any way extraordinary. A dog that capers about the room at the sight of its master preparing to take a walk is a familiar example.

This phenomenon is not as trivial as it might seem to be. In Canada, Siegel and his collaborators habituated rats to repeated injections of heroin, always given in the same laboratory. In the case of heroin, repeated injections usually produce a weakened reaction, which pharmacologists call "tolerance."[63] This tolerance is demonstrated by the fact that rats previously treated, unlike most untreated ones, are not killed by the effects of an elevated heroin dose. At the dose level used in the test, the mortality rate for untreated animals was 97%, as opposed to 32% for those that had developed a tolerance for heroin. However, the most important finding from Siegel's study showed that rats made tolerant but tested in a different room from the one in which they were given the heroin presented a mortality rate of 64% instead of 32%[64] (Fig. 4.20).

These data show that some of the tolerance developed by animals in response to repeated injections of heroin is affected by context. The term *behavioral tolerance* is used to distinguish it from classical pharmacological tolerance. The same phenomenon can be observed in treatments involving various other substances, such as alcohol, psychostimulants, and even hormones like insulin. To establish these facts, student volunteers in one of Siegel's studies each drank a liter and a half of beer in an hour and a half for four consecutive days. On the fifth day some of the volunteers were given the usual dose of beer and were left in the usual room for the usual period of time; others were given the usual dose in the usual time frame but were moved to a new room. In both groups, tests subsequently measured reaction times and cognitive capabilities. Subjects tested in an unfamiliar environment registered notably stronger reactions to alcohol than did those whose environment had not been changed.

The phenomenon of behavioral tolerance, therefore, is not an

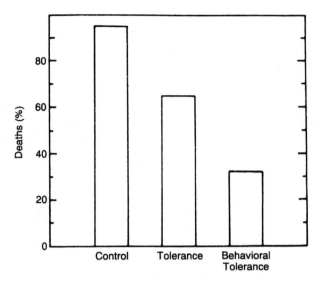

FIGURE 4.20.   Behavioral tolerance to toxic effects of heroin. After consecutively stronger heroin doses, rats are protected against toxic effects of a very strong dose—but only if the dose is administered in the same environment used for the previous treatments. The role of context in the pharmacological effects of medication and drugs defines behavioral tolerance (*adapted from Siegel et al., 1982*).

artifact. It is, however, difficult to interpret, and different theories collide when they attempt to explain it. Siegel's explanation postulates a subject's progressively stronger association between an environment and the effects of treatment received there. The conditioning he envisions is equivalent to that of Pavlov's dog—repeated exposures to the ticking of a metronome before delivery of a bowl of meat led the dog to associate that sound with meat and to salivate when it heard the ticking. In the case of behavioral tolerance, the environment in which treatment is normally administered becomes associated with the treatment's predictable effects; the subject adapts to or prepares for those effects by a compensatory response that will counter them. This compensatory response is specific, occurring only in the presence of stimuli associated with a particular treatment, just as Pavlov's dog had a salivary response to the sound of a metronome but not to other sounds.

This interpretation makes it possible to predict the conditions necessary for the development of behavioral tolerance. Thus, if tolerance is due to conditioning, one should be able to extinguish it by subjecting subjects to an extinction procedure, that is, by exposing them to an environment associated with the effects of treatment but without treatment. This is indeed what happened when the animals in the heroin experiment already cited were subjected to several injections of physiological saline in surroundings previously associated with the effects of heroin.

Let us consider for a moment the case of heroin and other drugs. These substances, if Siegel is correct, produce a phenomenon of behavioral tolerance due to the development of a conditioned compensatory response. And these compensatory responses are analogous to the withdrawal symptoms that replace euphoria when the active effects of a drug come to an end. Siegel holds that the withdrawal symptoms experienced by an addict placed in circumstances associated with the effects of a drug are the consequences of a compensatory conditioned response. Need for any particular drug arises because of this conditioning; consumption of the drug puts an end to the withdrawal symptoms. Addicts, therefore, are caught in a vicious circle whose single escape route requires a strict avoidance of circumstances that are similar to those that launched their addiction.

The possibility of such a relationship between behavioral tolerance and dependency provides an explanation for the widespread interest in that tolerance. Siegel had no hesitation in claiming that the example of heroin-tolerant rats tested in surroundings other than those in which the addiction developed could explain some cases of human death by drug overdose; that injection of a drug in unfamiliar surroundings would, in effect, be fatal for any addict who had developed a strong tolerance for it.

Further elaboration of this aspect of behavioral tolerance is not possible here. Siegel's hypothesis is only one of several possible explanations of dependency. Furthermore, it has the advantage of drawing attention to the various inevitable conditionings that occur between the rituals of drug taking and their effects, which include direct effects and withdrawal symptoms. These conditioning phenomena have been observed in human beings under rigorously controlled conditions and thus do not represent laboratory artifacts.[65]

Siegel's theory emphasizes the part played by conditioned compensatory responses in the development of both tolerance and dependency but does not advance our understanding of why such responses occur instead of conditioned responses analogous to

those produced by treatment. How can one explain Pavlov's observation that his dogs salivated on hearing the sound of a metronome that preceded injections of morphine (the conditioned
response in this case is analogous to the salivating response initiated by an injection of morphine) when, according to Siegel, they
should have salivated less than usual when placed in the environment associated with those injections?

Two Canadian researchers, Eikelboom and Stewart, have proposed an ingenious theory for demonstrating how a conditioned
response can sometimes oppose the effects of treatment[66] (Fig.
4.21). In their view, a drug is not the equivalent of a classic unconditioned stimulus like food because the effects of medication
are not directly perceived by the sense organs. If the treatment
alters the functioning of a physiological system regulated by the
nervous system, these changes will produce a counterreaction
aimed at reestablishing the essential balance that has been dis-

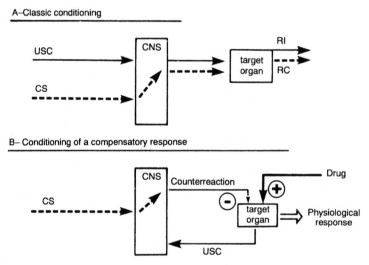

FIGURE 4.21.   Schema proposed by Eikelboom and Stewart to explain
why some medications provoke compensatory conditioned responses
that oppose their unconditioned effects. In the case of a medication acting
directly on a peripheral target organ the unconditioned stimulus (UCS) is
the perception by the central nervous system (CNS) of variations in the
state of this organ and the unconditioned response (RI) is the counterreaction reestablishing the initial state. The conditioned response (RC) provoked by the conditioned stimuli associated with the effects of medication
(CS) is therefore opposed to the effects of treatment.

turbed. In this case, the unconditioned response is not the direct effect of treatment on the organism but the reaction taken by the organism to correct the disturbance of which it is the object. Thus, the hypothermia induced by morphine would produce a compensating hyperthermia. This interpretation has the advantage of being testable; if the compensatory conditioned responses are in effect, one should be able to objectify them by exposing the subject to the situation associated with the effects of treatment but without those effects. But this is not the case, and it is very difficult, even impossible, to prove the hyperthermia or hyperglycemia previously mentioned.

How can behavioral tolerance be explained if there is no compensatory response? Some psychologists believe that an appeal to mechanisms that counter the effects of surprise is enough.[67] In his novel *Chronicle of an Announced Death*, Gabriel Garcia Marquez indicates to us, beginning on the first page, that the hero, Santiago Nasar, will be assassinated on the feast day celebrating the arrival of the bishop. This enables him to leisurely develop his extraordinary description of social relations in the small South American city that is the scene of the action while his readers are spared the troubling possibility that Nasar might escape the destiny that fate is weaving for him. An expected event is not surprising because it is the object of a mental representation even before it occurs. If the circumstances of the actual event are analogous to those anticipated, the consequences will be small; if, on the other hand, there is discord between expectation and reality, the reaction is amplified.

A first experience of the effects of treatment by medication can be surprising, as those taking hypnotic or anxiolytic drugs for the first time and suddenly experiencing their effects surely know. Repetitions of treatment can produce habituation; but this is not an automatic result[68] because, with some medications, this depends on the context in which the drug effects are tested. The whys and hows of such phenomena are not yet known.

Should one act or reflect? Human beings have always pondered the links between thought and action. Roger Martin du Gard made that subject one of the principal themes of his romantic narrative series *Les Thibault*. The two brothers are in opposition, essentially because of differing ideas about action. Jacques believes in acting in conformity with his ideas while Antoine tends to let life take its course.

Confronted by the diversity of means available to individuals for coming to grips with the difficulties of life, psychology for a long time remained impressionistic and incapable of reducing the complexity. Things began to change when it noticed that this complexity was subject to some elementary rules that hold that an organism has a need to master the events to which it is exposed, to act rather than submit, and to know rather than remain in ignorance. If an individual can effectively control a situation and if the necessary effort for achieving control is not too great, these attempts will have long-term beneficial results. Conversely, if control is difficult and the subject is unable to confront his problem, he will rapidly enter into a state of passivity that risks negative psychological and physiological consequences should the situation fail to improve. In both these cases, the attitude adopted for confronting the situation determines the mode of physiological response to it. In optimal conditions one would expect the coping strategy chosen by the subject to be adaptive, that is, to involve a lesser physiological arousal than that initially provoked by the stressor. Conversely, if the effort needed to control the situation is too great or can be controlled only with difficulty, physiological arousal should remain high.

This conceptualization is extremely appealing and has been quite successful in the hands of stress experts. Unfortunately, it has been understood for quite a while now that the idea of arousal is too simple to describe adequately an organism's reaction to its environment. The American psychophysiologist John Lacey has been one of its most vehement critics. Using a series of studies done principally on such indicators of arousal of the autonomic nervous system as heart rate and cutaneous conductance (an indirect indication of activity of the sweat glands that is the basis for the famous lie detector), Lacey showed that the important factor was not a hypothetical arousal but the attitude of the subject toward the situation: When the subject refused to acknowledge the situation, heart rate increased; conversely, when the subject accepted it and tried to obtain as much information as possible, heart rate diminished. This conception, however, is refuted by other writers, who claim that the dichotomy preached by Lacey reflects nothing more than the connection between the workings of the heart and the muscle activity of the subject.[69]

Let us leave these controversies to theoreticians. Describing the consequences of coping strategies in terms of arousal was a basis for identifying factors that determine the efficacy of those strategies. Wanting to go further without considering the multiplicity of reactive mechanisms an organism has available is equivalent to watching current television programs on an old black and white set. It can be done but it is not necessarily very instructive with respect to the chromatic richness of the world around us. At present there are enough elements for us to realize that the diversity of possible coping strategies corresponds to a whole range of physiological concomitants. The question is, How can we determine the possible associations between these two kinds of reactions? There are two ways to address this issue. The first is to determine the consequences of a given coping strategy on an individual's physiology; the second is to investigate how different individuals adapt to a given situation. It is this second approach that we shall now develop, because it gives greater emphasis to the individual variability that characterizes coping strategies.

THE MISFORTUNES OF INDIVIDUALITY

There are four basic types: the cretin, the imbecile,
the stupid, and the mad. Normality is
a balanced mixture of all four.

—UMBERTO ECO, *Foucault's Pendulum*

Popular belief clings firmly to the notion that several personalities coexist in each human being and define individuality by their more or less harmonious combination. A normal person inevitably lives his life in good health and dies of old age. An abnormal person, conversely, brings down on his own head all the ills of creation. Therefore, the ability to distinguish between normal and abnormal is all that is required for an accurate assessment of the pathological destiny of each and every person. In psychosomatic tradition, individuality determines vulnerability to specific illnesses.

For any reasonable test of that proposition, one must be able to characterize individuality by objective and verifiable methods. As the failure of psychosomatic medicine amply demonstrates, the answers supplied by traditional psychology are inadequate. But to conclude that there is nothing to gain from such an approach would be overly hasty. Evidence of important individual differences in coping strategies has given rise to new hopes. These differences, in turn, lead the way into the tangled jungle of the interrelationships between individuality and pathology.

THE PSYCHOLOGICAL APPROACH

For several decades psychiatrists have been refining a series of tests to define personality. These consist, essentially, of projective tests and of inventories presented as self-administered questionnaires.

The best-known projective test is the Rorschach, named after the Swiss psychiatrist who first proposed it.[1] It is said that when Rorschach was walking in the countryside with his family, he noticed that his children's descriptions of cloud shapes corresponded closely to their personalities. As it is difficult to standardize clouds, even in Swiss skies, Rorschach thought of using ink blots instead and asking patients what they perceived in them.

Projective tests pose serious problems of interpretation and reproducibility, and we already know that they can easily lead to illusory correlations.

The Weight of Discourse

Personality inventories are usually constructed in the form of a self-administered questionnaire. Subjects must reply to a series of assertions on various aspects of their beings, from physical condition to mental attitudes and social conduct. Answers are limited to "true" or "false" or "don't know." The test most frequently used is the *Minnesota Multiphasic Personality Inventory,* developed by American psychiatrists in the 1940s to facilitate the differential diagnosis of mental problems. Another personality inventory widely used in Europe was developed by Eysenck, at the Maudsley Institute in London.[2] The Maudsley inventory focuses on two dimensions: the introvert/extrovert dimension, which reflects tendencies to avoid or to seek out external stimulation, and the neurotic or impulsive/stable dimension, which expresses the temporal character of reactions to the environment. Four personality types are defined as follows: impulsive extrovert (choleric), stable extrovert (sanguine), impulsive introvert (melancholic), and stable introvert (phlegmatic) (Fig. 5.1).

To give these categories more of a biologic coloration, the English psychologist Jeffrey Gray tried to establish a correspondence between the personality categories defined by Eysenck and sensitivity to reward and punishment.[3] For Gray, individual behavior is the product of a dialectic between a tendency toward action, which is influenced by reward or stimuli associated with reward, and a tendency toward self-inhibition, which is influenced by punishment or signals associated with it. Neurotics make exaggerated responses to both reward and punishment, introverts are hypersensitive to punishment signals, and extroverts are hyperreactive to signals associated with reward. Consequently, the behavior of introverts is modified by punishment more readily than by reward whereas the opposite is true for extroverts. If one replaces the two dimensions defined by Eysenck with an anxiety axis measuring sensitivity to punishment and an impulsiveness axis measuring sensitivity to reward, Eysenck's neurotic extrovert becomes Gray's *impulse-driven subject* while the anxious person is a substitute for

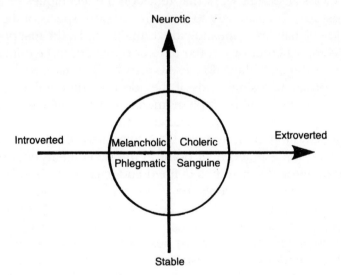

FIGURE 5.1.   The dimensions of introversion/extroversion and stable/ impulsive defined by Maudsley's personality inventory. An individual's personality is represented by a point in space determined by his position on each of the principal axes. Although it is tempting to seek similarities with Hippocrates' four temperaments, the Maudsley system distinguishes mainly pathologic personalities.

Eysenck's neurotic introvert. Those who haven't followed this argument needn't worry; Gray's scheme raises no doubts about the fundamentals of Eysenck's classification but is, instead, a set of variations on a single theme.

These personality tests have been widely accepted. Their current use by respectable and respected agents, whether psychologists or psychiatrists, tends to obscure two fundamental problems: the reality of the personalities so defined and the validity of the measurement scales, which are based directly on psychopathological features.

The Arbitrariness of the Method

The anxious, the impulsive, the choleric; the terms are expressive. We think that we know what they mean, and we therefore readily accept a system of classification using that terminology. The categories thus defined regroup in a totally arbitrary fashion the psychic and behavioral characteristics of various subsets of the population that was used to establish the classification. This is the work of a statistician, work that relies on the techniques of factor analysis. As it is customary to measure various aspects of the supposed personalities of the individuals under study, the first point to establish is whether or not the different tests do, in fact, measure the same thing. If they do, results can be summarized by their projection along a single axis; if they do not, the number of axes must match the number of phenomena in play. The axes of independent phenomena are perpendicular to each other; for clarity of representation, two or, at most, three axes are used. Each individual is then represented by a point in the two-dimensional or the multidimensional space thus defined and is characterized by projections of that point along the various axes (see Fig. 5.1). The definition of each axis is done *a posteriori* and is totally subjective; projecting the calculated measures along that axis involves conceptualizing what the factor that best explains the extremes of the population under study corresponds to. Concretely, this means that the introverted type does not exist: like the intelligence quotient, introversion is entirely defined by the way in which it is measured!

Personality tests also incorporate the major flaw of being based on pathology. No one would dream of describing the various modes of normal respiration in terms of the respiration of patients suffering from bronchitis or pneumonia or some other respiratory diseases. That, however, is what psychologists do when they use tests expressly developed to expose pathological personalities.

DIFFERENCES IN STRATEGY:
PASSIVE AND ACTIVE

Given the approximate and arbitrary character of the various psychological methods of approach, considering how each individual reacts to stress might make more sense. This reaction, as we have seen, occurs through the activation of a limited number of coping strategies, which involve a close link between a behavioral response and its corresponding physiological correlates. The simplest model incorporates two elementary and opposing strategies: attempts to maintain control, which are associated with activation of the sympathetic nervous system and the adrenal medulla, and resignation, associated with pituitary-adrenal activation (Fig. 5.2). This reactive dichotomy, pitting active against passive, was proposed in 1977 by James P. Henry at the University of Southern California, Los Angeles, in a remarkable synthesis of biological, social, and psychological data on the relationship between stress and illness.[4] Various strategies can be adopted in various situations

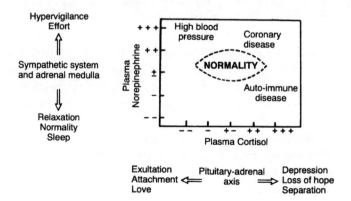

FIGURE 5.2.   Two-dimensional space opposing emotions associated with activation of the pituitary-adrenal axis to those associated with activation of the sympathetic nervous system and the adrenal medulla. Note that pathological risks occur when leaving the zone of normality (*adapted from Henry, 1986*).

by the same subject, or by different subjects, according to the subjects' attitude toward maintaining control.

Most studies of the active/passive dichotomy consider individuals whose mode of reaction (which psychologists call a trait) is determined primarily by the situation. Thus, when healthy volunteers are exposed to experimental situations in which they have to avoid electric shocks or to earn a monetary reward, they present, in the total absence of any physical exercise, a sympathetic reaction of a beta-adrenergic character, with accelerated heart rate and increased systolic pressure.[5] This sympathetic activation corresponds to the dimension of effort described in Sweden by Marianne Frankenhaeuser.[6] This dimension expresses the degree of involvement in a given task as well as the tension and concentration required for it. According to Frankenhaeuser, the dimension of effort associated with a sympathetic activation is balanced by a dimension of distress (understood in the sense of "dystress," as proposed by Selye) that corresponds to a subject's degree of dissatisfaction, boredom, impatience, and irritation and is associated with pituitary-adrenal activation.

As a function of his position in the two-dimensional space delineated by vectors representing effort and distress, a subject can move from the stage of effort without distress, corresponding to active control, to that of effort with distress, corresponding to thwarted control, or to a stage of distress, corresponding to lack of control. This model offers the advantage of being applicable to individual behavior in the workplace. Over the last 20 years Frankenhaeuser's research group has collected a great deal of data, covering various socioeconomic groups, that shows that one can link hormonal activity (measured by blood levels of cortisol and urinary excretion of catecholamines) to working conditions (e.g., demands imposed by the workplace, mental strain, imposed vs. chosen rhythms) (Fig. 5.3).

Such models are not only descriptive but predictive as well. If the appropriate physiological measures are taken, the predictions indicated can be tested on the spot. Thus, for motivated employees subjected to heavy work loads, the best way to alleviate symptoms of physical and psychic stress, while maintaining equal output, is to permit the worker to exercise his initiative, instead of requiring him to maintain a passive role.

In addition to its usefulness in defining roles, the active/passive dichotomy can also be helpful in discerning differences be-

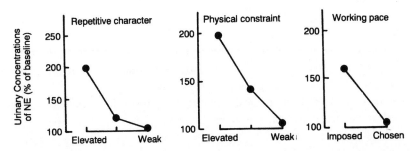

FIGURE 5.3. Influence of constraints imposed by the workplace on urinary excretion of norepinephrine in sawmill employees (*adapted from Frankenhaeuser, 1980*).

tween individuals. A factor analysis of the physiological and psychological reactions of parachutists at the time of their first jump from a training tower highlights two principal axes: an axis of active control, associated with sympathetic activation, and an axis of passive control, corresponding to the predominance of intrapsychic defense strategies over strategies of action and associated with activation of the pituitary-adrenal system.[7] A third axis associated with the testosterone factor is also prominent, but its significance is less clear and may correspond to the subjects' image of their own social status (the virile self-image of paratroopers!).

THE RIGID AND THE VERSATILE

The distinction just made between active and passive is not in itself enough to characterize an individual. To be more complete, one would have to anticipate what that individual would do in other circumstances, or in the same circumstances but at another time. The variability of strategies over time is a second criterion used in classifications. Confronted by particular circumstances, some individuals quickly develop a strategy to which they cling, even when circumstances change. Others are more versatile, changing strategies without hesitation, even when they have been successful.

Passive Mice and Aggressive Mice

Several experimental studies support a passive versus aggressive categorization. The most important work to date on individual variations in aggression, using laboratory rodents, was done by behaviorists at the Department of Animal Physiology at the University of Groningen, in the Netherlands.[8] As a function of their behavior toward an intruder crossing a territorial boundary, animals are classified as aggressive or passive.

In the case of mice, researchers used genetic selection based on that criterion to establish two inbred lines: one of aggressive animals and the other of passive ones. Under normal circumstances mice will only attack male strangers intruding in their territory. If the intruder is a familiar fellow or a female or if the encounter occurs in a new environment, the probability of attack is low. Aggressive mice, on the other hand, bred through genetic selection, no longer present these inhibitions. They vigorously attack all others, regardless of sex, familiarity, or place of encounter. Is this a sign of aggressiveness? Or is it a lack of sensitivity to those external stimuli that, in principle, modify behavioral expression?

A Delicate Balance

Individual behavior at any given instant is the product of interaction between two categories of factors: extrinsic factors, which initiate behavior and then guide it to fulfillment, and intrinsic factors, which organize that behavior during execution. The relative importance of each category of factors varies according to experience and circumstance; the playing of a novice pianist is far more affected by external stimuli than the playing of a seasoned virtuoso. Carrying out a behavior successfully requires the ability to pursue the corresponding activity to conclusion without being sensitive to interruption. And to achieve that ability the behavioral system in question (already referred to as a motivational system) must comprise a certain level of self-organization and the ability to inhibit other interfering activities. A hungry animal in search of food risks trouble if he stops to court a member of the opposite sex. In spite of that, behavior must preserve a certain degree of plasticity; confronting a threat that arises during a search for food may necessitate a change of plans, namely, a momentary abandonment of that search. And devouring a piece of rotten meat instead of the preferable fresh kill requires a sense of when to stop, in order to set out once again in search of something better. If, for one reason or another, this delicate balance is disturbed, this balance between a necessary sensitivity to external events and the mechanisms of self-organization, rigidity or flexibility will occur.

Sprinters and Loiterers

If the exaggerated attack behavior of so-called aggressive mice derives from a reduced sensitivity to external factors, this characteristic should also affect behavior other than aggression. Indeed, when mice are trained to find food at the end of a maze, "aggressive" animals run more quickly, as if they were paying less attention to other factors. If a researcher drops a scrap of paper at the end of a maze, these mice will keep on running as if nothing had happened. So-called passive mice, on the other hand, stop to sniff the new object before proceeding on their way, and, having yielded to distraction, they are subsequently disoriented rather more often than their single-minded peers (Fig. 5.4). In the same way, if one reorients the maze at a right angle to its initial position, so that the location of external points of reference used by the animals for orientation is changed in relation to the maze itself, the more passive mice make more mistakes than the others.

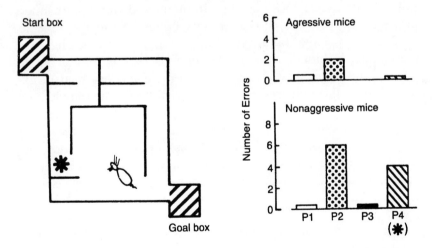

FIGURE 5.4.   Behavioral differences in a maze in mice bred for aggressiveness. When the animals have acquired some familiarity with the maze (P1), the device is turned 90° to alter the position of external reference points (P2). When the maze has been returned to its normal position (P3), a scrap of sticky paper is dropped on the course (P4). At each of these changes, the less aggressive mice are more seriously disturbed than the aggressive ones (*adapted from Benus et al., 1987*).

Differences of the same kind occur without any training. If the cycle of light and darkness is reversed, mice, which are nocturnal animals, require a certain amount of time to adapt themselves to the new lighting conditions and to reverse their rhythm of activity. For aggressive mice, this adaptation takes much longer than for the passive ones, as if the former were actually less sensitive to extrinsic factors of behavioral regulation.

Drinking Without Thirst

When animals are in situations of conflict or are in a state of frustration, their reactions demonstrate the importance of the balance between intrinsic and extrinsic factors. We have seen that when very small quantities of food are intermittently distributed to food-deprived rats, the animals will drink if they can find any water in the experimental cage. Not all rats do develop this behavior; however, in those rats that display it, drinking develops over time and is gradually manifested by identical behavioral sequences that are repeated in each interval between the food distributions. To drink, animals must lick a tube connected to a nursing bottle filled with water. At first, these lickings are infrequent and varied in manner. After several sessions, however, rats begin licking the tube as soon as they have eaten, and they continue this licking in a mechanical fashion for some ten seconds before setting out to explore the cage; finally, they head for the feeding dish in expectation of the pellet of food that will follow. The activities of the animals that do not become polydipsic are far more eclectic. They take a drink—but only from time to time—whereas their polydipsic companions are such prisoners of habit that they will drink any liquid that might be substituted for pure water, for instance, water fortified by alcohol or by quinine, which is how alcoholic rats are produced for studies of the effects of alcohol on behavior.

Other tests indicate similar differences between individuals. In the 1960s at the University of Michigan, Elliot Valenstein demonstrated that electrical stimulation of the lateral hypothalamus produces a condition of undifferentiated arousal in which, depending on the object present at the time, an animal will drink, eat, attack a congener, or mount a female. Once again, not all animals respond to stimulation in the same way. Some quickly focus their excitement on whatever object is present; others react in a more disorganized fashion. Those that drink in response to stimulation of the lateral hypothalamus also develop polydipsic behavior when intermittently fed.[9]

THE TRAPS OF RIGIDITY

It is not uncommon to see caged animals in zoos incessantly repeating gestures and activities. Bears rock back and forth or shake their heads, holding their forepaws widely separated, stepping in place as if to some sort of rhythm. Hyenas circle their cage for hours whereas other animals pursue invisible ellipses or figure eights. Birds nod their heads unceasingly or peck at imaginary objects. These repeated movements without any apparent aim, whose form and orientation remain relatively constant, are called stereotypies[10] (Fig. 5.5).

The catalogue of stereotypies in animals is not infinite, although the form of these activities can vary a great deal. They can be divided into two major categories, locomotor and oral. In human subjects stereotypies are common in several mental illnesses; before the introduction of neuroleptics, such stereotypies were among the most constant symptoms of schizophrenia.

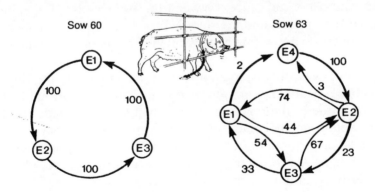

FIGURE 5.5.   Sequential descriptions of chewing stereotypies in confined sows. Figures correspond to the probability of transition from one element of the behavioral sequence to the next. The stereotypy for sow #60 is uniformly predictable (E1 = chewing the chain; E2 = licking the railings; E3 = chewing with an empty mouth) while the behavior for sow #63 is a great deal more variable (E4 = following the chain, without chewing it) (*adapted from Dantzer, 1986*).

Animals and Humans

For a long time the mechanisms by which stereotypies are expressed were poorly understood, because researchers often explained these signs by interpreting them symbolically. Here, for example, is an account of the behavior of an institutionalized schizophrenic. The patient usually went into the garden before meals, stood by the entrance for a while, and then walked back and forth for nearly half an hour.

> The door symbolizes for the patient a route to liberty, her sole stereotypical idea; the sole association the door expresses is return to the house. Because the large iron gates can be opened, they have for the patient a positive affective value. At the same time, this door—almost always closed—constitutes an obstacle that prevents the patient from realizing her objective, which is flight. The closed door therefore also has a negative value. The patient, who is seriously catatonic, reacts toward these opposing "values" with an affective tension that translates into movement. The stereotypical "back and forth" provoked by the door symbolizes her desire to escape, which in turn unequivocally demonstrates her ambivalent situation.[11]

Although many authors have noted a concordance, troubling in its symbolic significance, between the stereotypies of confinement in zoo animals and the stereotypies seen in human patients, practitioners do not normally draw on the first set of stereotypies to explain the second. The first group of symptoms, in fact, occurs only in captivity, that is, in an abnormal environment, and disappears once the animals are returned to their natural surroundings. And by virtue of the dualistic concept that leads to a radical separation between the brain and its product—both behavior and thought—one cannot draw on the normal functioning of the brain in an artificial environment to explain the abnormal functioning of another brain in normal surroundings.

Mechanical Animals

Yet the most detailed study of stereotypies in domestic animals, particularly pigs, indicates that the dual concept is unfounded; the stereotypies of confinement affect the functioning of the brain and permanently alter its properties.

On many commercial farms, sows are confined for the entire period of gestation; they are kept in collective or individual pens on a rationed diet that covers only their basic needs. Since the food is distributed in concentrated form, meals are rapidly consumed. The animals, therefore, are faced with hours in which there is nothing to do whereas in their natural state they spend most of their time snuffling and burrowing their snouts into the ground in search of something to eat. In the conditions of confinement that characterize commercial farms one can observe in a certain percentage of the animals oral stereotypies whose intensity increases with the length of confinement. The character of these stereotypies also varies with an animal's age. At first, when a sow chews or licks, she turns to the objects that surround her: railings, manger, drinking trough, chain. Then she gradually begins to chew or lick without any object. When the sow is moved, or gives birth, these stereotypies decrease, reappearing at their former level when the animal returns to the brood house after weaning and fresh impregnation.

The Brain Is Implicated

In these standardized conditions, one can verify the fact that stereotypical activity begins the moment the animal is introduced into the system (Fig. 5.6). If one lists the various activities in which a sow might engage from one moment to the next in the environment she is confined to, one can observe the progressive reduction of her behavioral repertoire to a few activities that will constitute the foundation for the stereotypical behaviors. These activities are manifested before or after the single important episode in the animal's daily life: the distribution of food. Later, when the stereotypy is fully developed, these activities will also occur at moments of intense excitement—as, for instance, when strangers visit the

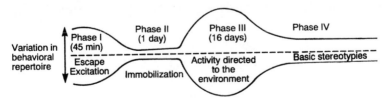

FIGURE 5.6.   Development of stereotypies in sows in their second pregnancy but tied up for the first time (*adapted from Dantzer, 1986*).

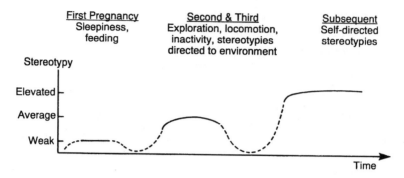

FIGURE 5.7.   Exaggeration of stereotypies in confined sows during successive pregnancies (*adapted from Dantzer, 1986*).

breeding pen. Stereotypical activities anticipating the distribution of food habitually extend to activities related to eating in general, whether these be chewings and lickings of the manger, aggressive gestures toward other sows, or efforts to catch the slop bucket or food wagon as these proceed past the animal. Stereotypies that occur after feeding initially incorporate objects, such as chains, bars of the cage, or drinking trough, but their expression deteriorates in proportion to the length of time the animal stays in the system.

One can demonstrate that stereotypies do not remain purely external but are accompanied by a gradual modification of the possibilities of brain functioning. If this were not true, if the brain did not retain some trace of stereotypical functioning, an animal returned to an abnormal environment would repeat every stage of the stereotypy's development. However, stereotypies recur at the levels that previously characterized them, and their subsequent development proceeds from that level (Fig. 5.7). Stereotypies therefore affect brain function and modify the brain in the sense that there is greater cognitive rigidity and a predominance of intrinsic factors in the organization of the animal's behaviors, characteristics already noted in the aggressive animals previously described.

AGAIN, SENSITIZATION

Why do some animals present stereotypical behavior in confinement while others remain indifferent to their surroundings? If we could understand what distinguishes them, we would have a better grasp of the biological foundations of rigidity and flexibility. It is, a priori, easier to analyze this from stereotypies than from aggressive behavior, since the determinants of the first activities must be simplier than those of the second.

The first clue in this inquiry is provided by the analogies that exist between stereotypies of confinement and those produced by psychostimulants administered in increasingly large doses. Amphetamine, perhaps the best known of these drugs, was widely used in the 1950s to facilitate performance and prevent drowsiness, before it was discovered that it could lead to abuse and could provoke true psychotic episodes in some individuals.

In animals, small doses of amphetamine stimulate locomotor activity. With larger doses, elementary movements are constantly repeated. These, for the most part, consist of chewing or licking or sniffing, defined as simple vertical and horizontal oscillations of the muzzle. The stereotypies of confinement, like those induced by amphetamines, are not arbitrary; their expression incorporates components of the dominant activity in any given situation.

To illustrate this idea, let us consider the case of a rat put into an unfamiliar cage whose cylindrical wall is pierced with holes that are too small to allow for escape. Under normal conditions the rat would explore this space by following the contours of the wall and poking its nose into each hole before passing along to the next one. After a weak dose of amphetamine, the rat's movements accelerate but their sequence does not change. With a somewhat stronger dose, the animal will explore only two or three holes. And when *that* dose is increased, it limits itself to one hole into and from which it repeatedly inserts and withdraws its muzzle, as if it no longer had time for the other holes. With a stronger dose still, the rat remains fixed in front of one hole, making truncated gestures with its head, up and down and to the right and left, but it does not put its muzzle in the hole.

This seems to suggest that under the influence of amphetamine the behavioral sequence accelerates in a space–time ratio that is itself compressed.[12] Thus, components of the sequence requiring the most time inexorably vanish. That is, the initial activity becomes fragmented, and the only behaviors that remain are those that require the least time. This phenomenon is almost identical to the previously described behavior in pigs, where the time frame necessary for development of the phenomenon was based on months instead of minutes. Nervous excitation produced by motor activity is not nearly so effective as that produced by amphetamine!

Psychiatrists are extremely interested in stereotypies. Depending on the school of thought, they regard amphetamine-induced stereotypies either as animal models of schizophrenia or, more modestly, as equivalents to the amphetamine psychoses observed in human subjects.[13] Since amphetamine induces behavioral changes by releasing brain dopamine and since this neurotransmitter is directly or indirectly implicated in schizophrenia, discussions of this subject inevitably include the validity of the dopaminergic theory of schizophrenia.

The description of stereotypies given here is not at that level. Stereotypies themselves are extremely diverse in their origins; they are as readily observed in schizophrenics as in autistic children, children blind since birth, and the mentally retarded. They certainly reflect a syndrome of cerebral dysfunction attributable, in these cases, to the brain's inability to process incoming information in any coherent fashion. The possibility therefore is small that stereotypies correlate with any specific group of cerebral neurons using any specific neurotransmitter. The fact that amphetamine-induced stereotypies are due to the effect of amphetamine on well-defined dopaminergic neurons in the brain does not necessarily mean that a functional anomaly of these neurons is responsible for the onset of non-amphetaminic stereotypies. However, one might very well use activity of these neurons as a way to assess the state of excitation of the brain of individuals exhibiting stereotypies.

In fact, when amphetamines are used to test the reactivity of dopaminergic neurons in animals, subjects that have developed stereotypies display a heightened behavioral response to the amphetamine challenge (Fig. 5.8). This phenomenon of sensitization can be observed in many different experimental situations. Rats that are made polydipsic by exposure to intermittent delivery of food, rats that eat or drink in response to electrical stimulation of the lateral hypothalamus, and rats that engage in oral behaviors when their tails are pinched are in the same way hypersensitive to amphetamine.[14]

There is a symmetrical relationship between behavior and sensitization since sensitization produced by repeated doses of amphetamine, especially under laboratory conditions, hastens the development of chewing and licking activities in response to electrical stimulation of the hypothalamus.

These results are important because they indicate that rigid

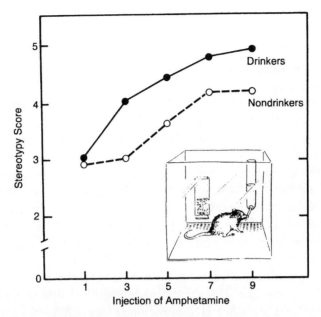

FIGURE 5.8.   Influence of oral displacement activities on the functional activity of brain dopaminergic neurons. Note that during the course of treatment rats that drink display greater sensitivity to amphetamine than those that do not (*adapted from Mittleman et al., 1986*).

individuals have sensitized neuronal systems. And, as seen in the previous chapter, neuronal sensitization is one of the consequences of exposure to uncontrollable stress. Rats exposed to inescapable electric shocks display a greater number of stereotypies in response to amphetamine challenge than do those exposed to controllable shocks.

SENSITIZATION EXPLAINS ALL AND THE REST

Sensitization is a general phenomenon and is not limited to dopaminergic neurons or psychostimulants. Electrical stimulation for some tens of seconds of certain areas of the brain like the amygdala, a structure involved in the regulation of emotions, produces only small effects (or none at all when the shocks are weak); during the passage of current a rat scarcely blinks. But if this stimulation is repeated regularly on a daily basis, neuronal activation will take place with increasing ease, first throughout the amygdala and then throughout the entire brain. After some ten days a general conflagration occurs (some writers use the term *kindling*), which produces a generalized convulsive crisis. Simultaneously, the animal's behavior changes; it becomes irritable and hard to handle. The modification of neuronal excitability produced in this way is permanent; animals tested several weeks after the experimental sequence ends present generalized epileptic seizures at the first electrical stimulation.[15]

Although mechanisms of sensitization in vertebrates[16] are not yet understood with any precision, there is some grasp of how analogous mechanisms function in invertebrates. The preferred subject of study for marine biologists is the *aplysia*, a marine snail conveniently equipped with a relatively small number of large, well-identified neurons. A retractable siphon extends from the external respiratory orifice of the aplysia. If one touches this siphon, the snail simultaneously retracts both siphon and gills. Repeated stimulation rapidly produces habituation; the intensity of the response diminishes and ultimately disappears. Conversely, if the experimenter sharply taps the head of the aplysia, the intensity of the withdrawal reflex of the gills when touched shows considerable increase, as if cutaneous stimulation had become painful.

The withdrawal of the gills by the aplysia involves a simple neuronal circuit (Fig. 5.9) consisting of three categories of neurons, whose cellular structures are all located in the abdominal ganglion. There are 6 motor neurons innervating the muscles of the gills; 24 sensory neurons that innervate the cutaneous surface of the siphon and make monosynaptic connections with the motor neurons; and interneurons, 1 inhibitory and 5 excitatory, which modulate the intensity of the reflex. For the aplysia, the effects of a strong noxious stimulus to the head are transmitted to this circuit by facilitatory neurons that augment the effectiveness of transmission within the circuit. These neurons establish what neurobiologists call "presynaptic connections" on endings of sensory neurons on motor neurons and excitatory neurons.

Eric Kandel and his colleagues at Columbia University have elucidated the molecular mechanisms of this facilitation of neuronal transmission. In particular, Kandel has shown that neuronal transmission is accompanied by changes in the conformation of the channels that permit the passage of potassium ions through the

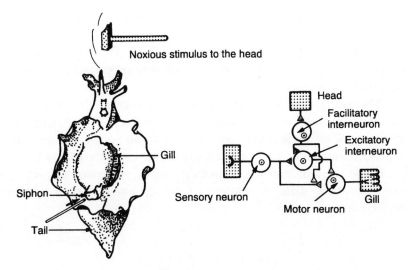

FIGURE 5.9.   Neuronal circuit involved in the sensitization of the gill-withdrawal reflex in aplysia (*adapted from Kandel, 1983*).

neuronal membrane and by morphologic changes at the level of the synapses.

In a lecture given at Yale University in 1982 for an audience of psychiatrists, Eric Kandel, whose work in invertebrate cellular and molecular biology is considered worthy of the Nobel prize, expressly compared the sensitization of the gill-withdrawal reaction in the aplysia to chronic clinical anxiety, claiming that the mechanisms of sensitization and of anxiety are the same.[17]

In the same vein, the American psychiatrist Robert Post argued that the kindling provoked by chemical or electrical stimulation of the brain could explain manic-depressive psychoses.[18] Seymour Antelman, in the psychiatry department of the University of Pittsburgh, after studying the neurochemical mechanisms of amphetamine sensitization in rats that compulsively rip and tear with their teeth anything they can reach when their tails are pinched, developed a theory of stress applicable to depression, anxiety, schizophrenia, obesity, and immune system disorders.[19]

Although the desire to explain everything by sensitization is not always sound, the enthusiasm of researchers is understandable. They feel that they have found a plausible biological explanation for vulnerability to mental and somatic illnesses. Experimental studies of laboratory rats show that amphetamine sensitization, the best-known instance of sensitization at the present time, varies according to characteristics of the animal (individual, sexual, and genetic), environmental factors, and exposure to controllable versus uncontrollable stress. Sensitization can also result from positive feedback from the sensorimotor stimulation produced by performance of the stereotypy itself.

The studies we have described unquestionably demonstrate that the processes of sensitization are capable of modifying the efficiency of synaptic transmission in the brain and, consequently, of conditioning the state of excitation and reactivity of the brain. But in the present state of knowledge these processes still represent more of a *deus ex machina* than an actual explanation of illness.

THE PANIC ATTACK

Without any warning, some persons may experience a sudden sense of smothering, accompanied by tachycardia, palpitations, trembling, sweating, and alternating hot and cold flashes; they also have the impression of a splitting of the personality. Confronting such symptoms for the first time, subjects who think of themselves as already at the point of death are seized by intense panic. Fortunately, the duration of such crises rarely exceeds some 10-odd minutes. Nonetheless, persons experiencing them are deeply affected, especially since a subsequent medical examination usually reveals nothing abnormal.

Episodes like this can end at this point but very often recur, at increasingly frequent intervals. Subjects rapidly develop a secondary anxiety, either diffuse or specific, directed toward events or situations associated with the panic attack and perceived as threatening. Fear of a new acute anxiety attack in full view and knowledge of the general public is so strong that subjects will scrupulously avoid any situation in which security is felt to be less than absolute. This can, of course, mean all public places or confined spaces (elevators, trains, stores, airplanes). Subjects afflicted by these anxieties present what specialists call *phobias*. Thus, agoraphobia corresponds to the fear of being alone in an unfamiliar space. In that situation and in the absence of physical or moral support, the agoraphobic patient may well experience a fresh attack.[20]

Those who have experienced several episodes of this kind live in a state of permanent apprehension. From then on, the fear of fear is so strong that subjects regress affectively and intellectually. In their efforts to surmount these difficulties, patients turn to self-medication, even to alcohol. Typically, there is no consultation with a psychiatrist, the doctor of mental disorders, until several years have elapsed. And by that time the patient's personal and social situation has been seriously and adversely affected by the illness.

Panic attacks are not exceptional. They affect nearly 3 percent of the adult population of the United States and produce a recognized pathology in roughly half of these cases. Initial episodes occur in adolescence or among young adults. Women seem to be affected far more often than men.

Biological Predisposition

The importance that American psychiatrists ascribed to panic attacks provoked a great deal of comment during the 1970s, as if the subject were a new one not previously identified. Without entering the quarrels of the various schools of thought that are passionately followed by many psychiatrists, it is nonetheless necessary to concede that the protean nature of panic attacks has undoubtedly led to the identification of different pathological entities depending on the particular symptoms manifested. In the space of a century, panic attacks have traveled throughout the body—beginning with the cardiovascular system, rising to the head, and then sinking down again to the parathyroids and the intestines. During this game of yo-yo, the medical vocabulary has been enriched by terms like Krishaber's cerebrocardiac neuropathy, Da Costa's irritable heart syndrome, Westphal's agoraphobia, pre-Freudian neurasthenia, Freud's anxiety neurosis, neurocirculatory asthenia, spasmophilia, and irritable bowel syndrome.

In all of these cases, the most remarkable phenomenon, at least for the psychiatrist, is the profoundly biological character of panic attacks. A panic attack is a specific experience that occurs in subjects possibly predisposed to such events as part of the aftermath of a period of difficulty. But identifying in these patients events that are objectively more important than those experienced by the general population is not, in fact, possible, and although there is no shortage of explanatory hypotheses, the basic biological phenomenon of these attacks is not yet understood. The possibility of a subclinical somatic pathology that becomes overt on the occasion of some hyperactivity of the autonomic nervous system is often mentioned—perhaps a mitral valve prolapse; an attack of *angina pectoris;* intestinal spasms; or, closer to the brain, a hypersensitivity of chemoreceptors in the brain stem (chemoreceptors are specialized nerve cells that control breathing by responding to variations in the content of carbon dioxide in the blood).

Identification of these factors of individual predisposition would represent an important advance toward understanding the pathophysiology of panic attack. But this objective is made extremely difficult by the progressive intervention of retroactive processes that add to the original trouble. Such processes involve interoceptive conditioning phenomena and avoidance behaviors.[21]

Retroactive Anxiety

The somatic symptoms experienced by patients during panic attacks are associated with the anxiety itself, so much so that an onset of these symptoms for any one of a number of reasons—a moderate episode of anxiety, for example—is, through generalization or the snowball effect, enough to initiate a complete attack episode (Fig. 5.10). The most striking illustration of this phenomenon is provided by the possibility of artificially inducing a state of panic in

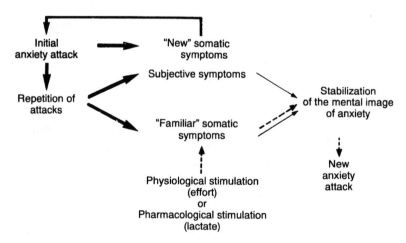

FIGURE 5.10.   The association between somatic symptoms and subjective symptoms of anxiety in panic attacks.

the laboratory in patients, by means of stimuli as diverse as muscular effort, hyperventilation, or the injection of lactate, caffeine, or epinephrine. In each of these cases the resulting physiological symptoms resemble those of spontaneous attacks, and their perception by patients leads ineluctably to a subjective state of anxiety or anguish.

There is nothing unusual about a phenomenon of this kind. Although emotions have long been categorized as purely cognitive, it is now clear that the mental representation of an emotional experience includes motor and visceral components as well as cognitive ones. The intensity and the paroxysmic nature of an anxiety attack are in fact the only peculiarities. These might originate in sensitization affecting the neuronal systems implicated in fear. In view of our previous comments on the strong contribution made by uncertainty and the lack of control to the onset of sensitization, the possibility that a first experience of panic would produce such a phenomenon is not surprising. Sensitization would favor the repetition of attacks, which by itself would reinforce sensitization.

However, a form of pseudoequilibrium may develop if the subject is able to prevent a repetition of attacks by means of a behavioral adjustment. Thus, a person who carefully avoids situations he incorrectly or correctly indentifies as anxiety-provoking, surrounds himself with a protective world in which he finds himself with the impression of control (since uncertainty favors affective judgments at the expense of rationality). So long as this behavior is not challenged by some unanticipated attack or external event (as, for example, when a company employing an office worker who has a phobic fear of elevators decides to move to new quarters on the 50th floor of the Tour Montparnasse in Paris), the sensitization that originated with the first crisis will dissipate, and the probability of a relapse will diminish. Avoidance behavior is thus functionally effective, which suffices to ensure its persistence.

For many psychiatrists such an analysis is heretical. For the heterogeneity of anxiety disorders observed in practice it substitutes a unitary concept that postulates an apparently common biological vulnerability to the anxious and depressive states that the process of sensitization, which has already been described, reveals and amplifies. But this hypothesis, seductive though it may be, cannot claim to provide a total explanation. Instead of launching into impassioned controversy, it is wiser to try and understand what the components of sensitization are and what are its consequences for neuronal function, efforts that are the object of several ongoing studies.

THE FRAGILE HEART OF STRIVERS

In the late 1950s two American cardiologists, Meyer Friedman and Ray Rosenman, provided an explanation of coronary illness that, one might say, hit the jackpot: "We feel that a complex of emotional reactions which we categorize as Type A behavior is the principal cause of coronary illness." In a book written for the general public, *Type A Behavior and Your Heart*,[22] Friedman and Rosenman describe their disenchantment with the standard cardiological practices of the day and the generally ineffective nostrums proffered to patients (avoid animal fats and cholesterol, increase consumption of unsaturated lipids, exercise, give up smoking). Participating in yet another study on the importance of diet, this one comparing the consumption of cholesterol and animal fats by office employees with that of their wives (who seemed to present a reduced risk of coronary disease), Rosenman and Friedman were struck by a repeated comment made by the wives about their husbands: "It's not what they eat that matters; it's the pressure they're under at work." This refrain triggered a thousand memories of patient complaints about the daily problems of life—and reminded them of the upholsterer's comment when the chairs in the waiting room were redone: "You must have an odd bunch of patients; only the edge of the seat shows any wear." The rest of the account is a sequence of attempts to demonstrate that the typical candidate for a myocardial infarct tends to "engage in more or less constant struggle to obtain from his surroundings an unlimited number of objectives as quickly as possible, despite whatever obstacles may lie in his path, including the active opposition of other people in the same environment." This behavior, known as Type A, is the quintessential product of a society that establishes confident, dynamic, ambitious, and aggressive behavior as a model to be emulated. Not everyone is equally apt to conform to this model; the incidence of Type A behavior depends on the interaction between certain individual characteristics and the environment (Fig. 5.11).

FIGURE 5.11.   Type A and Type B behavior and the risk of heart disease.

A Correspondence Recognized Early . . .

Type A individuals present several prominent characteristics. They all intend to accomplish whatever task they have set for themselves and to make progress despite any difficulties that may lie in the way. They are driven by a sharp sense of urgency and are notably lacking in patience; in short, they are workaholics who trample unhesitatingly on family life to accomplish whatever goal they have set for themselves, a drive made all the more urgent by a general conviction held by each of them, namely, that he or she is the only one capable of doing the job properly. Type B individuals, conversely, confront every challenge with placid nonchalance. It seems that persons belonging to Type A are driven by an imperious need to control every contingency.

To claim association between Type A behavioral characteristics and coronary risk is not in itself particularly original; the annals of psychosomatic medicine contain ample documentation of this fact. But Friedman and Rosenman's work had the merit of probing beyond the anecdotal quality of standard psychosomatic studies and attempting to prove the association using the methods of epidemiological research. To achieve this proof they needed an instrument for measuring the behaviors of both the Type A and the Type B person.

To assess a subject's ambitions, competitiveness, hostility, and sense of time, Friedman and Rosenman used structured interviews conducted by trained researchers. Questions focused on the subjects' reactions to various inconvenient situations: sleeping late because one didn't hear the alarm clock, being caught in a traffic jam, waiting for an appointment because the other party is late. Some of these questions were carefully formulated to elicit from interviewees either impatience, manifested by a tendency to answer before a question has been formally completed, or hostility in response to deliberate provocation. As an element in these exchanges, an interviewer would freely accuse a subject of cheating if it seemed that he always had the goal of winning whenever he indulged in sports or played games.

But this kind of structured interview perfected by Rosenman and his colleagues is not the only available method for identifying Type A behavior. A self-administered questionnaire elaborated by Jenkins, a psychologist, can also be used, although it is less reliable.

. . . and Proved During the Seventies

Many epidemiological studies conducted with these instruments show a strong association between Type A behavior and coronary disease.[23] The Western Collaborative Group Study (WCGS), for instance, in the late sixties and early seventies followed over three thousand men in good health, aged 39 to 59, for eight and a half years. Two-thirds of the 7 percent who developed myocardial infarcts were Type A, one-third Type B, a result that corresponds to a risk factor of 2, independent of other factors such as arterial hypertension, tobacco use, or obesity. A second study using coronary arteriography confirms that Type A people have a greater number of coronary lesions.

Classification of individuals as Type A or Type B is not, of course, enough in itself to determine who is or is not at risk of developing an infarct. In any given population some 30 to 70 percent are Type A. More detailed studies on the relationship between Type A behavior and coronary risk show that factors like age, sex, and occupation are also important. Furthermore, not all characteristics of type A behavior have the same effect; the association between characteristics and disease is most pronounced in regard to a competitive spirit and hostility.

A recent review of the body of studies on the relationship between the Type A profile and coronary risk reveals two interesting trends:[24] First, the importance of this association seems to be lessening, since it was less marked in the 1980s than in the 1970s and 1960s. There are several possible explanations for this development. After initial enthusiasm for the importance of Type A behavior, there emerged a more critical attitude toward it. As a result, negative results are now published more readily whereas they would previously have been imputed to methodological error. Nor do negative results necessarily contradict the initial theory. For example, researchers at the University of Berkeley have reconsidered the data of the WCGS study and have shown that the risks of recidivism and mortality in people who have experienced a first coronary accident are half as strong in individuals of Type A as in those of Type B.[25] This study had considerable impact and was thought by some researchers to invalidate Friedman and Rosenman's classification. One might, however, assume that an initial coronary accident is experienced entirely differently by Type A and Type B patients and that a Type A patient is able to invest much more in his desire to survive than can a Type B patient and will, for example, follow his doctor's orders far more scrupulously. Furthermore, a decrease in the importance of the association between behavioral factors and illness may simply indicate the fact that lifestyles since the 1950s have changed. The greater importance accorded to leisure activities and relaxation may in some way counter the deleterious effects of Type A behavior.

. . . Which Makes Room for Other Factors

Another interesting point that emerges from an analysis of various studies on the link between myocardial infarct and psychological factors is that depressive tendencies and, to a lesser degree, anxiety represent risk factors that are as important as a Type A profile. These are independent factors and not simply supplementary facets of the Type A profile.

These considerations indicate that, contrary to what Friedman and Rosenman initially proposed, restricting intervention only to patients with Type A profiles would not constitute a judicious approach to the reduction of coronary disease. Prevention programs organized by some American centers, such as the Duke University Medical Center in North Carolina, emphasize treatment of the whole individual, essentially through regular participation in a structured sports program.

A Biological Component

The value of Friedman and Rosenman's work is not confined to epidemiology. As soon as one has a simple method of classification, like the A and B categories, one can begin a more systematic study of the characteristics that might be responsible for the increased coronary risk in subjects with a Type A profile. Friedman and Rosenman's classification, therefore, has had a normative influence on studies of the relationship between physiology and behavioral factors. Most of the work on this subject has been done in the United States. In a typical study, students were assigned to one or the other category (Type A or Type B) as a result of their replies in a structured interview and their responses to a self-administered questionnaire (two references being superior to one) and to more-or-less elaborate psychological tests that were accompanied by a simultaneous checking of cardiovascular reaction.

Undergraduate students, already divided into Types A and B, were given a test of mental arithmetic and a test of reaction time.[26] In the first test students were asked to subtract the number 13 from 7683 and then to continue subtracting it from each result until a number less than 13 was reached. The first student to reach this point would win a cash prize. The second test involved pressing a button as quickly as possible at the sound of a tone. Performance on both tests proved to be unrelated to profile. At the physiological level, Type A subjects exhibited a greater release of catecholamines and cortisol than people of Type B only during the mental arithmetic test, which was also the more competitive one. In a test with a video game against an opponent who in fact was a stooge for the experimenter, Type A individuals reacted normally as long as the game was going well. However, if they felt harassed by an opponent who not only played better but who directed a stream of sarcasm at each instance of weakness, they presented a heightened physiological arousal, whereas Type B subjects were unaffected[27] (Fig. 5.12).

Physiological studies indicate that family factors play an important role in the autonomic hyperactivity characterizing Type A

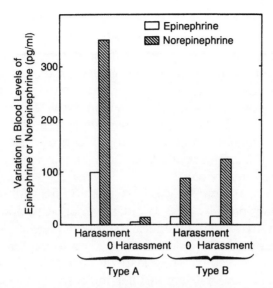

FIGURE 5.12.   Influence of behavioral type on hormonal reaction. Students of Type A or Type B play an electronic game with a superior opponent who either does or does not subject them to sarcastic comment. Blood levels of epinephrine and norepinephrine are measured before and after the test, with the differences recorded on the vertical axis (*adapted from Glass et al., 1980*).

individuals. In the experiments just described,[27] a relationship was established between the intensity of the Type A profile and the physiological data obtained during tests of reaction times only in subjects with a family history of coronary disease. Indeed, a recent study of adrenergic receptors in medical students with Type A profiles indicates a reduction of beta-adrenergic tone (which affects the possibility of vasodilation) only in subjects whose genealogy includes at least one forebear who developed a myocardial infarct before the age of 65.[28]

SEXUAL DIFFERENCES

In the various pathologies that we have tried to link to individuality, women do not present the same risks of developing illness that men do. Women pay a heavy price with respect to anxiety and depression, but they are far less subject to coronary disease.

It seems somewhat paradoxical to claim to elucidate associations between personality and pathological risk when we do not yet understand the explanation for these differences between the sexes, but such is the case. By wishing to make women in every way equal to men, we have overlooked biological singularity. A great many works considering correlations between psychopathology and personality do not even mention sexual differences, as if they were negligible. And when the influence of such factors is mentioned, it is not explained, as if the subject were overwhelmingly ordinary and banal.

In laboratory animals it is easy to show that the reactions of females confronted by tests of adaptive capacity and hormonal response to stress are not identical to those of males.[29] As a general rule, females seem to be less reactive, and to explore new environments more readily. They learn more quickly how to avoid electric shocks and present smaller increases in blood levels of corticosteroids in response to various stressors.

However, categorizations of this kind have no great significance. Tests for measuring emotional reactivity are highly conventional and do not necessarily match the range of female competence. Females react with particular vehemence to any menace that threatens their young.

Sexual differences in reactions to stress have been noted in human subjects as well.[30] To use Marianne Frankenhaeuser's terminology, women are not as strongly activated as men on the effort axis. Despite comparable baseline levels of epinephrine and norepinephrine and given identical performance on psychological tests, the hormonal response of male subjects is stronger than that of females. Furthermore, engagement in a given task and intensity of motivation are often weaker in females than in males. However, one cannot draw a general rule from these data. When the problem involves hospitalization of a child, mothers exhibit more intense disturbance than fathers. But when roles are identical—when both subjects are students at engineering school, for example, or when a woman occupies a position of responsibility in a traditionally male environment—the differences previously observed tend to blur.

It must also be recognized that our view of female behavior in comparison to that of males is not always entirely objective. A typical example can be found in our perceptions of aggressive behavior, a type of behavior that is popularly believed to be characteristically male. And, in fact, attacking an intruder is generally a male activity, at least among rodents. Therefore, it is not surprising that most experiments on the hormonal basis of aggression have focused on this paradigm. However, closer study of aggressive manifestations among animals reveals that females are not always the gentle creatures we might choose to imagine.[31] Even among mice, when no male is present, females—including nursing mothers—will vigorously attack intruders.

From Cliché to Biological Truth

The mechanisms by which sex hormones act on the brain are beginning to be well understood.[32] Development takes place in two phases: During the perinatal period, when the brain is maturing, hormones contribute to the neuronal differentiation, and their action leads to the structuring of a brain of either a masculine or feminine type depending on the hormonal state and the nature of the undifferentiated primary material. (In rodents, the initial organism is feminine, and male differentiation occurs as a process of defeminization; in primates, masculinization is more important than defeminization, so that males retain the potentialities of both sexes to a greater degree than is the case among rodents.) The neural structures established in this way are activated at puberty and at maturity by circulating hormones, resulting in the expression of normal sexual behavior.

Realization of this schema is not an all-or-nothing matter. As indicated in studies of mice, strength of sexual differentiation is related to the hormonal composition of the amniotic fluid that surrounds the fetus.[33] In the mouse uterus a male fetus may be situated between two males (fetus 2M), between two females (fetus 0M), or between a male and a female. The hormones secreted by his brothers and sisters spread sufficiently to modify the hormonal concentrations to which he is exposed, so that an 0M fetus will be defeminized to a lesser degree than one that is 2M. By mechanisms that are not very well understood, stress applied during gestation also reduces defeminization.[34]

These data indicate that behavioral differences between the sexes, or between individuals of the same sex, have a biological basis. For example, a male attack against an intruder depends on the activating effect of androgens on a brain of the male type; a rat castrated at birth and treated with androgens at maturity does not attack.

In functional terms, hormones sensitize all of the nerve structures that are involved in the execution of a new behavior pattern (the reading of a new program). They also cause variation in the intensity with which preexisting behavior patterns are expressed (an already functioning program is read differently).[35] This sensitization modifies the system's intensity of reaction, predetermining the direction of its mode of reaction. A subject will, for example, present behavior of a male or of a female type or will be attracted to a newborn rather than attack it. This bias appears within a few minutes, or a few days, and lasts for a variable length of time depending on the dominant hormones, the behavior, and the species. The net result is that the organism responds differently to certain configurations of signals.

There is no question here of describing in greater detail what is already known, for example, the fact that a castrated male that does not attack intruders will attack as soon as he has received his dose of testosterone. The model proposed has a certain number of implications: specifically, modification of the properties of a neuronal network by hormonal stimulation can affect behavioral patterns other than those normally supported by the hormonal system in question because of the interdependence of behavioral modules. Two experimental examples illustrate this idea: The first, already discussed in this chapter, is the aggressive male, either rat or mouse, that presents both behavioral and cognitive rigidity. Aggression in these animals is highly correlated with blood levels of testosterone. The relationship is not just unidirectional, from the hormones to the brain; engaging in aggressive behavior produces in the dominant animal a rise in blood levels of testosterone. One might, therefore, very well imagine that the behavior of these animals is nothing more than the functional consequence of neuronal activation produced by testosterone excess. This hypothesis has not yet been tested, but it is already known that in rodents testosterone does in fact promote behavioral persistence.[36] Furthermore, aggressive rats present symptoms of sympathetic hyperactivity, especially elevated arterial pressure.[37]

The second example is that of differences between the sexes in the sensitization of dopaminergic neurons that is produced by repeated injections of amphetamine or repeated exposure to uncontrollable stress.[38] In both cases the female reaction, both behavioral and neurochemcial, is stronger than that of males (Fig. 5.13). These differences are not due to ovarian hormones but to the absence of male hormones. The behavior of neutered females is indistinguishable from that of unaltered females, while the behavior of castrated males resembles that of females.

It is tempting to extrapolate from aggressive rats to persons of Type A behavior with respect to coronary illness, and from sensitized female animals to anxious or depressed women. Under present circumstances that would be moving somewhat too fast, since the mechanisms of sexual differentiation in the brains of

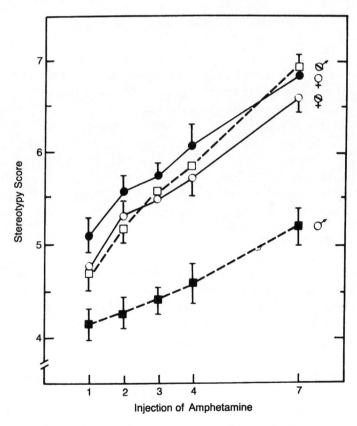

FIGURE 5.13.   Sexual differences in the sensitizing effects of amphetamine. As injections are repeated, intensity of stereotypies increases, a phenomenon more marked in females than in males. With castration, this difference disappears in males, but the neutering of females has no discernible effect in this regard (*adapted from Camp and Robinson, 1988*).

primates and rodents are not precisely congruent. But the study of sexual differences in adaptive capacities nonetheless offers a fascinating perspective toward understanding individuality.

In concluding this study of the biological foundations of individuality and their pathological implications, it seems wise to return to the original objective, that is, to inquire whether or not any real progress has been made in understanding psychosomatic illness.

In his work on psychosomatic medicine, Franz Alexander already recognized two distinct categories of "neurotic responses of vegetative functions":[39]

- Problems related to sympathetic hyperactivity: These occur when an aggressive or hostile action in which the subject would normally have engaged is not possible. This circumstance, if frequently repeated, exacts its price in the form of migraine, hypertension, hyperthyroid activity, neurotic cardiac disorder, arthritis, or diabetes.
- Problems related to parasympathetic hyperactivity: These occur in cases of flight from reality and when a subject regresses toward attitudes of maternal dependency. These problems affect gastrointestinal function (ulcers, constipation, diarrhea), bronchial function (asthma), and the mind (psychasthenia or mental fatigue).

On a more abstract level, the distinction established by theoreticians at the Institut de Psychosomatique in Paris between problems created by a surcharge of excitement and those related to inadequate engagement reflects a duality of the same kind.[40]

Analogies undoubtedly exist as well between these categorizations and Henry's active/passive types, Frankenhaeuser's categories of effort and distress, Eysenck's extrovert and introvert, and Friedman and Rosenman's Types A and B.

One could engage in lengthy speculation over the similarities and dissimilarities of these various points of view. To do so, however, would overlook the central point. In actual situations one must try to identify as precisely as possible both the underlying pathogenic factors and the intermediary mechanisms brought into play.

And one must certainly recognize that despite all the progress that has been made, attitudes have not fundamentally changed.

The progress itself reflects new technical and methodological possibilities (essentially, epidemiological resources and more accurate hormonal assays, thanks to the progress in neuroendocrinology) rather than any revolutionary concepts. A great deal of time is still lost attempting to identify putative psychic factors, and the idea that the psyche dominates the physical body is still so dominant that bodily events (it seems) can only be explained by psychic factors: "I'm having a heart attack because I possess all the characteristics of type A." In coronary illness, Type A behavior is determined, at least in part, by autonomic hyperactivity. Although the behavior is certainly not the root cause of the hyperactivity, it does contribute to its maintenance, a function made all the easier by the fact that Type A individuals put themselves in difficult situations, thereby creating their own problems[41] (Fig. 5.14). In panic attacks the primary event is probably organic; psychological aspects are secondary and are responsible for the diversity of modes of expression assumed by the illness.

By pushing this argument to the limit, one could make the case that individuality is a matter of biological, rather than psychological, variables. This does not mean turning to what biological psychiatrists call indicators, that is, indices measured at the periph-

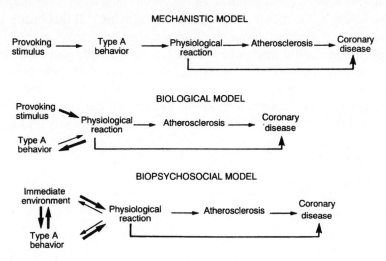

FIGURE 5.14.   Models of the relationship between type A behavior and coronary disease. The biopsychosocial model depicts the complex interactions among physiology, behavior, and the environment better than the mechanistic model or the biological model (*adapted from Smith and Anderson, 1986*).

ery and thought to provide an image of what is happening in the brain. (An example of this is the "neuroendocrine window" strategy, the study of blood levels of pituitary hormones, which indirectly reflects the activity of neurotransmitters modulating the release of these hormones or their hypothalamic releasing factors. Another example is the study of the binding characteristics of neurotransmitter receptors present on various blood cells such as platelets, lymphocytes, and red blood cells). Given that a reactive module is a complex of psychological and physiological characteristics, it should be possible to trace psychological characteristics from physiological components. A whole body of work has, for example, already been done with dogs simply by studying the ability of experimental animals to control an overload of fluid when exposed to a tense emotional situation. Dogs that might be characterized, to use the vernacular, as "easy pissers" adapt easily to a variety of circumstances, especially to inescapable electric shocks. They rapidly accept a situation as it occurs and readily condition themselves to meet it. Conversely, "non-pisser" dogs display exaggerated responses to similar situations: as soon as they enter the room in which they will receive electric shock, they develop major symptoms of autonomic arousal (tachycardia, accelerated respiration, increased consumption of oxygen, increased salivation), which persist for the duration of the experiment.[42] If this group is given the ability to control the shocks, these reactions return to normal. One could discourse at length on the quality and intensity of anxiety experienced by these animals or on their various personality traits. But it remains the case that the problems they encounter can be summarized quite simply as the interaction of external events and the constitutional variables of ordinary biology.

MIND AND IMMUNITY

Of course doctors know a lot about cancer, but they don't know what it really is. I think that cancer is a sickness of the soul in which a person who devours his own sorrow is eventually devoured himself, by that inner sorrow.

—FRITZ ZORN, *Mars*

Clay as a remedy for AIDS? Perhaps that makes you smile, but all of these natural remedies strengthen natural immunity. They make possible a sustained production of T.8, and other cells which kill viruses.

—RIKA ZARAI, *Mes secrets naturals pour guérirs réussirs*
[Natural Secrets for Successful Cures]

On March 19, 1878, during a session of the Academy of Medicine in Paris, Louis Pasteur presented his esteemed colleagues with two chickens. One of these was in perfect health, the other blackened and dead. Both birds had been inoculated with the blood of a third bird that had died of anthrax, an infectious disease relatively common at the time. The living bird, however, had received its inoculation without prior treatment; the dead bird had been exposed to cold before getting its shot. This observation is important because it shows that infection by a microbial germ, in this case the anthrax bacillus, is not in itself enough to produce illness. Microbes develop only on favorable terrain—the one offered by an organism already weakened by an external stress. Louis Pasteur, therefore,

155

was able to assert forcefully, "A microbe is nothing; the terrain, everything."

However, research into verifiable methods of vaccination and the characterization of the various categories of immunological response initiated by an organism to resist germs was supposed to have relegated, for over a century now, this notion of terrain to the background. Although it was generally agreed that an organism's resistance to infection is affected by attendant circumstances, such as a patient's state of fatigue or the degree of stress bearing on him, the reasons for this were not understood for a long time. It must also be granted that such a topic was scarcely tempting as a subject for research. With respect to the mechanism involved, it was difficult to see how an organism could be aware of stress from its surroundings, especially when immunologists, for their part, were exerting themselves to prove that the immune system functions autonomously, entirely independent of any passions that may stir the host organism. Further, the study of the links between stress and illness related to the functioning of the immune system—infectious diseases, cancers, or autoimmune disorders—seemed only to satisfy the prejudices of the imagination. The nineteenth century embraced the idea that tuberculosis was associated with a bohemian lifestyle. Our period accepts no less tenaciously the view that cancer progresses more swiftly in patients who surrender to despair and resignation than in those who fight it.

As with other branches of psychosomatics, progress in understanding psychosomatic illness has come from elsewhere, specifically, from an understanding of the interactions between the nervous system and the immune system. This understanding has led to an entirely new discipline—psychoneuroimmunology—which has made prodigious gains in the last five years. The history of this discipline certainly merits telling, since it encompasses the entire field of psychosomatic study, from the influence of psychological factors on illness to the reverberations of illness in the psyche.

THE NERVOUS SYSTEM COMMUNICATES
WITH THE IMMUNE SYSTEM

A Perfectly Self-Regulated System

Immunologists use the imagery of warfare to describe the mobilization of the immune system to fight infection. The attackers, known as antigens, are pathogenic agents—viruses, bacteria, parasites, or the body's own cells that, for reasons still not known, are recognized as foreign (not-self). The defenders are various kinds of white corpuscles circulating through the blood and lymph systems or fixed in the tissues. The first line of defense is represented by the macrophages in the skin and organ walls. These cells capture microbes, digest them, and present them to the lymphocytes in tiny fragments. The T lymphocytes (so designated because they are differentiated in the thymus before being stocked in the spleen and the lymphoid ganglia) are the first to be activated. On contact with the macrophages, they multiply and destroy the infected cells (in which case they are called cytotoxic lymphocytes) or help other lymphocytes to intervene. This is particularly true of B lymphocytes (B stands for bone marrow, from which they issue directly, without passing through the thymus), which become capable of producing antibodies, which fix specifically on the antigen, making its destruction possible through a series of complex reactions. This experience is not lost. Lymphocytes involved in an immune reaction "remember" the characteristics of the antigen and intervene rapidly in any subsequent contact with it. Other cells—called natural killer cells—specialize in the destruction of tumor cells. And, finally, some antigens provoke the manufacture of specialized antibodies, the E immunoglobulins, or *IgE*, which attach themselves to the surface of mastocytes and basophils. Recognition of an antigen or allergen by IgE attached in this manner induces a degranulation, that is, a release of the various mediators that are contained in the secretion granules of mastocytes and basophils and are responsible for an allergic reaction.

The various cells involved in immune reactions do not charge into battle in random disorder, unaware of what has already been accomplished. Cytokines, messenger substances secreted by the lymphocytes and macrophages, work to coordinate and strengthen defense. All these elements constitute a perfectly regulated system, one that can function in the laboratory test tube independent of the organism that nurtured it. It is for this reason that the possibility of nervous system influence on the functioning of the immune system had long been thought negligible.

Extrinsic Innervation

Things began to change in the early 1980s when anatomists became interested in the innervation of lymphoid organs. The primary lymphoid organ (the thymus) and the secondary ones (the spleen and the lymphoid ganglia) are innervated by the sympathetic nervous system, an innervation that is not limited to the course followed by the blood vessels irrigating these organs; the nerve filaments dissociate themselves more or less quickly from the vascular branches to innervate areas in which the maturing lymphocytes are stocked.[1] Thus, nerve endings are abundant in the white pulp of the spleen, where T and B lymphocytes are concentrated.

The sympathetic nerves innervating the lymphoid organs release catecholamines as well as various peptides that they contain in abundance, such as substance P, enkephalins, cholecystokinin, neurotensin, and the vasointestinal peptide. For this reason, the chemical composition of the microenvironment in which the lymphocytes are immersed is profoundly influenced by the level of activity of the sympathetic nervous system. But let there be no confusion here; this is not a claim that nerve endings form synapses with lymphocytes, as they would other neuronal elements. In contrast, David Felten, an anatomist specializing in this type of study, thinks that the autonomic nervous system is capable of extremely close contact with mastocytes, the cells that effect allergic reactions.

Immune cells can also be reached by various hormones released into the blood on occasions of stress: glucocorticoids, epinephrine, endorphins, and pituitary peptides.

Sensitivity to Hormones and Neurotransmitters

These various routes of communication linking the nervous and immune system would not be particularly useful if recipient cells were insensitive to the messengers dispatched. Studies completed in recent years show that lymphocytes possess membrane recep-

tors for most of the known neurotransmitters, as well as intracellular receptors for steroid hormones. These receptors have
biochemical characteristics comparable to those of receptors situated on the traditional target cells of the various neurotransmitters
in question. This suggests that when these receptors are activated,
they are capable of modifying the functioning of immune cells.[2]
This is, in fact, the case, since immune responses are altered if one
changes the quantity of transmitters present in an organism or in
cultures of lymphocytes. Thus, the selective destruction of sympathetic nerve endings innervating the spleen reduces the production
of antibodies against bacterial or viral antigens whereas administration of drugs that stimulate the alpha-adrenergic receptors located in the membranes of B lymphocytes increases the synthesis
of antibodies.[3] The endorphins also have complex effects on immunity according to the substance and quantities used, the response tested, and the timing of treatment in relation to phase of
immune reaction. However, the presence of specific receptors for
opioids on the lymphocytes has not been established with any
certainty.[4] As for the corticoids, they have immunodepressive effects but only in heavy doses. They inhibit production of most
cytokines elaborated by the immune cells. Weak doses of corticoids can stimulate response in certain cases. In some species,
particularly rodents, corticoids have direct cytolytic effects on the T
lymphocytes and on the thymocytes, their precursors in the thymus.[5]

As with the other cells whose function is affected by various
transmitters, lymphocytes have ionic channels in their membranes
that modulate transmembrane movements of sodium, calcium, and
potassium. Their role in lymphocyte reactions is not yet known
with any precision. In the case of T lymphocytes, potassium channels are instrumental in lymphocyte proliferation.[6]

THE BRAIN AND IMMUNITY

From the preceding pages, it should be recalled that the immune
system possesses all the machinery necessary to be influenced by
the brain. That various changes in brain function can affect immunity indicates that this potential is certainly real.

As there is no convenient index of immunocompetence, that
is, the immune system's ability to confront pathogenic agents, con-

ducting studies of this type is far from easy; each category of response must be studied separately in various tests conducted *in vivo* or *in vitro*.

A classic method of studying the influence of the brain on organic function is to injure or stimulate strictly delineated structures in the brain. For example, in mice a lesion in the median eminence at the base of the hypothalamus hastens the growth of experimental tumors and suppresses for a considerable period the cytotoxic activity of natural killer cells but has no effect on the macrophages or the T and B lymphocytes.[7] That degree of specificity of action is, however, unusual. More often, lesions modify cellular or humoral immune responses, as well as the expression of allergic reactions (immediate hypersensitivity).[8] The importance of these effects varies, depending on which structures are affected. They are distinct when lesions are made in the visceral brain, particularly in the region of the hypothalamus, which is involved in the control of autonomic and hormonal functions. Electric stimulation of various brain structures is also capable of modifying the functioning of various immune responses.

Differences Between Right-handers and Left-handers

One of the most spectacular results of recent years concerning the relationship between the brain and immunity has been the demonstration of interhemispheric asymmetry in the modulating effects of the brain on the immune system. The design of the human brain includes hemispheric specialization: the left hemisphere, dominant in right-handed people, is the seat of language and the capacity to abstract while the right hemisphere controls spatial representation. Negative emotions (fear, sorrow, pain) involve the right hemisphere, positive emotions (joy, pleasure) the left. As the number of right-handed people exceeds that of left-handed people, the search for anomalies tends to gravitate toward the ranks of the latter. In immunity studies, several retrospective studies do, in fact, suggest that the risk of autoimmune disorders is greater in left-handed subjects. Geschwind and Behan, for example, did a systematic study of illness in patrons of a shop in Glasgow, Scotland, that specializes in items specifically designed for left-handed people. In this group, they observed an incidence of autoimmune disorder two and a half times greater than that of a control group composed exclusively of right-handed subjects.[9]

The first experimental work in this area, however, took an entirely different tack. During the 1970s, in the course of her hospital residency, a neurologist, Kathleen Bizière, noticed that patients who had suffered a cerebrovascular accident affecting the left hemisphere presented a higher incidence of infectious complication than those with damage to the right hemisphere. With Gérard Renoux, an immunologist from Tours, Bizière launched a series of experiments testing repercussions for the immune system from unilateral lesions of the cerebral cortex in mice. A project of this kind implied a certain limitation of knowledge because at the time it was still thought that cerebral lateralization was a specifically human attribute. In conformity with their thesis, Bizière and Renoux noted that lesions of the left cortex depressed the cellular immune response while those of the right hemisphere were either without effect or increased cellular immunity.[10]

These results were reproduced in Bordeaux by Pierre Neveu. Cortical lateralization is not limited to cellular immunity but also affects the production of antibodies and the oxidative activity of the macrophages. Even more interesting, Neveu has recently shown that the cellular immune responses of mice identified as "lefties" or "righties," by the paw used to reach a pellet of food at the bottom of a tube, are different: under the influence of a nonspecific mitogen, the proliferation of T lymphocytes is greater in left-pawed mice[11] (Fig. 6.1). Although the intermediary mechanisms are not yet known, this difference in the working of the immune system linked to the dominant hemisphere could have functional consequences. In a model of the autoimmune disorder lupus erythematosus, biological signs of illness appeared more rapidly in "left-handed" than in "right-handed" mice.

STRESS AND IMMUNITY

It is customary to expect a reduced level of immune defense in individuals under stress. In recent years studies of students during an exam period (Table 6.1) or of men and women at moments of marital difficulty (divorce), familial troubles (illness or death of a close relative), or professional stress (the restructuring or breaking up of a business) indicate as a general rule a reduction in cellular immunity and an increase in antibodies against viruses like herpes, which are already chronically infecting most of the general popu-

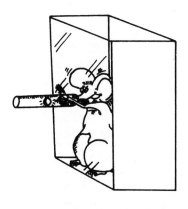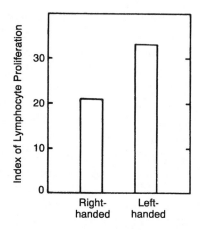

FIGURE 6.1.   Influence of manual preference on immune response. Mice are classified as "righties" or "lefties" according to paw used to retrieve a pellet of food from a tube. The index of lymphocyte stimulation corresponds to the relationship between the quantity of radioactive thymidine incorporated by splenocytes stimulated by a mitogen, compared to that incorporated by splenocytes that were not stimulated. Under the influence of a mitogen, the proliferation of T lymphocytes is greater in "left-paw" mice than it is in "right-paw" mice (*adapted from Neveu et al., 1988*).

lation.[12] This last category of change signals a failure of the humoral immune processes defending against a proliferation of viral organisms. In most of these studies, researchers have made sure that these effects are not due to the influence of other factors such as medications, tobacco, alcohol, or nutritional deficits.

There is not always a straightforward temporal link between life events and their consequences for the immune system. American accountants, for instance, confronting the annual overload caused by tax returns due on April 15, experience heightened immune reactions during the crisis period. These subsequently sink below baseline value before returning to normal.[13]

A diminution in cellular immune response has been noted in patients suffering from depression. This seems to be relatively specific to a depressive pathology since it does not occur in conjunction with other psychiatric disorders or in hospital patients. Such an effect on the immune system might be thought to constitute an argument of some weight supporting viral theories of mental illness. The most recent studies, however, do not favor these views; effects on the immune system are extremely uneven, and when

TABLE 6.1

The Influence of Life Events on Immunity

Forty second-year medical students were tested six weeks before end-of-year exams (baseline) and on the first day of exams. Note the extreme reduction in interferon production by activated blood white cells and the decrease in the number and the cytotoxic activity of natural killer cells.

	Leukocyte Interferon (units/ml)	Natural Killer Cells	
		% Circulating	Cytotoxic Activity (%)
baseline	2000	16.3	45
exam	80	9.1	30

(Adapted from Glaser et al., 1986)

they occur, they seem more closely related to life events preceding the onset of depression rather than to the depression *per se*.[14]

A General Tendency Toward Depression . . .

Despite their controversial character, several epidemiological studies suggest an association between psychological factors and the onset or progress of certain cancers, such as breast cancer or melanoma. Studies have attempted to supply specific information about the effects of stress on cellular elements that might play a part in the surveillance and control of tumor growth—either cytotoxic lymphocytes or natural killer cells. Exposure to life events is accompanied by a reduction in the cytotoxic activity of natural killer cells, but this is not a constant. In a direct study of breast cancer patients, Levy and his collaborators at the Cancer Research Institute in Pittsburgh recently noted that this biological index is affected by psychological factors—passive acceptance of the illness, apathy, and the absence of social support.[15]

Taken as a whole, these studies on human subjects suggest an association between stress and reduced immune defense capacity. But to claim that this association plays a causal role in the increased probablity of infectious disease and other pathology linked to a weakening of the immune system is a leap of faith. What is still needed is to show that the observed changes in the immune response are representative of what happens in the immune system and that they are strong enough to result in an actual deterioration in the resistance to infectious agents.

Experimental studies on animals have the advantage of offering more rigorous conditions of observation. One can note more precisely the ways in which the immune system is affected, and possible biases are more easily controlled. As with human subjects, the first observations in animals of the effect of stress on immunity concentrated on deleterious effects. For example, mice subjected to electric shock or intense sound rejected heterogeneous grafts less readily, were more susceptible to pathogenic viruses, and in cases of infection synthesized less interferon, a cytokine of lymphocyte origin with antiviral properties.[16]

... Which Is Not Always the Case

The effects of stress on immunity are, however, far more complex; in some cases one can see an increase in resistance to pathogenic agents and a stimulation of immune responses. For instance, instability in the social hierarchy, caused by the systematic rotation of chickens from one flock to another, reduces resistance to mycoplasmas and viruses but increases resistance to bacterial infections and *coccidiosis*, a parasitic illness common in poultry.[17] Mice subjected to forced immobility show a decrease in the delayed hypersensitivity response to sheep red blood cells, an immune response due to T lymphocytes and similar to the tuberculin test. Conversely, the same stress increases the intensity of another form of response mediated by cellular immunity, hypersensivity to dinitrofluorobenzene (DNFB), a chemical substance that on contact with the skin provokes the formation of DFNB–epidermal protein complexes that act as antigens.[18]

We saw in Chapter 4 that the effects of stress on an organism depend on the subject's ability to predict or control what happens. This should also be true for the effects of stress on immunity. In 1979 Sklar and Anisman showed that tumor cells injected into mice proliferate more rapidly and cause significantly higher rates of mortality if the animals are also exposed to inescapable electric shock. Mice able to control shocks do not differ significantly from control animals not exposed to shock.[19] This is also true for the mitogen-induced proliferation of T lymphocytes.[20] Conversely, the production of antibodies in rats able to avoid shock is depressed, in comparison to that of yoked rats unable to avoid the electric shocks they are exposed to[21] (Fig. 6.2). These results confirm the importance of control over external events with regard to their impact on immune responses.

As for prediction: exposure to unpredictable electric shock impairs the lymphoproliferation of T cells in rats whereas exposure to predictable electric shock has no consequence.[21]

In all these experiments, researchers used electric shock or some other physical stressor that is easy to arrange in a laboratory setting. Their artificial nature, however, precludes extrapolating these results to more natural circumstances. Stress occurring in a social context is far more pertinent. Various experiments with rodents show that subordinate animals present reduced cellular and

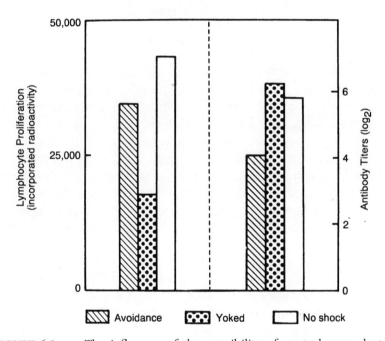

FIGURE 6.2.   The influence of the possibility of control over electric shocks on cellular and humoral immunity in rats. Rats that had learned to avoid electric shocks (avoidance condition) were compared with rats whose behavioral attempts to avoid the shocks were ineffective (yoked condition) and with control animals (no shock) after ten sessions of conditioning. Cellular immunity is measured by lymphocyte proliferation in response to a mitogen (indicated by the amount of incorporated radioactivity in cultured splenocytes), whereas humoral immunity is estimated by the titer in antibodies against sheep red blood cells injected on the fifth day of the experiment (*adapted from Mormède et al., 1988*).

humoral immune responses.[22] In primates, breaking the bonds of attachment between a young animal and its companions in captivity has consequences for the immune system that are far from negligible. Once again, it is difficult to speak of a generalized suppression of the immune system, since certain aspects of the immune response are depressed (the number of lymphocytes and circulating eosinophils, the serum levels of G immunoglobulins, and the primary humoral response to a viral antigen), while others are simultaneously augmented (the hemolytic activity of complement, the oxidative activity of macrophages, and certain responses that are mediated by cellular immunity).[23]

Why These Variations?

Although it is well established that various physical and psychological stressors can affect immunity, this does not always imply a full immunodepression. The reasons for these variations are not well understood. There is first of all the question of measurement relativity: the effects of stress on immunity remain within the range of normal testing variations, and a lowering of response relative to what is observed in nonstressed individuals does not necessarily indicate a collapse of immune defenses. Thus, rats returned to a setting in which they had received electric shock a day earlier present a reduction of humoral immunity that one might attribute *a priori* to the immunosuppressant effects of fear. This reduction is observed in relation to values measured in a group of control animals manipulated in the same way as the experimental animals but without receiving shock. Nonetheless, the immune response of the experimental animals is superior to that of animals that were not handled and were left in their home cages for the duration of the various experiments. These results mean that, when all is said and done, the immune levels of animals exposed to shock do not necessarily differ from those of "normal" animals[24] (Fig. 6.3).

Another difficulty arises from the fact that in a majority of studies to the present day, immunity has been measured in a relatively global way, involving circulating lymphocytes or splenocytes. The modifications that have been demonstrated are not necessarily representative of what happens in the rest of the immune system, in particular, in target organs, such as the respiratory apparatus in cases of bronchopulmonary infections. Further, the impact of stress on the immune system reflects not only the effects

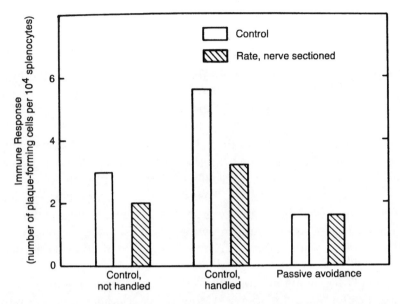

FIGURE 6.3.   The influence of stress on the humoral immunity of rats immunized against sheep red blood cells. Immune response is measured by the number of plaque-forming cells observed after placement of splenocytes in culture. Simple handling of the animals is enough to increase the immune response compared with the immune response of rats left in their housing cages (control, not handled). This effect is due to activation of the autonomic nervous system, since it disappears after surgical nerve section of the spleen. Passive avoidance conditioning reduced the immune response in comparison with that of the handled controls but not in comparison with that of the unhandled controls. Nerve section of the spleen does not affect this influence of stress (*adapted from Croiset, 1989*).

of hormones and transmitters on immune cells. Stress also affects the permeability of the organic barriers that contain ambient pathogens. Thus, administration of inescapable electric shock favors the formation of gastrointestinal ulcers and, consequently, the passage of germs through the gut mucosa. Since intestinal flora vary according to the environment and the individual, it is easy to understand why reproducing the results of experimental studies of stress isn't always possible—between laboratories or even within the same laboratory. To progress in our understanding of the stress–immunity connection, we need to carry out studies in animals that have controlled flora and are kept in strictly defined environments.

MECHANISMS OF THE EFFECTS
OF STRESS ON IMMUNITY

When an immunosuppressant effect of stress is observed, the first explanation that suggests itself is the intervention of glucocorticoids released in response to stress. There are various ways of verifying this possibility, from ablation of the adrenal or the pituitary or injection of drugs that slow the synthesis of corticoids, blocking the effects of stress, to administration of ACTH or glucocorticoids to mimic hormonal effects. For example, an American researcher, Robert Sapolsky, has shown that chronic stress increases the possibility of tumor growth in rats and that this effect is stronger in old, as opposed to young, animals. Since the response of the pituitary-adrenal axis to stress is more marked in older rats, he gave younger rats supplementary synthetic corticosterone immediately following an episode of stress in order to equalize hormonal differences due to age. Under these conditions, young rats became as sensitive as older animals to the effects of stress on tumor growth[25] (Fig. 6.4)

Intermediates of the Effects of Stress on Immunity

Pituitary-adrenal hormones are not the intermediary agents for all effects of stress on immunity. Ablation of the adrenals or injection of drugs reducing synthesis of glucocorticoids blocks reduction of the delayed hypersensitivity reaction produced in mice by forced immobilization but does not modify increased contact sensitivity.[20] In the same way, adrenalectomy does not reduce the abrupt fall of lymphocyte proliferation responses observed in rats exposed to intense electric shock.[26]

Several intermediary hormones other than the glucocorticoids may intervene, particularly the catecholamines, endorphins, and growth hormone.

The catecholamines released during moments of stress produce consequences for immunity that are far from negligible. In volunteers exposed to various psychological tests and physical exercise, the distribution of lymphocyte subsets in circulating blood changes simultaneously with changes in plasma concentrations of epinephrine. This is not simple coincidence; the effects of injected epinephrine are comparable to those observed in the tests.[27] This

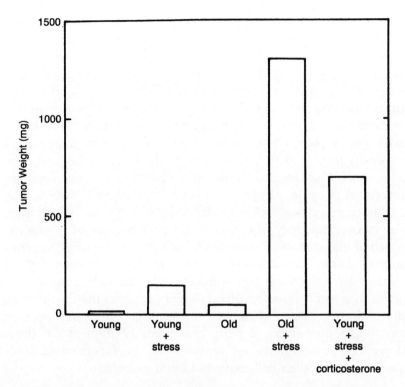

FIGURE 6.4.   Role of glucocorticoids in the influence of age on the sensitivity to stress of tumor growth in rats. Tumor growth, measured by the weight of the tumor 15 days after inoculation, is significantly increased by stress in older, but not in younger, rats. If younger rats receive injections of corticosteroid following stress, mimicking the adrenocortical response to stress of older rats, the effects of stress on tumor growth are increased (*adapted from Sapolsky and Donnelly, 1985*).

treatment also reduces lymphocyte proliferation induced by non-specific mitogens. Catecholamines block the oxidative activity of the macrophages through the intermediary of alpha-adrenergic receptors. In the case of antigens normally controlled by phagocytosis, this deficit may require the activation of compensatory mechanisms, for example, the production of antibodies directed against these antigens, which explains the increased number of antibodies against herpes viruses observed in human subjects exposed to various life events. In experiments done on mice, exposure to intense noise facilitates production of antibodies against a vaccinal antigen. The injection of epinephrine in unstressed mice mimics the effects of stress on immunity, and stress effects are blocked by the injection of an antagonist of alpha-adrenergic receptors.[28]

The involvement of endorphins has been demonstrated in a series of ingenious experiments conducted by Shavit and Liebeskind at the University of California, Los Angeles, on rats exposed to intermittent or continuous inescapable electric shock.[29] As shown in Chapter 3, intermittent shock produces a transitory reduction of sensitivity to pain. This effect is due to the release of opiate peptides, since it is blocked by the administration of naltrexone, an antagonist of opiate receptors. Conversely, analgesia provoked by continuous electric shock is mediated by non-opioid mechanisms. The cytotoxic activity of natural killer cells is reduced in rats exposed to intermittent electric shock but not in those receiving continuous shock. The effects of intermittent shock on immunity are blocked by naltrexone and reproduced by the injection of morphine. The mechanisms involved are central rather than peripheral, since injection into the brain of very weak quantities of morphine reproduces the effects of peripheral administration of the drug. However, the intermediaries between endogenous cerebral opioids and natural killer cells have not been identified.

Those That Favor Recuperation

Negative effects are often opposed by positive ones. Besides the mediators responsible for the effects of stress on immunity, there are other factors that promote recuperation, that is, the return to normal of immune functions. As shown by Gisler's experiments in Switzerland between 1960 and 1970, now ancient history, growth hormone belongs to this second category of mediators; the immunosuppressant effect of glucocorticoids in mice is increased by ablation of the pituitary, and injection of growth hormone counters this deterioration in resistance. Numerous studies have since confirmed the immunostimulant effect of growth hormone and similar hormones, like prolactin. Growth hormone activates the macrophages as effectively as interferon-γ, the classic mediator for activation of the macrophages. It also restores the thymus and cellular immunity in aged rats.[30] Prolactin normalizes immune responses depressed by the administration of corticoids or morphine. Animals made hypoprolactinemic by various treatments present an immunodepression affecting both cellular and humoral immunity.[31]

Cyclosporine, an immunodepressant medication used in hospitals to prevent rejection of grafts and to slow the development of autoimmune disorders, binds on prolactin receptors present on the membranes of lymphocytes and may, at least in part, act as an antiprolactin. Its immunodepressant action can actually be reduced by the concomitant administration of prolactin.[32]

Despite these favorable results, one should be aware of the methodological limits to any complete study of the intermediary mechanisms of stress effects on immunity. The immune system is sensitive to a whole series of mediators whose profile is modified in a complex way during stress. When one artifically adjusts the level of one of these mediators in order to understand its role, one has only a partial view of what is happening. The exercise of simultaneous control over several factors is even more difficult to achieve. However, the few experiments in simultaneous variation of more than one mediator have all confirmed the importance of the interactions among molecular factors capable of acting on lymphoid cells.[33]

THE CONDITIONING OF IMMUNE RESPONSES

Pavlov's dog quickly began to salivate at the sound of a metronome when this sound regularly preceded the serving of food. In psychological jargon, food is an unconditioned stimulus that releases unconditioned salivation, and the sound of a metronome is a conditioned stimulus that produces a conditioned response after a sufficient number of associations. Innervation of the salivary glands and the brain's ability to establish a link between two successive temporal events are all that is needed for the production of a conditioned salivary response. Since the lymphoid organs are innervated and since functioning of the immune system can be modified by nervous activity, there is no *a priori* reason why this should not also be true of immune function.

If the immune system can be conditioned, stimuli initially without effect on immunity should become effective through regular association with an immunomodulating treatment. The first experiments on this subject were done during the 1920s by Metalnikov and Chorine at the Pasteur Institute in Paris. Along the lines developed by the school of Pavlov, these researchers tried to condition various aspects of an animal's response to infection, such as modification of the white blood cell count and the secretion of anti-bodies.[34]

How Cells Acquire Memory

When the experimenter blows a trumpet or systematically scratches a rabbit's ear before an intraperitoneal injection of germs attenu-ated by heat, the afflux of leukocytes produced by this treatment eventually appears as soon as the conditioned stimulus is pre-sented. In the same way, application of a curling iron to the ear of a rabbit or guinea pig (without burning the skin) or scratching its side is enough to increase the number of antibodies against a microbial antigen if the vaccinal injection has been repeatedly as-sociated with these sensory stimuli.

Attentive reading of Metalnikov and Chorine's original publi-cations shows, however, that their results were excessively incon-stant. This, however, did not stop these authors, who believed in the correctness of their findings, from proclaiming that immune responses could be conditioned and that the nervous system is responsible for sensitizing the immune system:

> After immunization, the nervous system acquires a new fac-ulty: to heighten cellular sensitivity, that is to say, to act in a specific manner against a given antigen. This new faculty is often retained for a considerable time, sometimes for months and even years, after the antibodies have vanished. And this fact that immunity, the ability to react vigorously against a specific challenge, functions long after relevant antibodies have disappeared can be explained only by memory. Which is why we say, when we immunize an animal, that we have immunized its nervous system.

This manner of explaining how the mind—or, more precisely, the memory—affects the immune cells made no great impression on immunologists or neurophysiologists, and the possibility of im-mune conditioning was neglected for some 50 years.

The conditioning of immune responses was rediscovered by chance by Robert Ader, an American psychologist working on learned taste aversion at the University of Rochester. Conditioned taste aversion is the ability possessed by several species to attribute to a newly consumed aliment all the poisoning that may ensue. Several toxic substances can be used to provoke aversion. For convenience, Ader chose cyclophosphamide, a chemical immuno-suppressant with important secondary effects. He was surprised to find unusually high mortality rates in rats presented with the new food that had been paired with the intoxication induced by cyclo-phosphamide. As mortality was due to apparently common infections, Ader wondered if the conditioned rats had not in fact associated immunosuppression induced by cyclophosphamide (unconditioned stimulus) with the new food—in this instance, a saccharin solution with a sweet taste (conditioned stimulus). That would have indicated that presentation of saccharin during the test was enough to depress immunity even further, producing a collapse of resistance to commonly encountered germs.

In a series of experiments Ader demonstrated that this was indeed the case and that the presentation of saccharin to animals that associated the taste of this drink with immunosuppressant treatment resulted in decreased production of antibodies against various vaccinal antigens[35] (Fig. 6.5).

In the Absence of All Smell

Similar phenomena are encountered in the realm of allergic reactions, such as the anecdote of the young woman who was sensitive to the smell of roses and who sneezed when she saw a paper rose (an account that appears in many volumes dedicated to the study of allergy without any precise information about when and where this woman lived). Apparently Proust reacted in precisely this way when he saw Van Gogh's celebrated painting *Sunflowers*. Researchers at the University of California, San Francisco, have shown that guinea pigs sensitized to ovalbumin, a foreign protein, so thoroughly associate a smell present during conditioning with the allergen that the smell alone precipitates an allergic reaction that can be measured by the release of histamine, one of the mediators of shock.[36] However, in this experiment, the histamine was assayed in the blood, so that it was unclear whether it came from cells implicated in the hypersensitivity reaction, that is, the mastocytes. In a recent study Canadian researchers made use of the fact that during the course of degranulation the mastocytes of intestinal mucosa release a specific enzyme. They sensitized to ovalbumin rats previously infested with digestive parasites, in order to stimulate local production of IgE, and then achieved a conditioning that consisted of an aller-

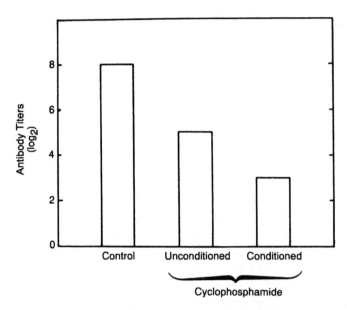

FIGURE 6.5.   Influence of conditioning on the humoral immune response of rats. Rats immunized against sheep red blood cells normally
present elevated titers of antibodies. When they are treated by cyclophosphamide, an immunodepressant, synthesis of antibodies is reduced. In
conditioned animals (i.e., those that received cyclophosphamide after
ingestion of a saccharin solution) antibody titers were depressed even
further after presentation of the saccharin solution paired with cyclophosphamide (*adapted from Ader and Cohen, 1985*).

gic reaction provoked by administration of the allergen following
a stay in a cage equipped with a blinking light. After three such
associations a stay in the cage with the light produced a release
of an enzyme of mastocyte origin comparable to that produced
by the allergen[37] (Fig. 6.6).

This is not a matter of isolated experiments. Many studies
done in various European and American laboratories during the
course of the last eight years show that the following kinds of
immune response can be conditioned: humoral immunity, cell-
mediated immunity, and the cytotoxic activity of natural killer cells.
Conditioning can even affect the course of an illness, as shown by
the slowed progress of an animal model of disseminated lupus
erythematosus produced by repeated exposure of mice to a saccharin solution associated with cyclophosphamide.[35]

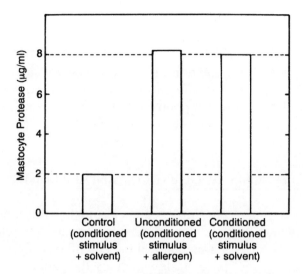

FIGURE 6.6.   Conditioning of allergic reactions in rats. The allergic reaction is measured by the circulating concentrations of a protease released by mastocytes. In conditioned rats, the presentation of a conditioned stimulus is enough in itself to provoke a degranulation of intestinal mastocytes comparable to that observed in nonconditioned animals exposed to the allergen (*adapted from MacQueen et al., 1989*).

Conditioning or Artifact?

On the basis of so many concordant arguments, claims that the phenomena does not exist or is an artifact would seem incongruous. Can one nonetheless conclude that exposing a patient to the white coat of the doctor or nurse who vaccinated him will in itself spur his humoral immunity into action in case of infection? And, less spectacular but just as useful, might one conceivably reduce doses of immunosuppressive drugs and their attendant problems of toxicity by the use of conditioning? There are strong possibilities that answers to these questions will be negative. Despite the claims of researchers, it is not at all clear that the modifications of immunity observed in conditioned animals are due to genuine conditioning. The reason for doubt is simple: in the vast majority of experiments on conditioned immune responses, the conditioning procedure itself is very taxing, because of the important secondary effects of the immunomodulating treatments that are used as unconditioned stimuli. Conditioned animals, in fact, are equipped with an alarm signal that warns them of the miseries to be inflicted. The situation of these animals, therefore, is comparable to that of animals exposed to predictable electric shock. As seen in Chapter 4, the physiological condition of an individual anticipating a disagreeable experience is different from that of an individual who cannot predict what will happen, and the former's immune system will very probably be affected by this physiological state.[38]

HYPNOSIS, SUGGESTION, AND IMMUNITY

Nicholas Hall, an American researcher studying the interactions between the nervous and the immune systems, likes to refer in his lectures to the case of a mentally ill patient afflicted with multiple personalities. In the space of a few minutes, the patient (who is still a young man) becomes a fearful small boy, a lewd street urchin, or a senile old woman. One of these personalities was allergic to wool and would sneeze and weep allergic tears in Hall's presence, because Hall kept on his wool jacket during the interview. A change of personality invariably resulted in the immediate disappearance of these symptoms.

Warts Sensitive to Hypnosis

To study the influence of mental states on immunity, it is easier to work with subjects who have been hypnotized, or subjected to suggestion, than to wait for the personality changes of patients with multiple personalities.[39] The experiment of Sinclair-Gieben and Chalmers, done at the end of the 1950s, on ten patients with flat warts on various parts of their bodies is often used to illustrate the power of hypnosis over immunity. Warts are benign tumors of the skin caused by viruses and are well known to be sensitive to suggestion. To better prove the effects of suggestion, the authors decided to tell their subjects, under hypnosis, that their warts would all regress, not just all at once but from whatever side of the body the hypnotist indicated! If Sinclair-Gieben and Chalmers can be believed, the results were positive in nine cases out of ten, the tenth case having responded bilaterally to the treatment.[40] This was too good to be true; since the side of the body chosen by the experimenter was the side most heavily endowed with warts, the probability of noting effects was biased from the start. As one would expect, many subsequent studies have confirmed that warts are sensitive to hypnosis, without, however, encountering lateralization of the effects[41] (Fig. 6.7).

Proof of the effectiveness of hypnosis extends beyond warts. The intensity of a passive cutaneous anaphylaxis reaction (a local form of immediate hypersensitivity obtained in a normal individual who is injected at one or several points in the skin with the serum of an allergic patient and then by the antigen)—like the extent of a tuberculin reaction (a form of delayed hypersensitivity deriving from T lymphocytes)—is reduced in subjects told under hypnosis not to respond.[42] In this last experiment, a biopsy of the indurated area indicated that infiltration of the injection site by T lymphocytes was not altered but that the inflammatory reaction was reduced. In

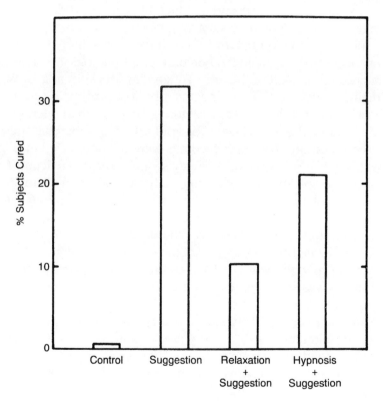

FIGURE 6.7.   Influence of suggestion, alone and combined with relaxation and hypnosis, on the development of warts. Each group consisted of 19 subjects. Note that hypnosis or relaxation was not more effective than suggestion alone (*adapted from Spanos et al., 1988*).

terms of mechanisms, this observation is important because it allows one to think that hypnosis (or suggestion) does not alter the development of the immune response but does interfere with the release of inflammatory mediators.

The Effects of Suggestion

Studies of the effects of hypnosis on immunity are part of a series of observations on physiological and psychological changes that occur under hypnotic conditions, either spontaneously or under the influence of suggestion. Detailed examination of individual results (in the rare cases available) show, moreover, that a patient's sensitivity to hypnosis is of little importance, in contrast to his suggestibility. One can, therefore, set aside everything deriving from hypnotic techniques and conduct this kind of work simply by using suggestion. Volunteers reacting positively to tuberculin were the subject of an experiment in which their sensitivity was tested every month by applying tuberculin or physiological saline on scratches in the skin of the arm. Tuberculin was kept in a jar with a highly visible red label, and the physiological saline in a jar whose label, equally visible, was green. Scratches had been made in both arms, the arm chosen for application of tuberculin being chosen randomly. These proceedings were repeated five times. As might have been expected, a delayed inflammatory reaction (24 hours) was observed each time only in the immediate area swabbed with tuberculin. During the sixth test, done a month later, contents of the jars were switched, without either patient or nurse being told. In these circumstances the delayed hypersensitivity reaction was greatly diminished, as if the fact of "knowing" that what was in the jar with the green label could not be responsible for the induration was sufficient to interfere with the development of the immune reaction.[43]

In this experiment the subjective measure of intensity of reaction to tuberculin by a nurse who, because of the green label, was persuaded not to have a reaction introduces an important bias. Other observations, however, strengthen the hypothesis that suggestion influences immune response. This is particularly clear in allergic attacks. Luparello and his colleagues have shown that asthmatic patients inhaling an aerosol believed to contain the allergen to which they are sensitive develop bronchial constriction. This rapidly vanishes if the doctor tells them that Isuprel, a broncho-

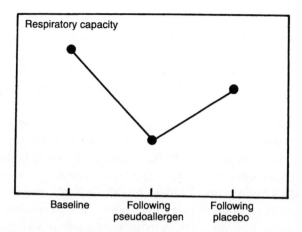

FIGURE 6.8. Influence of suggestion on bronchial reactions in some asthmatic patients. Respiratory capacity is measured by plethysmography (*adapted from Luparello, 1971*).

dilator with whose efficacy in a crisis the patient is well acquainted, has been added to the aerosol. However, in both these cases, the allergen and the bronchodilator are both physiological saline, which is totally innocuous (Fig. 6.8). Furthermore, if after bronchial constriction has been induced by a pseudoallergen, the doctor tells the patient that he is going to see if a puff of pure air will dissipate his symptoms and then adds Isuprel to the aerosol, this last treatment will have slight if any effect.[44]

Too Spectacular to Be Systematic

The bronchoconstriction developed by asthmatic patients under the influence of suggestion is due to variations of the parasympathetic vagal tonus, since it is blocked by atropine, an anticholinergic medication. Not all patients are equally sensitive to suggestion; the phenomenon is observed in roughly 50% of cases. Some go so far as to develop a genuine asthmatic attack analogous to the asthmatic attack developed in the presence of the allergen. Contrary to what one might suppose, the reactions to suggestion by asthmatics do not differ qualitatively from those presented by normal subjects; indeed, one can point to modifications of the respiratory tract in this last group in response to suggestion.[45]

Most studies on hypnosis and suggestion were done between the 1950s and the 1970s, well before the renewal of interest in the links between the immune and nervous systems. The results of these studies are spectacular in appearance only; there is considerable individual variability of response, without conclusive knowledge of the cause. Furthermore, it seems that the phenomena observed cannot be directly imputed to alterations in immunity but, rather, to changing intensities of the inflammatory reaction consequent to an immune response. Despite these restrictions, many people continue to believe in the possibility of direct action on the immune system by thought. Some American physicians, like Carl and Stephanie Simonton, in Dallas, offer their patients anticancer therapies based on relaxation and mental imaging: patients must visualize their own natural killer cells vigorously attacking weakened tumor cells. But, as of now, none of the studies recently undertaken in this area has proved that such practices actually strengthen immune defenses.

THE IMMUNE SYSTEM COMMUNICATES
WITH THE NERVOUS SYSTEM

Despite the random nature of studies attempting to link psychology and the immune system, the ability of the nervous system to affect the immune system is beyond question. How should this phenomenon be interpreted? Intervention in organic function by the nervous system assures effective regulation, since this arrangement permits a coordinated response in case of disturbance. For example, both the reduction of blood volume consequent to hemorrhage and the blood hyperosmolarity that accompanies dehydration involve neurohormonal responses: secreted vasopressin reduces urinary excretion, and the angiotensin that is released augments arterial pressure and initiates the search for and intake of water. The nervous system also assures a linkage between mental and physiological conditions. Fear and anger do not remain purely subjective but lead to action that is only possible if the following corresponding physiological adjustments take place: cardiac rhythm augments, arterial pressure mounts, respiration accelerates and deepens, large quantities of oxygen are directed toward the muscles and brain, and available energy is mobilized.

An analogous concept applied to the immune system suggests that neural influences on immunity are not due to chance; they

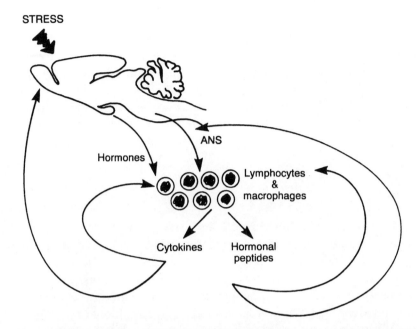

STRESS

Hormones

ANS

Lymphocytes & macrophages

Cytokines

Hormonal peptides

FIGURE 6.9.   Communication pathways between the immune system and the nervous system. The influences of stress on the immune system are mediated by the autonomic nervous system (ANS) and the hormonal paths that normally regulate the immune system, in response to information provided by the latter and transmitted via cytokines and peptides elaborated by immune cells (*adapted from Dantzer and Kelley, 1989*).

represent the inevitable correlation of extrinsic regulation of the functioning of lymphoid organs and cells by the nervous system[46] (Fig. 6.9).

The first essential condition for immune cells to be sensitive to neural influences is that the lymphoid organs in which they are stocked should themselves be objects of extrinsic innervation and should be equipped with all the mechanisms necessary for responding to mediators of the nervous system and to hormones. And we have seen that this is, in fact, the case.

Immune Cells Inform the Brain . . .

However, effective regulation cannot be assured by a simple system linking the brain to a regulated system. To respond in a manner adapted to needs, the brain must receive information about the system it is supposed to regulate. And this means a difference in system design analogous to the difference between a heating apparatus that one lights and then turns off when the desired temperature is reached and a radiator equipped with a thermostat. Transposed to the immune system, an apparatus of the latter type informs the brain of its functioning condition. The classic means available for this communication are, on the one hand, the nerve afferences from appropriate transducing receptors and, on the other hand, humoral factors. It is to this latter group that research is oriented.

... Through the Cytokines

Historically, it was the work of Besedovsky and Sorkin, in Davos, Switzerland, that first drew attention to the existence of influences of the immune system on neuroendocrine systems. In the 1970s, these authors observed that during antibody production in response to the injection of a standard antigen (the equivalent of a vaccinal response) laboratory animals, at the moment of maximum response, show a marked increase in blood levels of corticosterone and decreased levels of norepinephrine in the spleen (Fig. 6.10). These modifications are not the product of local influences but the result of a reflex, since a simultaneous augmentation is observed in the frequency of neuronal discharge in certain areas of the hypothalamus of immunized rats.[47]

Subsequently, efforts were made to identify the humoral factor or factors responsible. A first approach resulted from the observation that a soluble factor, provisionally called GIF (for Glucocorticoid Increasing Factor) and released by lymphocytes cultivated in the presence of mitogen, has the same hormonal and neural effects as those observed in the course of an immune response. This factor has not yet been identified. A second approach derives from the development of biotechnology, more precisely, from the possibility of synthesizing in large numbers and at relatively low cost the cytokines produced by immune cells. Interleukin-1 (IL-1), one of the principal inflammatory mediators synthesized and released by activated macrophages, activates the pituitary-adrenal axis by a direct action on the pituitary or the CRF neurons in the paraventricular nucleus of the hypothalamus.[48]

Each of these mediators can intervene as part of a regulatory network of communication signals. According to Besedovsky, GIF, that factor of lymphocyte origin elaborated during the course of a

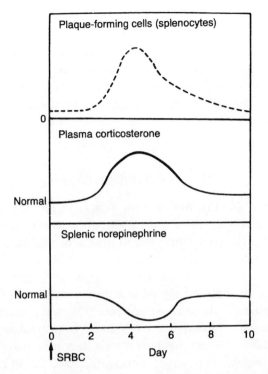

FIGURE 6.10. Relation between immune response as measured by the number of new plaque-forming cells in cultured splenocytes, the activation of the pituitary-adrenal axis as indicated by blood concentrations of corticosterone, and the activity of the sympathetic nervous system as measured by splenic concentrations of norepinephrine, in rats immunized from day 0 with sheep red blood cells (SRBC) (*adapted from Besedovsky and Sorkin, 1977*).

humoral immune response, acts on the hypothalamus and provokes in consequence an elevation of circulating corticosteroids, which are responsible for the phenomenon of antigenic competition. And we know, in fact, that the production of antibodies directed against a second antigen is very weak when the second antigen is injected several days after the first. This would be due to the fact that corticosteroids reduce the capacity for activation in lymphocytes not yet activated while they have very little effect on lymphocytes already activated. As for IL-1, it is produced by the macrophages during infection or antigenic stimulation and exercises a variety of immune (lymphocyte activation), vascular (inflammation), metabolic (negative nitrogen balance), and neural (fever) actions. These effects favor the struggle against infection but, if overly prolonged, risk becoming noxious. Since IL-1 also stimulates the pituitary-adrenal axis and since the production of IL-1 by the macrophages is reduced by glucocorticoids, one might suppose that the hormonal action of IL-1 represents the efferent pathway of a negative feedback loop on the macrophages, which limits the possibility of an excessive reaction to infection (cf. Fig. 3.3).

ACTH of Immune Origin

Edwin Blalock and Eric Smith at the School of Medicine, University of Texas, Galveston, set out in a direction totally different from Besedovsky's. By comparing the amino acid sequences of ACTH (the pituitary peptide that stimulates the secretion of glucocorticoids) and of interferon (an antiviral protein synthesized by the lymphocytes during viral infection), they were struck by the analogous structures of these two peptides.[49] They therefore proposed the hypothesis that interferon exercises a hormonal action similar to that of ACTH. To test this hypothesis they inoculated mice with Newcastle disease. This virus, pathogenic to fowl but not to mice, nonetheless provokes in mice a synthesis of interferon by the lymphocytes. As expected, the infected mice produced elevated concentrations of circulating glucocorticoids, which were present even in hypophysectomized animals, in principle deprived of all sources of ACTH (Fig. 6.11). These results, therefore, tended to prove that lymphocytes secrete a mediator with an action comparable to that of ACTH. However, this mediator was quickly revealed to be not interferon but ACTH itself; the lymphocytes activated by the Newcastle virus synthesize proopiomelanocortin, the prohormone also present in the anterior pituitary. As it is in the pituitary, this precursor is divided into several constituent fragments, including ACTH and β-endorphin. Furthermore, production of lymphocyte ACTH is stimulated by CRF and vasopressin and blocked by the glucocorticoids.[50]

These results have given rise to several controversies. Although the reality of production of peptides derived from proopiomelanocortin by the lymphocytes is scarcely a matter of doubt, the same cannot be said of their possible hormonal role. The experiments of Smith and Blalock were roundly criticized; the authors

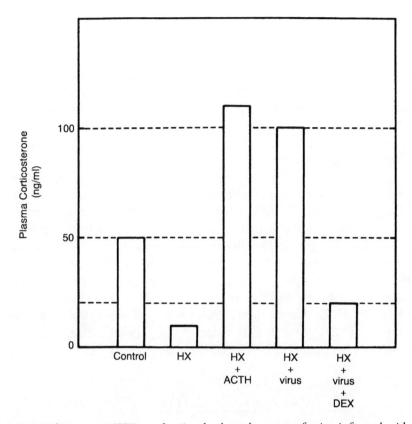

FIGURE 6.11.   ACTH production by lymphocytes of mice infected with the Newcastle disease virus. In mice whose pituitary gland has been removed (hypophysectomy, Hx)—that is, who have been deprived of endogenous ACTH—plasma corticosterone concentration is very low. Nevertheless the adrenal cortex is still able to respond to ACTH injected by the experimenter (Hx + ACTH). In hypophysectomized mice also infected with the virus, the existence of another source of ACTH is suggested by an increase in plasma corticosterone (Hx + virus) and the disappearance of this increase after treatment with a synthetic corticoid, dexamethasone (Hx + virus + DEX) (*adapted from Smith et al., 1982*).

had not verified the extent of hypophysectomy in mice infected by the Newcastle disease virus and presenting adrenal activation. In fact, with even a small fragment of the pituitary, ACTH can be secreted. Other teams were unable to find increases of circulating ACTH in totally hypophysectomized animals.[51] In any case, as quantities of peptides produced by lymphocytes remain minimal compared to those of pituitary origin, it seems probable that peptides released in this manner do not act at a distance but serve as local communication within the immune system.[52] To the credit of Smith and Blalock, it must be conceded that their work stimulated a series of research efforts on the possibilities of synthesizing other peptides by the immune cells. The valuable nature of this research was borne out by discovery in the lymphocytes of an arsenal of peptides including the thyroid-stimulating hormone, growth hormone, and proenkephalin.

From these results concerning the possibilities of communication between the immune and nervous systems, it must be stressed that the immune cells release two major categories of mediators: on the one hand, cytokines like interleukin-1, which in addition to acting as mediator within the immune system also affect nervous targets at a distance and, on the other, peptides analogous to those in the nervous system and capable of intervention in cellular communication within the immune system. In this latter instance, the presence of the same mediators in the neuroendocrine and immune systems constitutes an additional argument favoring the possibilities of interaction between the two systems.

THE IMMUNOLOGICAL BASIS OF ILLNESS

The condition of being sick is not limited to the presentation of a certain number of specific symptoms in the affected organs, for example, coughing for respiratory difficulties or a runny nose in bronchopulmonary illness; it also means feeling miserable, with fever, perhaps, and a lack of desire for food and drink, lethargy, a reduced inclination to interact with others, sleepiness, and lack of interest in one's external appearance.

Fever is certainly the best known of these nonspecific symptoms. In physiological terms, fever corresponds to an upward adjustment of the thermoregulatory reference point of central temperature. A feverish subject feels cold in normal temperatures. To reduce heat loss, peripheral blood circulation is reduced, and animals without hair or fur are in a state of piloerection. Affected individuals seek warmth, and if they fail to find it, they curl up to reduce surface areas subject to thermal exchange. If these measures prove insufficient, mechanisms of thermogenesis are activated, which is when shivering occurs.

Fever: A Mechanism of Defense

We tend to think of fever as a harmful reaction, to be fought energetically. This is true of the powerful hyperthermias that can produce convulsions and cerebral lesions in the newborn, but it is not the case with moderate hyperthermias. Fever constitutes a useful defense mechanism since many pathogenic agents suffer reduced rates of proliferation at temperatures that are above normal. Falling levels of plasmatic zinc and iron during febrile episodes also contribute to the inhibition of growth in germs. Finally, temperatures that are slightly higher than normal activate the immune responses. As the American physiologist Kluger[52] has shown, lizards or fish exposed to bacterial infection survive less well under cold than under warm conditions. And the same tendency exists in homeotherms; ferrets become more sensitive to the human flu virus when they are shaved or treated with aspirin. In elderly people, the fever response is attenuated, and sensitivity to infectious agents is often heightened.

Fever mobilizes all an organism's resources to resist infection. A fight against illness is not a matter of a few moments but, rather, of days and even weeks. During this time energy demands are made on internal resources, and the physiology of the entire organism is oriented toward rest. Activities requiring high expenditures of energy are banned; seeking food or drink not only exposes individuals to attack from predators at a moment when they are weakened but also squanders energy. It should therefore be no surprise that fever is accompanied by weakness, hypersomnia, and a raised threshold of response to stimuli of hunger and thirst.[53]

Fever Mechanisms

Fever mechanisms have only recently been elucidated, and it is to be noted that mediators at the origin of fever are also responsible for coordination between the various immune, vascular, metabolic, and neural elements of the organic response to infection. The first stage of this research was completed in the 1950s when it was shown that fever is not caused by direct action on thermoregulation by the infectious agent but, in fact, occurs through release of an endogenous pyrogen by the phagocytic cells, particularly the monocytes and macrophages. We then had to wait until the beginning of this decade to clarify the exact nature of the endogenous pyrogen and to show that it and interleukin-1, already identified by immunologists, were one and the same. Until 1985 fever mechanisms could only be studied through the administration of bacterial endotoxins (still known as lipopolysaccharides because of their chemical structure) and, less often, of the endogenous pyrogen, more or less purified. Isolation of the IL-1 gene (there are actually two genes encoding two different molecules, IL-1 alpha and IL-1 beta, but their activities are very closely related) has made it possible to produce IL-1 with bacteria into whose genomes the IL-1 gene has been inserted, and thus to obtain the pure product in quantities adequate for experimentation.

Interleukin-1 forms part of many factors of growth and cellular differentiation secreted by the immune cells. Injection of interleukin-1 produces an elevation of central temperature and the appearance of biological signs of fever, which involve the acute phase reaction (reduction of plasma zinc and iron, the synthesis of specific proteins by the liver, and an increase in fibrinogenesis), the activation of immune responses, vascular modifications characteristic of inflammation, and metabolic alterations (degradation of organic proteins and a shift to negative nitrogen balance). Interleukin-1, therefore, is a genuine hormone that acts on several target cells (lymphocytes, hepatic cells, muscle cells, vascular endothelium, and hypothalamic neurons)[54] (Fig. 6.12). Some of these

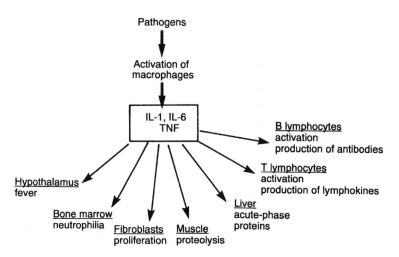

FIGURE 6.12.   The many actions of interleukin-1, interleukin-6, and tumoral necrosis factor.

effects are due to the synthesis of prostaglandin E. This is true of fever since it is reduced by administration of an inhibitor of the synthesis of prostaglandins, such as aspirin or indomethacin.

IL-1 Acts on the Brain

The pyrogenic action of IL-1 occurs in the hypothalamus. However, how IL-1 reaches the hypothalamus is not yet understood with precision, especially as it is not of a size and chemical nature to pass through the blood-brain barrier, which limits penetration of the brain by large molecules and nonlipophilic substances.

Direct injection of IL-1 into the brain provokes fever, although less intense than fevers observed subsequent to intravenous injection. Indomethacin administered to the brain has no effect on fever induced by intravenous injection of IL-1, but it can block fever caused by the intracerebral injection of IL-1. Similarly, intravenous injection of indomethacin is effective only when IL-1 is administered in the same way. These results indicate that IL-1 acts outside the blood-brain barrier, probably in what are called the circumventricular organs (because of their location around the cerebral ventricles). IL-1 induces a synthesis of prostaglandins in one of these organs, the organum vasculosum of the lamina terminalis, and the prostaglandins that are then released diffuse as far as the hypothalamic areas involved in the central regulation of body temperature.[55]

In addition to fever, IL-1 produces a reduction of motor activity, an increase in sleep, diminished intake of water and food, a sense of discomfort, and reduced sociability. These symptoms are similar to those that accompany illness and do not derive from prostaglandins, since they are not affected by indomethacin or aspirin. The mechanisms by which they are manifested are not yet known[56] (Fig. 6.13).

The organism does not passively submit to the effects of IL-1. We have already seen that it releases glucocorticoids to inhibit the synthesis and release of this cytokine in the producer cells. It also has available other means for calming things down: vasopressin and alpha-melanotropin, a melanotropic hormone. In sheep, fever produced by the administration of endotoxin entails a release of vasopressin in the septum, a structure of the limbic system. Local administration of vasopressin reduces fever while the injection of antibodies that neutralize vasopressin has the reverse effect.[57]

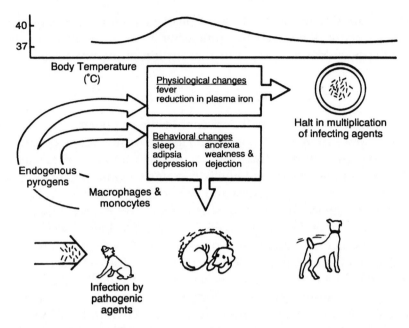

FIGURE 6.13. Endogenous pyrogens (IL-1, IL-6, and TNF) released by the immune system are responsible for the behavioral and psychological disturbances that accompany the response to infection in a nonspecific fashion (*adapted from Hart, 1988*).

TNF and Other Mediators of Sickness

The actions of other cytokines produced by the immune cells are similar to those of IL-1 and increase its possible effects. This is true of the tumor necrosis factor (TNF), of interferon-alpha, and of interleukin-6.

The tumor necrosis factor is named for its antitumoral action.[58] The first indications that such a factor exists were collected at the end of the last century by William Coley, a physician in New York. After noticing that tumor regression occurred in the course of some bacterial illnesses, he thought of deliberately infecting his patients, with all the risks and caveats such an approach entailed at that time. This approach met with some success, and Coley moved on to a systematic use of vaccines made with dead bacteria (Coley toxins). Although this effort produced mixed results, it led to the identification of the active component of bacteria, lipopolysaccharide or endotoxin, and of the cells responsible for the synthesis and release of TNF, that is, macrophages. As with IL–1, it was not until

1984 that TFN could be cloned, sequenced, and produced by recombinant biotechnology. This work also enabled us to discover that TFN is identical to cachectin, a molecule that had been characterized by parasitologists as being released by macrophages during parasitic infections and being responsible for the wasting syndrome of severe parasitic infections. Injections of TNF to laboratory rodents confirmed that this cytokine has cytotoxic effects on certain tumoral cells and that, like IL–1, it is an important component of the response to infection and inflammation. TNF plays a pivotal role in the pathogenesis of septic shock because it profoundly affects blood vessels and coagulation. Cachexia, another consequence of TNF, is due to the inhibition of the lipoprotein lipase enzyme, which is normally responsible for lipid storage.

Interferons are produced by white blood cells and fibroblasts (interferon α and β) and T lymphocytes (interferon γ). These cytokines induce the synthesis of antiviral proteins by cells infected with viruses. Interferon γ is a potent activating factor of macrophages. It also stimulates the cytotoxic activity of natural killer cells. All interferons produce fever and have effects on the nervous system similar to those of IL–1 and TNF.[59]

The story of the mediators of disease does not stop there. Cytokines are also present in the brain and, furthermore, brain peptides are present in immune cells. In the first instance, recent studies show that glial cells, which surround neurons and contribute to their functioning, can synthesize and release various cytokines including IL–1 and TNF. This is particularly true of microglial cells and astrocytes. The exact physiological role of cytokines in the brain is not yet known. They modulate the growth as well as the differentiation of neurons and glial cells. Several elements suggest that these cytokines may play an important part in the pathological processes of infections and tumors within the nervous system, considerations that constitute a new domain in neurology.[60]

The second case of note is illustrated by the muramyl peptides. These peptides were initially isolated from the membranes of bacteria in an attempt to find adjuvants of immunity capable of stimulating immune responses in a nonspecific way. In an entirely independent effort, neurophysiologists discovered in the cerebrospinal fluid, blood, and urine of sleep-deprived animals a protein factor that produces sleep in normal animals. Chemical analysis revealed that this somnogenic factor was, in fact, a derivative of the muramyl peptides. When small quantities of these peptides are injected directly into the brain, they raise brain temperature and induce sleep, apparently by local release of IL-1.[61] Since peptides of this kind cannot be synthesized by mammals, just how they appear in the nervous system is not yet understood.

When All Becomes Clear—Almost

The rapid evolution of knowledge about the interaction between the nervous and immune systems exemplifies the basic perspective of psychosomatics, for it concerns an area in which the possible links between psychological factors and pathology have been at the root of several controversies—in the total absence of elements supporting arguments one way or the other. During the last eight years, this situation has completely changed. We can now explain how mental states affect the functioning of the immune system and how illness affects the psyche. The enthusiasm that accompanies major discoveries is always a generator of excess: A California psychotherapist recently wrote me claiming that he had been able to make a patient in analysis understand that the tumor in his left lung was a product of his professional problems. Firmly persuaded of this diagnosis, he had instituted a psychotherapeutic regimen designed to make the tumor vanish, and he was already envisioning getting his patient to reexpose himself to the same set of professional problems to see if the tumor would grow back!

The Rehabilitation of Psychology

In regard to psychological influences on immunity, research in psychoneuroimmunology has not yet managed to identify a psychological profile that would be considered a risk factor and that would be the equivalent of Type A behavior for coronary diseases. It is clear that life events affect the functioning of immune responses. However, results are not always in the direction of immunodepression. Furthermore, many immunologists consider the observed variations to be marginal and unlikely to lead to an established pathology. The most remarkable fact in this area is not so much the results that have been obtained but the attitude beginning to emerge in medical circles. This attitude is apparent in ordinary, as well as exceptional, circumstances. Thus, in the first place, at some cancer clinics the psychology of the patient is taken into consideration, and there is no reluctance to treat the depression that is bound to arise sooner or later, especially since some antidepressants may actually strengthen immune defenses. And in the second place, it is no longer startling to see a small group of Dutch clinicians—led, one must concede, by a retired professor of medicine—adopt as their objective the discovery of the explanation for spontaneous remission in cancer cases diagnosed as uncurable.

Neural Influences on Inflammation

We are now beginning to understand, in biological terms, how neural influences can modify the evolution of diseases with an immune component. These neural influences principally affect the inflammatory processes consequent to an immune response. Rheumatoid arthritis is a typical example. This disease, affecting women far more often than men, is characterized by chronic inflammation of the joints, with attendant stiffness, swelling, and redness. After several years, it leads to deformation of the bones and gradual restriction of movement. Rheumatoid arthritis has a strong psychological component; according to Alexander, it develops in people who, having been the objects of excessive parental solicitude during childhood, try in vain during childhood and adolescence to revolt, expressing themselves in physical activities before developing a neurotic tendency to wish to control their surroundings.

Immunologists have shown that rheumatoid arthritis is, in fact, an illness with an immune component in which, for reasons not yet understood, some cells of the synovial membrane begin to manifest on their membrane class II molecules of the major histocompatibility complex. While doing this, they behave like macrophages presenting an antigen to lymphocytes. They therefore initiate a local immune response with a subsequent release of IL-1, TNF, and interferon. The consequent inflammatory reaction irritates the nerve endings innervating the synovial membrane. This irritation translates into a release of the peptides contained in nerve fibers, particularly substance P, a peptide that exacerbates the inflammatory process by stimulating proliferation of synovial cells and promoting the release of prostaglandin E and collagenase, an enzyme that attacks collagen.[62] Many experiments done on models of rheumatoid arthritis in rats confirm the importance of the neurogenic component in the development of this illness; a lesion of sympathetic nerve fibers innervating the joints reduces the intensity of symptoms. This remains the case during the course of treatment by antagonists of substance P. Conversely, injection of substance P into the joint increases the severity of the arthritis[63] (Fig. 6.14).

The mechanisms we have just described apply also in other cases of interaction between the nervous and the immune systems. Physiologists have long been acquainted with the *axon* reflex, the part played by the nervous system in the inflammatory reaction: mechanical or chemical stimulation of a sensory nerve ending in the skin provokes a moderate inflammatory reaction in the area innervated by the neuron to which that ending is attached. This is called an axon reflex because nerve impulses do not need to travel up to the neuronal cell body to invade the nerve collaterals (axons) that are stimulated. The release of substance P and other vasodilatory peptides is responsible for the local inflammatory reaction.

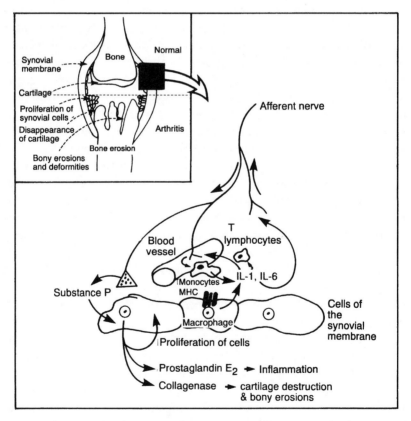

FIGURE 6.14.   Mechanisms of neurogenic inflammation in rheumatoid arthritis.

Substance P provokes vasodilation, increased capillary permeability, and a local release of inflammatory cytokines (IL-1, TNF, and IL-6) by the macrophages and circulating monocytes.[64] The ubiquitous distribution of vasodilator peptides like substance P in the nerve endings innervating various visceral territories, from nasal mucosa to gastric and intestinal mucosa, leads one to suppose that these are important defense mechanisms in the local reaction to pathogens. How or if such mechanisms become sensitive to supraspinal influences is not yet known.

The Cytokines Reverse the Perspective

Although it is clear that the nervous system can modify the development of diseases with immune components, that is not the end of the matter. Through the cytokines, the immune system is also able to alter the functioning of the nervous system. Here are molecules that, in addition to their effects on the immune system, provoke turmoil in the organic economy and dramatic changes of behavior. The disordered conditions during an attack of flu can readily be imagined!

The idea that cytokines can be mediators not only of reactions to infection but also of neural and psychological components of illness leads to a genuine change of perspective in our conception of psychosomatic diseases. One might, in fact, readily imagine that cytokines are released into the organism at the moment of the initial defense reaction to a pathogenic agent—long before the illness has been diagnosed in its own right. Therefore, the psychological modifications that occur in consequence actually precede the disease. Since one cannot divine that these are another facet of the disease, one naturally tends to give them a causal role, although they are, in fact, simple correlates. In the same way, one can assume that during the course of a disease the effects of releasing cytokines will be greater when the immune system is more affected. Thus, the more serious the illness, the more intense are the psychological symptoms produced by the cytokines. Here again, there is a tendency in all good faith to see in psychology a factor that explains the development of disease. This is not simply a speculative matter. It has been possible to show in human subjects that episodes of flu are accompanied by sensorimotor and cognitive disturbances that extend beyond the episode and that can be reproduced by simple injection of interferon α.[65]

THE
EXPERIENCE
OF ILLNESS

Illness is a behavior of negative value for a living
individual. It is concrete and in a relation
of polar opposition to its milieu.

—GEORGES CANGUILHEM, *The Normal and the Pathological*

In making an in-depth study of the modalities of the stress reaction and of the details of interaction among the different defense systems of the organism facing stress, one risks losing sight of the singularity of illness as an experience lived through by the afflicted person. Furthermore, an essential notion is involved here. Psychoanalysts were quick to realize this, distinguishing between *sign, symptom,* and *word.* More prosaically, a sick person is first and foremost someone who does not feel well. He consults a doctor to discover what is wrong with him and what might be done to treat him. But what is diagnosed and treated by the medical establishment is not identical to what is experienced by the patient. English has two expressions to designate these phenomena: *disease* and *illness,* respectively.

The increasing complexity of diagnostic methods and methods of care introduces a growing distance between these two representations of illness. This tendency is aggravated by the relative unimportance accorded to human qualities and to psychology in the training of doctors and medical personnel.

Various voices have already been raised in protest against this expansion of medical power over the rest of life and the dehumanization resulting from it.[1] Modern technologically oriented medicine stumbles over the human being—who is not a machine. Between the headlong rush forward into an ever more rigid technology and the attraction of what Alain de Sédouy, in a highly impressionistic work,[2] calls *magouillothérapie* (dishonest medical practices), there is certainly room for the responsible practice of medicine, one that is as much concerned with the sufferings of life as with organic dysfunction. For the restoration of psychosomatics, what goal could be nobler than the establishment of a genuine behavioral medicine, beyond the sterile battles of conflicting schools?

HEALTH AND ILLNESS

In his doctoral thesis presented to the Faculty of Medicine at Strasbourg in 1943,[3] the philosopher Georges Canguilhem stresses the importance of the conceptual rupture introduced by Claude Bernard in the understanding of illness. Before Bernard, the patient lying in his bed was the focus of the doctor's interest. Doctors observed their patients, noted symptoms, looked for connections; when they finally decided to open a few cadavers, they discovered pathological anatomy and "in the clarity of death"[4] could return to their patients to establish in living bodies sensory markers denoting the affected organs.

For Claude Bernard and his successors, the pathological proceeds from the normal and is the physiology of the sick person (Victor Pachon). It is not possible to understand diabetes mellitus without knowing the means of metabolic regulation of glucose and other carbon hydrates and the role of insulin. A future doctor, therefore, should begin by studying physiology (the normal functioning of organs) before undertaking pathology. The way in which medical studies are organized translates this idea.

As Georges Canguilhem notes, the risk in medicine of confusing illness with cellular or organic dysfunction is a serious one. "To seek out an illness at the cellular level is to confuse the realm of real life, in which biologic polarity makes the difference between health and illness, with that of abstract science, in which problems receive solutions." Illness exists only in the realm of a patient's relationship to his body and to the world around him and not at the level of a specific organ, much less a specific cell.

In an attempt to respond to this preoccupation, the World Health Organization defined health as a state of physical and mental well-being, rather than as the absence of illness. But this definition, although seductive, has the gross defect of not being operational at any level other than that of the health authorities. Well-being is an ideal of life defined by society; it is essentially a sociocultural norm. Instead of this idealistic conception of health, a more pragmatic view might be preferable, a view that is also more personal since it involves the outlook of the patient himself: "Health is life accompanied by silence from the vital organs." This admirable maxim was produced by Leriche, who succeeded Claude Bernard to the Chair of Experimental Medicine at the Collège de France. "A state of health is a subject's unawareness of his body. Inversely, awareness of the body derives from a sense of limits, threats, obstacles to health." Such a definition is correct because it expresses the point of view of the person who is ill and not that of the physician or of society. Once again let us quote Canguilhem: "It is, therefore, first of all because people feel ill that we have medicine. It is only secondary that people, because medicine exists, know what their illnesses are."

GENETIC DISEASES

Canguilhem's thesis, that understanding of the illness must come from consideration of the patient, is largely ignored by modern medicine, a tendency that is intensified by the growing importance accorded to molecular genetics. As James Watson (winner of the 1953 Nobel prize for his work on the structure of the double helix of DNA, deoxyribonucleic acid) freely volunteers, the destiny of the human species is inscribed not in the stars but in human genes.

Mapping the human genome, that is, determining the location on the chromosomes of the genes, which code for various constituents of human heredity, has become for biologists an adventure analogous to that of the space shuttle for American astronauts in the 1970s, an undertaking of depth and breadth backed by a lavish commitment of material and human resources. Susceptibility to disease, like eye color, is a matter of genes. Identifying the defective genes at the root of disease is, therefore, the best way to determine the probability of an individual's developing a particular disease and the indispensable preliminary step in instituting a regimen to prevent its onset.[5] This is not a utopian proposal. It has already been proved by a reference model: phenylpyruvic oligophrenia, a profound mental retardation caused by a genetic anomaly affecting the synthesis of phenylalanine hydroxylase, an enzyme indispensable to the metabolism of amino acids. This enzymatic insufficiency is without consequence so long as the patient's diet remains free of phenylalanine.

This is not a question of the merits or limitations of the genetic approach, not to mention the ethical problems to which this approach inevitably leads. Returning to his thesis of 1943 and the light shed by discoveries about the genetic origin of some diseases, Canguilhem stressed in 1966 the problems raised by the new medical orientation:

> One can nonetheless maintain that the idea of organic error is nothing if not reassuring. It requires a great deal of clarity combined with courage not to favor an idea of illness in which there is still room for some sense of individual guilt over an explanation that pulverizes that sense and disseminates causality in the familial genome, in an inheritance that the heir cannot refuse because inheritance and inheritor are one and the same. . . . Linked to the refusal of death, of pain, and of suffering, that is, to the fundamental reasons for medicine's existence, enzymatic misreadings are lived by human beings who must pay the consequences, as for an error of driving in which the driver is not at fault.

Canguilhem, with remarkable foresight, formulated these problems very early, problems that normally would mobilize the energies of psychosomaticians preoccupied with the unity of mind and body. And it seems that the was preaching to a void.

ILLNESS AS A BEHAVIOR

The example of pain provides a better understanding of the limitations of present attitudes toward illness. Until recently, all pain research was based on a very simple model, the nociceptive reflex described by Sherrington, an English physiologist in the early years of this century. An individual exposed to a nociceptive stimulus—that is, to something painful, such as scalding water, a needle prick, or some direct excitation of the nerve fibers that convey pain—will feel nothing if neural transmission is blocked at some point along the sensory circuit involved. And the intensity of his reaction to pain is reduced if an antalgic medication like aspirin or, in serious cases, morphine is administered to him.

But, as Leriche had already noted, "physical pain is not a simple matter of nerve impulse proceeding along a nerve at fixed speed. It is the product of conflict between a stimulus and the entire individual."

This is the idea that Bolles and Fanselow rediscovered without realizing it when, as shown in Chapter 3, they suggested viewing pain as a central motivational state, that is, a perception and set of motivated behaviors rather than a simple sensation. To feel pain or discomfort is to perceive an abnormal sensation at the surface or in the interior of one's body and to act in ways that attempt to minimize that perception. Viewing pain as a motivational state makes possible an interpretive system for recognizing what is not working within the self. Further, it makes available the means inherent to that motivational system so that, if need be, an individual can use them to achieve what would otherwise be impossible.

André Gide, who was a sickly, pampered child, has written eloquently about the mixed feelings of a sufferer who grasps only too well the power over others that is conferred by his situation.[6] For everyone near him, the sufferer is the center of attention. He is allowed to lie back and rest until his ability to function returns. If his professional circumstances displease him, he may be tempted to exaggerate his discomfort and extend his period of recuperation. Conversely, a patient who is overly concerned about his professional life but handicapped by his pain may try to minimize his discomfort in order to continue working.

Explanations of pain behavior, therefore, are no longer confined to the immediate effects of the painful sensation. As in the case of Skinner's hungry rat pressing on a lever to obtain food, the initial motivation is still there to determine behavior, but the form assumed has nothing to do with motivation. One might make the rat press the lever a hundred times before he receives food or one might allow one minute to elapse and then reward the first effort. In each case the rat's behavior depends entirely on the link between the response, what he does, and the reward, what he obtains. For an external observer, an examination of the response curve does not, by itself, make clear whether the animal is responding in order to obtain food or drink or to avoid electric shock. Furthermore, when a rat is well trained, it may continue to press the lever to obtain a pellet of food even if other food is freely available in the corner of the cage!

Yet Skinnerian psychologists have made the same conceptual mistake as stress theoreticians; they have emphasized the importance of the stimulus–response relationship to such an extent that they have denied the existence of mental states. For them, anxiety and pleasure do not exist, and the directly observable is all that counts. We now know that this qualified conception of behaviorism[7] is inadequate; economizing with the idea of internal representation will not produce an understanding of behavior, even the behavior of animals. When a rat runs in a radial maze that has food at the end of each branch, he does so methodically, never making two consecutive trips to the same branch. As he explores, he constructs in his brain the equivalent of a map of his surroundings, which psychologists call a cognitive map.

Internal representations are usually multidimensional. When these are well established, perception of a single dimension is enough to reconstitute the whole. The taste of a little madeleine, even diluted in tea, resurrects the entire universe of Combray in the mind of Marcel Proust!

If the same schema is applied to pain, it would mean that a patient suffering chronic pain would experience all its discomforts from perceptions associated with it, in the absence of any directly painful stimulation. Clinical data support this reading: many cases of chronic pain persist even after the specifically relevant nerve fibers have been blocked.

The implications of this concept are important. If pain gradually becomes autonomous, independent of the painful stimulus, recourse to antalgic therapies is useless. Inducing the patient to acquire new behaviors contradicting those he previously embraced is the best way to reduce suffering. This cannot be done in isolated fashion; the contribution of the setting to pain-provoking behavior must also be considered.

At this point we can perceive the principles of what is called behavioral medicine, a medical practice inspired by methodological behaviorism.[8] This practice considers the patient in his relationship to illness and attempts to influence that relationship by adding to the treatment of the symptom or cause a correction of the patient's behaviors (and the behaviors of those around him) that may support his injurious way of living.

TO RECONCILE PATIENT AND CURE

The behavioral approach also implies a knowledge of the patient's experience of the illness and an understanding on the part of medical practitioners that this is not a question of an instantly accessible fact but involves aspects of the illness whose proof requires as much skill as any other medical undertaking. The ultimate goal is to improve the patient's condition, helping him to function normally, despite his handicap, by understanding the nature of his complaint and incorporating it into his psychoaffective life.

One of the key elements of this question is the patient–therapist relationship. Recent work by psychologists and sociologists has considerably furthered our knowledge of this aspect of illness and care.[9] We can now move beyond generalities and deal with specific problems, such as the following: What precisely impels a patient to seek professional help? What elements external to the illness determine the way in which consultation is conducted? How satisfied does the patient feel? And how does he translate his feelings of satisfaction (or dissatisfaction) into adherence to (or disregard of) the suggested treatment (a problem known as compliance)?

English psychologists followed 79 women, aged 16 to 44, for six weeks, asking them to note systematically every instance of indisposition during the course of a day. In the period delineated there were, on average, some 11 instances per subject, with an average length of some two days but with fewer than one professional consultation. The most frequent symptoms were headaches and fatigue (one-third of the total). These, however, produced almost no consultations (only 6 percent) while skin problems, representing only 1 percent of problems, motivated a full quarter of the consultations. A decision to visit the doctor was usually not entirely individual but was a product of discussion with someone in the patient's immediate circle, a husband or a friend. These facts are important because they indicate that one cannot disregard the social dimension of illness.

What happens once a patient decides to visit a doctor? Psychologists at London University, attempting to schematize their understanding of how these visits were organized, made detailed analyses of over two thousand consultations. Social inequality was the primary and most obvious element; an average consultation lasted six minutes in the case of a member of the professional class, as opposed to just over four minutes for working-class patients. This difference bore no relation to the severity of the medical problem, nor did it relate to a patient's verbal facility (or lack thereof). Three-quarters of these consultations were led entirely by the doctor, who asked questions without searching for what really motivated the patient. Experience seems to play a small part in this regard; differences between established and novice physicians were minimal. However, when patients are asked why they are consulting a doctor, it is clear that an enormous majority have something specific to say but only 37 percent do this spontaneously, while another 26 percent will speak out if their input is solicited.

In research done at Children's Hospital, Los Angeles, mothers who came to the emergency room were systematically questioned on how they perceived their child's illness, what they hoped to get from the doctor, and the degree of satisfaction obtained. For 800 consultations, the balance at first glance seems encouraging, with three out of four patients declaring themselves satisfied. However, detailed analysis reveals a picture that is considerably more complicated. At the end of their visits, a full 50 percent still did not know the nature of their child's complaint, and one in five imputed this ignorance to a total lack of information from the doctor. As these women did not know the nature of their child's illness, it is not surprising that in 38 percent of cases the mother herself felt guilty. In terms of observance, the results were disastrous: in the two weeks subsequent to consultation only four in ten mothers followed prescribed treatments to the letter; a similar proportion made some form of compromise effort, and one in ten did nothing at all. As might be expected, compliance was weakest among those least satisfied by the consultation.

Failure to observe prescribed treatment is one of the major limitations on any medical action. All research concurs that only 50 percent of patients follow medical advice and that at least nine of ten doctors are largely unaware of this problem. Imperfect observance of the doctor's orders is not necessarily an act of defiance by the patient. In that case, too, detailed analysis of consultation content suggests a failure of communication. Since the vocabulary used by doctors is two to three times more specialized than that of the average patient, there is a strong possibility that patients simply do not grasp what the doctor is trying to tell them. As partial proof, researchers point to the fact that by the end of a consultation 40 percent of what was said has already been forgotten and one or two in every ten patients still don't know what the problem is.

This analysis at least has the advantage of supplying concrete data for intervention with a view toward improving the situation. And it is known that various aspects of the patient–doctor relationship are markedly improved by the presence of adequate attendant staff. French medical schools teach a subject known as medical psychology; this would be a splendid opportunity to revive it!

THE ATTRACTION OF ALTERNATIVE MEDICINE

It is paradoxical, if not even disquieting, to note a tendency in the direction of mysticism instead of objective consideration of an illness and the pragmatism such objectivity fosters. To paraphrase Michel Foucault, there is no question here of supporting one theory over another or of militating against medical treatment or in favor of inaction.[4] The point here is to isolate a few elements for reflection.

The medical literature for the lay public includes a growing number of books that stress general cosmic influences on health, the power of the mind over the body, and the power of natural defense systems. Thinking and feeling "right" constitutes a popular rallying cry; "negative" emotions are held responsible for sickness and death while "positive" emotions heal and protect.[10] Add to this mixture a flavoring of ecology and physical narcissism, and you have all the elements of a best seller. That doctors themselves are

responsible for a considerable number of these books is not without significance.

On behalf of doctors, it should be said that the present crisis of
medical practice derives from the dissatisfaction so many of them
feel. Armed only with the tools of etiological therapy (e.g., antibi-
otics for cases of infection) or symptomatic therapy (tranquilizers
for anxiety), doctors must confront the uniqueness of the illness
experienced by the patient. Physicians sufficiently clear-sighted to
recognize their inability to cure the distress expressed by so many
patients, and aware of the risks of iatrogenic illness provoked by
assaultive prescriptions, find themselves highly desirable prey for
the so-called holistic therapies.

What could be more seductive than a practice based on a
philosophy whose specific intention—whether the immediate concern be nutritional, social, or cosmic—is to return the individual to
the complexity of his relationship with the environment? Philo-
sophical support for such a position is readily available. In English-
speaking countries holism, the doctrine which has most affected
medical practice, was proposed early in the century by Jan Chris-
tiaan Smuts, a South African politician who attempted to integrate
the Darwinian theory of evolution into the complexity of the universe.[11] The world, according to this view, is organized in structures of increasing complexity, from physicochemical structures
(the realm of physical and chemical relationships) to psychophysical structures (the realm of mind, spirit, and personality) by way of
organisms and biochemical structures (the realm of life). At each
level new properties that cannot be reduced to elementary components emerge. Creativity, the generating engine of evolution (not
to be confused with Creationism and its belief in an external di-
vinity), is therefore a characteristic property of the essential structures of life itself.

Applied to illness, holistic theory refutes the identity between
organic dysfunction affecting the biochemical structure and the
illness affecting the psychophysical structure. Holism, or more exactly a caricature of it, has become the justification for a heterogeneous collection of medical practices ranging from iridology to
acupuncture.[12] Some of these treatments—like homeopathy in
France and chiropractic in the United States—are institutionalized,
so that guarantees of respectability are implied. The fact that different countries have reached different conclusions about the non-

scientific medical practices that have become institutionalized in itself suggests the relative character of such respectability.

Why are such practices so popular, given that they have no serious scientific foundation and that they are probably no more effective than any placebo? One can suggest several possible reasons:

- The basic principles are simple and can be grasped without study.
- These principles make a greater appeal to intuition than to reason (e.g., strengthening natural defenses is better than engaging in exaggerated measures to struggle against the cause of the difficulty).
- From a limited number of principles one can attain a universal vision.
- The field of endeavor is pertinent because it involves problems that affect all of us, either intimately or from a distance, and that are neglected by scientific disciplines.

In this view, there is no basic difference between holistic medicine, astrology, parapsychology, and all the other forms of pseudoscience that clutter the scene. Which to adhere to is a simple matter of preference.

A COHERENT THEORETICAL FRAMEWORK

Mysticism is the classic refuge of those who doubt and can no longer support the materialism that surrounds us. Sir John Eccles, the esteemed English neurophysiologist, believed that he could reach an understanding of how the brain functions by studying the properties of the single neuron. Despite his best efforts, however, he could never find any spirit residing in the neuron and concluded that the mind was not a material substance but a gift from heaven.[13]

By stressing the primacy of the mind, monism, dualism, mentalism, materialism, and all the other "isms" forget—as the great scientific philosopher Mario Bunge[14] points out—that there is no reason for the relationship of the mind to the brain to be fundamentally different from that of gait to legs or digestion to gastrointestinal tract. Abilities to remember, learn, perceive, and think are emergent properties of the networks of neurons that constitute the brain. The term *emergent properties* here means that the properties in question are present only in regard to the whole network, not at the level of its constituents, just as the transparency or viscosity of a liquid is not a property of its constituent molecules or atoms. The relationship in question is not fixed, since it is subject to the influences of evolution and development.

The doctrine that should inspire the study of the relationships between body and mind, between the physiological and the psychological, corresponds to what Bunge calls an emergent reductionism. This is no simple return to holism but a systemic approach. The brain is a system composed of mutually interactive subsystems. Each mental process has affective and cognitive components, as well as sensorimotor, visceral, and endocrinological components. A sense of fear is no longer simply a matter of emotion but also involves plasma concentrations of epinephrine. And attempts to explain individual behavior entirely by mental states are as flawed as those that limit the question to cardiac rhythm and hormone levels.

The biological sciences, psychology, and the social sciences— all are needed for a proper understanding of illness, and all have long existed in mutual unawareness. The growth of knowledge comes from the integration of disciplines rather than from overspecialization. Molecular biology draws its strength from the integration of biochemistry and genetics. But for that integration to be fruitful, the two domains must share a certain number of referents and concepts, and there must be a structure of tested formula bridges linking the concepts of one field to those of another. Categories like "astromedicine," purporting to combine astrology and medicine, are only caricatures of integration. As Mario Bunge elegantly remarks, a coupling of psychoanalysis and psychology is no more promising than one of astrology and astronomy. An understanding of mental and behavioral phenomena will be achieved only through a synthesis of psychology, biology, and the social sciences. That is what psychobiology is trying to achieve, an excellent substitute for mysticism!

CONCLUSION

TO DISPEL
THE ILLUSION

A tradition of thought well rooted in our culture, which shapes minds beginning in primary school, teaches us to know the world by "clear and distinct ideas." It enjoins us to reduce the complex to the simple, that is, to separate connected pieces into parts, to unify multiplicities, to eliminate everything that brings disorder or contradiction to our understanding. And the crucial problem of our time is the necessity of a thinking that can highlight challenge within the complexity of reality, one that is capable of grasping the connections, interactions, and mutual implications that constitute multidimensional phenomena.

—EDGAR MORIN, *Le grand dessein*[1]

Can one maintain health or at least recover it by optimism and good nature? Do fatalism and exaggerated pessimism precipitate a fatal outcome? One man's fantasy is another's reality where, between the two, can one find the truth?

At the beginning of this century psychosomaticians thought they had found the answer when they identified illnesses that were neither entirely organic nor truly mental, that is, troubles whose onset and development seemed to keep pace with the mood and psychological history of the patient. But they were opposed by specialized medicine, which, with tranquil confidence, has absorbed in its practice the so-called psychosomatic diseases. Rheumatology appropriated rheumatoid arthritis while gastroenterology subsumed gastroduodenal ulcers and hemorrhagic rectocolitis; asthma went to allergology, neurodermatitis to dermatology, essential hypertension to cardiology, and thyrotoxicosis and diabetes mellitus to endocrinology. Meanwhile, since institutional medicine had divided up all the bodily segments and subsegments, psychosomatic medicine found that its sole viaticum was the originality of its psychological view of pathology. When it became cumbersome and institutionally unclassifiable, this branch of medicine was condemned to extinction.

But banishing psychosomatic medicine did not get rid of psychosomatic diseases. Imbued with a despair of life that no one dares to qualify as "psychosomatic" (so pejorative has that epithet become), these diseases are simultaneously and respectively the despair and delight of modern technical medicine and of alternative medicine.

Norman Cousins's laugh or the anguished fury of Fritz Zorn? How does one escape illusion and dare to finally confront reality? Making the effort to understand how beliefs are formed and maintained can in itself lead to a considerable degree of understanding, which also happens when one borrows the perspective of the epidemiologist in appreciating the role of psychological factors.[2] That the end of such an analysis leaves psychosomaticians and their detractors back to back is somehow comforting; there must be some reason for illusion, since getting rid of it is far from easy.

If one cannot escape appearances, it is better to use them as props with which to confront reality instead of rejecting them. If some illnesses are engendered by psychological factors, one should at least be able to show that modalities of communication between the mind and the body do in fact exist. This question is not new; specialists of emotion and stress have long been trying to decipher the language of passions and to determine how it is understood by the body. But quitting the cloudy terrain of psychosomatic medicine for the equally cloudy realm of stress and emotions cannot automatically be defined as progress. Blame lies with the biologists, whose vision was long obscured by the study of the mechanisms of hormonal and nervous reactions to arbitrary situations and who therefore were slow to appreciate that organisms were not reacting reflexively.

The situation only began to change in the 1970s and 1980s, thanks to the influence of the behavioral sciences. We now understand that adaptation is not submission but action, and that action for an individual confronted by a fluctuating environment is not confined to the mobilization of resources so that a challenge may be resisted, but can also mean attempting to look ahead, calculating the chances of success in order to launch a sound strategy. This was a heavy charge for a brain already occupied by surveillance of the automatisms of visceral functioning. To detach itself from reactive stereotypes, the brain had to acquire the capacity to create information, that is, to interpret the signals received by the sense organs: thought is born from the necessities of action.[3]

And what point have we reached now? The nebulous realm of the mind–body relationship has yielded to a complex of interactions between the psychological and the physiological. The complexity of these interactions is not random; it was selected by evolution to confer a decisive advantage on organisms capable of using it to master the problems they must confront. This evolutionary advantage carries a risk: the possibility of dysfunction of the regulatory mechanisms, rather than the ordinary alteration of the constituent elements. The new challenge facing us is to dare to confront that complexity and to seek understanding of the mechanisms involved.

> The overlap of the psychological and the spiritual, of physiology and psychology, their reconciliation in an acceptance of their respective specificities and interaction is beginning to promote a concept that will prove rich in promise. This is the idea of interdependence, of reasoning in terms of connections and not oppositions, of both "this" and "that"—without rejection, opposition, or exclusion.[4]

In this garden of chimeras that is the domain of health, the experimental approach and a courageous grasp of the real constitute the only viaticum offered by modern biology in the quest for that *telos* ignored by scholars—happiness.

NOTES AND REFERENCES

INTRODUCTION TO THE AMERICAN EDITION

1. Too many books belong in this category to attempt to cite all of them; however, the truly useful guides are those that provide a step-by-step program of exercises that individuals can complete at their own pace while monitoring their progress. A recent text with such an objective is E. Peper and C. F. Holt, *Creating wholeness: A self-healing workbook using dynamic relaxation, images and thoughts* (New York: Plenum, 1993).

2. A typical example of such a recourse to old medical practices is J. Eden, *Energetic healing: The merging of ancient and modern medical practices* (New York: Plenum, 1993).

3. See for example E. L. Rossi, *The psychobiology of mind-body healing* (New York: Norton, 1986).

4. A good example of this belief can be found in N. Hodgkinson, *Will to be well: The real alternative medicine* (London: Hutchinson, 1984). See also B. S. Siegel, *Love, medicine and miracles: Lessons learned about self-healing from a surgeon's experience with exceptional patients* (New York: Harper Collins, 1988).

5. B. Moyers, *Healing and the mind* (New York: Doubleday, 1993).

INTRODUCTION

1. F. B. Michel, *Le souffle coupé* (Paris: Gallimard, 1984).

2. M. Bunge and Ardila, R., *Philosophy of psychiatry* (Berlin: Springer-Verlag, 1987).

3. N. Cousins, *Anatomy of an illness as perceived by the patient* (New York: Norton, 1979).

4. F. Zorn, *Mars* (Paris: Gallimard, 1988).

CHAPTER 1. ABERRATIONS OF BODY AND MIND

1. S. Freud, From the history of an infantile neurosis, in *Standard Edition,* vol. 17, J. Strachey, ed. (London: Hogarth Press), 1–122.

2. G. Groddeck, *Au fond de l'homme, cela* (Paris: Gallimard, 1963); *La maladie, l'art et le symbole* (Paris: Gallimard, 1969). Groddeck's therapy, based on diet, hydrotherapy, and massage, relied on the absolute

submission of patient to doctor—a far cry from the passive role of "comprehending presence" the therapist is supposed to play!

3. F. Alexander, *Psychosomatic medicine: Principles and applications* (New York: Norton, 1950).

4. F. Dunbar, *Emotions and bodily changes: A survey of the literature on psychosomatic interrelationships* (New York: Columbia University Press, 1935).

5. Alexander, *Psychosomatic medicine.*

6. P. Marty, de M'Uzan, M., and David, C., *L'investigation psychosomatique* (Paris: PUF, 1963).

7. J. C. Nemiah and Sifneos, P. E., Affect and fantasy in patients with psychosomatic disorders, in O. Hill, ed., *Modern trends in psychosomatic medicine* (London: Butterworth, 1970).

8. For a more complete review of work by Walter Cannon and Hans Selye, see R. Dantzer, *Les émotions: Que sais-je?* #238 (Paris: PUF, 1988).

9. P. D. Maclean, Psychosomatic disease and "the visceral brain": Recent development bearing on the Papez theory of emotions, *Psychol. Med.* 11 (1949): 338–53.

10. J. Gray, *The psychology of fear and stress* (London: Weidenfeld & Nicholson, 1971). The second edition of this work, extensively rewritten, was published by Cambridge University Press, Cambridge, in 1987.

11. H. Laborit, *L'inhibition de l'action,* 2d ed. (Paris: Masson, 1986).

12. L. Levi, Psychosocial factors in preventive medicine, in D. A. Hamburg, E. O. Nightingale, and V. Kalmar, eds. *Healthy people: The Surgeon General's report on health promotion and disease prevention* (Background papers, #79-55071A) (Washington, DC: U.S. Government Printing Office, 1979).

13. H. Selye, *The stress of life* (New York: McGraw-Hill, 1956).

CHAPTER 2. BETWEEN THE IMAGINARY AND THE REAL

1. S. Sontag, *Illness as metaphor* (New York: Farrar, Straus & Giroux, 1978).

2. M. Bourgeois, *La médicine dite psychosomatique et ses mythes,* *Ann. Medico-Psychol.* 47 (1989): 311–17.

3. R. A. Kirkpatrick, Witchcraft and lupus erythematosus, *JAMA* 245 (1981): 1937.

4. S. Greer, Morris, T., and Pettingale, K. W., Psychological response to breast cancer: Effect on outcome, *Lancet* ii (1979): 785–87.

5. Theoretically, the phenomenon known as "autoshaping" (the disk-pecking response activated without intervention by the experimenter) is important because it demonstrates that associations established by an individual do not belong to the stimulus–response category (the

pigeon does not peck the luminous disk because this behavior produces food) but, rather, to the stimulus–stimulus category (the pigeon pecks the disk because it associates it with food and reacts to it as it would to grain). This means that it would not peck a disk associated with grain in precisely the same way used to peck a disk associated with water. For a more complete analysis of "autoshaping," see B. Schwartz and Gamzu, E., Pavlovian control of operant behavior, in W. K. Honig and J. E. R. Staddon, eds., *Handbook of operant behavior* (New York: Prentice-Hall, 1977), 53–97.

6. J. Garcia, Hankins, W. G., and Rusiniak, K. W., Behavioral regulation of the milieu interne in Man and Rat, *Science* 185 (1974): 824–31.

7. For a more complete discussion of the links between learning and acquiring knowledge, see J. E. R. Staddon, *Adaptive behaviour and learning* (Cambridge: Cambridge University Press, 1983).

8. For a general review of how the human subject treats information in terms of beliefs and assumptions, see E. T. Higgins and Bargh, J. A., Social cognition and social perception, *Ann. Rev. Psychol.* 38 (1987): 369–425. The example of cards is taken from P. C. Wason and Johnson-Laird, P. N., *Psychology of reasoning: Structure and content* (London: Batsford, 1972).

9. W. R. Kunst-Wilson and Zajonc, R. B., Affective discrimination of stimuli that cannot be recognized, *Science* 207 (1980): 557–58.

10. According to an IPSOS poll, the French fear drugs even more than a nuclear accident. *Le Monde,* 23 Feb. 1989.

11. L. J. Chapman and Chapman, J. P., Genesis of popular but erroneous psycho-diagnostic observations, *J. Abnorm. Psychol.* 72 (1967): 193–204.

12. R. Fitzpatrick, Lay concepts of illness, in R. Fitzpatrick, J. Hinton, S. Newman, G. Scrambler, and J. Thompson, eds., *The experience of illness* (London: Tavistock, 1984), 11–31.

13. Michel Foucault in *La naissance de la clinique* (Paris: PUF, 1963) speaks of the logic of degeneration.

14. Jean-Didier Vincent in *Biologie des Passions* (Paris: Odile Jacob, 1986) shows how the logic of equilibrium is supported by pairings of opposite moods.

15. P. Watzlawik (ed.), *L'invention de la réalité: Contributions au constructivisme* (Paris: Seuil, 1988).

16. C. Lévi-Strauss, *Le cru et le cuit* (Paris: Plon, 1964).

17. E. Durkheim, *De la division du travail social,* 11th ed. (Paris: PUF, 1986), 1st ed., 1893; *Le suicide: Étude sociologique,* 10th ed. (Paris: PUF, 1986), 1st ed. 1897.

18. R. K. Merton, *Social theory and social structure* (New York: Free Press, 1949).

19. A notable exception is the use of the concept of anomie by a

sociologist, Ellen L. Maher, to explain the difficulties of re-adaptation experienced by patients cured of cancer: Anomic aspects of recovery from cancer, *Soc. Sci. Med.* 16 (1982): 907–12.

20. M. Marmot and Winkelstein, W., Jr., Epidemiologic observation on intervention trials for prevention of coronary heart disease, *Amer. J. Epidemiol.* 101 (1975): 177–81.

21. R. Schwartz and Geyser, S., Social and psychological differences between cancer and non-cancer patients: Cause or consequence of the disease? *Psychother. Psychosom.* 41 (1984): 195–99.

22. R. H. Rosenman, Brand, R. J., Jenkins, C. D., Friedman, M., Strauss, R., and Wurm, M., Coronary heart disease in the Western Collaborative Group Study: Final follow-up experience of 8.5 years, *JAMA* 233 (1975): 872–77. See Chapter 5 for a more detailed discussion of Type A behavior.

23. The Minnesota Multiphasic Personality Inventory is a scale developed in the United States during the 1940s as a tool for the systematic diagnosis of mental disorders. It is given in the form of a self-administered questionnaire.

24. L. R. Derogatis, Abeloff, M. D., and Melisaratos, N., Psychological coping mechanisms and survival time in metastatic breast cancer, *JAMA* 242 (1979): 1504–8.

25. L. Temoshok and Heller, B. W., On comparing apples, oranges, and fruit salad: A methodological overview of medical outcome studies in psychological oncology, in C. L. Cooper, ed., *Psychological stress and cancer* (London: Wiley, 1984) 231–60.

26. M. Friedman and Rosenman, R. H., Association of specific overt behavior pattern with blood and cardiovascular findings: Blood cholesterol level, blood clotting time, incidence of arcus senilis and clinical coronary artery disease, *JAMA* 169 (1959): 1286–96.

27. R. H. Rosenman, The interview method of assessment of the coronary-prone behavior pattern, in T. M. Dembroski, S. M. Weiss, J. L. Shields, S. G. Haynes, and M. Feinleib, eds., *Coronary-prone behavior* (New York: Springer Verlag, 1978).

28. J. P. Harrell, Psychological factors and hypertension: A status report, *Psychol. Bull.* 87 (1980): 482–501.

29. W. D. Gentry, Chesney, A. P., Gary, H. E., Hall, R. P., and Harburg, E., Habitual anger-coping styles: I. Effect on mean blood pressure and risk for essential hypertension, *Psychosom. Med.* 44 (1982): 195–202.

30. T. H. Holmes and Rahe, R. H., The Social Readjustment Rating Scale, *J. Psychosom. Res.* 11 (1967): 213–18.

31. D. J. Cooke and Hole, D. J., The aetiological importance of stressful life events, *Br. J. Psychiatry* 143 (1983): 397–400.

32. F. Amiel-Lebigre, Événements stressants de la vie et l'identification de sujets à risque, *Actualites Psychiat.* 9 (1986): 149–54.

33. M. B. Marx, Garrity, T. F., and Bowers, F. R., The influence of recent life experience on the health of college freshmen, *J. Psychosom. Res.* 19 (1975): 87–9.

34. R. H. Rahe, Romo, M., Bennett, L., and Siltanen, P., Recent life changes, myocardial infarction, and abrupt coronary death, *Arch. Int. Med.* 133 (1974): 221–28.

35. C. M. Parkes, Benjamin, B., and Fitzgerald, R. G., Broken heart: A study of increased mortality among widowers, *Br. Med. J.* 1 (1969): 740–43.

36. G. W. Brown and Harris, T. O., *Social origins of depression: A study of psychiatric disorder in women* (New York: Free Press, 1978).

37. J. S. House, Robbins, C., and Metzner, H. L., The association of social relationships and activities with mortality: Prospective evidence from the Tecumseh Health Study, *Am. J. Epidemiol.* 116 (1982): 123–40.

38. J. S. House, Landis, K. R., and Umbertson, D., Social relationships and health, *Science* 241 (1988): 540–45.

39. M. Peters-Golden, Breast cancer: Varied perceptions of social support in the illness experience, *Soc. Sci. Med.* 16 (1982): 483–91.

40. L. E. Cluff, Canter, A., and Imboden, J. B., Asian influenza: Infection, disease, and psychological factors, *Arch. Int. Med.* 117 (1966): 159–63.

41. R. A. Depue and Monroe, S. M., Conceptualization and measurement of human disorder in life stress research: The problem of chronic disturbance. *Psychol. Bull.* 99 (1988): 36–51.

42. T. Lecomte, *Aspects socio-éconimiques de la depression,* Center de Recherches, d'Étude et de Documentation en Économie de la Santé, 1988.

CHAPTER 3. THE LABYRINTH OF STRESS

1. K. Vonnegut, Jr., *Breakfast of champions* (New York: Dell, 1973).

2. W. Vale and Greer, M., Corticotropin releasing factor, *Fed. Proc.* 44 (1985): 45–263.

3. J. Axelrod and Resine, T. D., Stress hormones: Their interaction and regulation, *Science* 224 (1984): 452–59; T. D. Resine, Affolter, H. U., Rougon, G., and Barbet, J., New insights into the molecular mechanisms of stress, *Trends Neurosci.* 9 (1986): 574–79.

4. L. W. Swanson, The hypothalamus, in A. Bjorkland, T. Hokfelt, and L. W. Swanson, eds., *Handbook of chemical neuroanatomy: Vol. 5. Integrated systems of the CNS: Part 1. Hypothalamus, hippocampus, amygdala, retina* (Amsterdam: Elsevier, 1987), 1–124.

5. R. M. Sapolsky, Glucocorticoids and hippocampal damage,

Trends Neurosci. 10 (1987): 346–49; M. J. Meaney, Aitken, D. H., Van Berkel, C., Bhatnagar, S., and Sapolsky, R. M., Effect of neonatal handling on age-related impairments associated with the hippocampus, *Science* 239 (1988): 766–68.

6. A. Munck, Guyre, P. M., and Holbrook, N. J., Physiological functions of glucocorticoids in stress and their relation to pharmacological actions, *Endocrine Rev.* 5 (1986): 25–44.

7. A. I. Leshner, The role of hormones in control of submissiveness, in O. F. Brain and D. Benton, eds., *A multidisciplinary approach to aggression research* (Amsterdam: Elsevier, 1981), 131–55.

8. J. L. McGaugh, Hormonal influences on memory, *Ann. Rev. Psychol.* 34 (1983): 297–323.

9. B. Bohus, De Kloet, E. R., and Veldhuis, H. D., Adrenal steroids and behavioral adaptation: Relationship to brain corticoid receptors, in D. Ganten and D. Pfaff, eds., *Adrenal actions in brain* (New York: Springer-Verlag, 1982), 107–48; E. R. De Kloet, Function of steroid receptor systems in the central nervous system, *Clin. Neuropharmacol.* 7 (1984): 272–80; J. W. Funder and Sheppard, K., Adrenalcortical steroids and the brain, *Ann. Rev. Physiol.* 49 (1987): 397–411.

10. D. De Wied, Pituitary-adrenal system hormones and behavior, *Acta Endocrinol.* 85, suppl. 214 (1977): 9–18.

11. M. R. Brown and Fisher, L. A., Corticotropin-releasing factor: Effects on the autonomic nervous system and visceral systems, *Fed. Proc.* 44 (1985): 243–48.

12. K. T. Britton and G. F. Koob, Behavioral effects of the corticotropin-releasing factor, in A. F. Schatzberg and C. B. Nemeroff, eds., *The hypothalamic-pituitary-adrenal axis: Physiology, pathophysiology and psychiatric implications* (New York: Raven Press, 1988).

13. D. D. Krahn, Gosnelle, B. A., Grace, M., and Levine, A. S., CRF antagonist partially reverses CRF and stress-induced effects on feeding, *Brain Res. Bull.* 17 (1986): 285–89.

14. C. L. Rivier and Plotsky, O. M., Mediation by corticotropin releasing factor (CRF) of adrenohypophysial hormone secretion, *Ann. Rev. Physiol.* 48 (1986): 475–94.

15. J. Rossier and Chapouthier, G., Enkephalines et endorphines, *La Recherche* 13 (1982): 1296–1306; H. Khatchaturian, Lewis, M. E., Schafer, M. K. H, and Watson, S. J., Anatomy of the CNS opioid systems, *Trends Neurosci.* 8 (1985): 111–19.

16. L. R. Watkins and Mayer, D. J., Organization of endogenous opiate and non-opiate pain control systems, *Science* 216 (1982): 1185–92; G. W. Terman, Shavit, Y., Lewis, J. W., Cannon, J. T., and Liebeskind, J. C., Intrinsic mechanisms of pain inhibition: Activation by stress, *Science* 226 (1984): 1270–77; Z. Amit and Galina, Z. H., Stress-induced analgesis: Adaptive pain suppression, *Physiol. Rev.* 66 (1986): 1091–1120.

17. The differing character of analgesia, opioid or non-opioid, depending on the area of the body exposed to electric shock, is certainly related to the distance (and hence the nerve route) separating the stimulated area from the area in which analgesia is tested. In acupuncture, stimulation close to the painful area produces a non-opioid analgesia while a distant stimulation produces an opioid analgesia.

18. R. C. Bolles and Faneslow, M. S., A perceptual-defensive-recuperative model of fear and pain, *Behav. Brain Sci.* 3 (1980): 291–323.

19. M. S. Faneslow, Odors released by stressed rats produce opioid analgesia in unstressed rats, *Behav. Neurosci.* 99 (1985): 185–200.

20. R. J. Rodgers and Randall, J. I., On the mechanisms and adaptive significance of intrinsic analgesia systems, *Rev. Neurosci.* 1 (1987): 185–200.

21. I. Izquierdo, Beta-endorphin and forgetting, *Trends Neurosci.* 5 (1982): 455–57.

22. J. Panskepp, A neurochemical theory of autism, *Trends Neurosci.* 2 (1979): 174–76.

23. J. J. Christian, Social subordination, population density and mammalian evolution, *Science* 168 (1970): 84–90.

24. R. V. Andrews, The physiology of crowding, *Comp. Biochem. Physiol.* 63A (1979): 1–6.

25. J. B. Calhoun, The social aspects of population dynamics, *J. Mammal* 33 (1952): 139–59.

26. E. O. Wilson, *Sociobiology: The new synthesis* (Cambridge, MA: Belknap, 1975).

27. M. K. McClintock, Social control of the ovarian cycle and the function of estrous synchrony, *Amer. Zool.* 21 (1981): 243–56.

28. J. A. French, Abbott, D. H., and Snowdon, C. T., The effect of social environment on estrogen excretion, scent marking, and sociosexual behavior in tamarins (*Saguinis oedipus*), *Amer. J. Primatol.* 6 (1984): 155–67; A. Savage, Ziegler, T. E., and Snowdon, C. T., Sociosexual development, pair bond formation, and mechanisms of fertility suppression in female cotton-top tamarins (*Saguinis oedipus oedipus*), *Amer. J. Primatol.* 14 (1988): 345–59.

29. D. H. Abbott, Hodges, J. K., and George, L. M., Social status controls LH secretion and ovulation in female marmoset monkeys (*Callithrix jacchus*), *J. Endocr.* 117 (1988): 329–39.

30. M. Perret, Social influences on estrus cycle length and plasma progesterone concentrations in the female lesser mouse lemur (*Microcebus murinus*), *J. Reprod. Fert.* 77 (1986): 143–51.

31. L. A. Bowman, Dilley, S. R., and Keverne, E. B., Suppression of estrogen-induced LH surges by social subordination in female talapoin monkeys, *Nature* 275 (1978): 56–8.

32. D. Von Holst, Renal failure as the cause of death in *Tupaia*

belangeri exposed to persistent social stress, *J. Comp. Physiol.* 78 (1972): 236–73.

33. E. B. Keverne, Sexual and aggressive behavior in social groups of talapoin monkeys, in *Sex, hormones and behavior* (Amsterdam: Ciba Foundation Symposium, Excerpta Medica 62, 1979), 271–86.

34. L. R. Jarrett, Psychosocial and biological influences on menstruation: Synchrony, cycle length, and regularity, *Psychoneuroendocrinology* 9 (1984): 21–8.

35. J. W. Mason, A re-evaluation of the concept of "non-specificity" in stress theory. *J. Psychiat. Res.* 8 (1971): 323–33. This article is important because it is the first to propose the hypothesis of emotional intervention in pituitary-adrenal activation. It is also the first to test this hypothesis specifically.

36. J. W. Hennesy and Levine, S., Stress, arousal and the pituitary-adrenal system: A psychendocrine hypothesis, *Progr. Psychobiol. Physiol. Psychol.* 8 (1979): 133–78. In this article the authors summarize a series of experiments on laboratory rodents. These indicate that intensity of pituitary-adrenal activation is affected by novelty, by uncertainty, and by conflict engendered by the situation.

CHAPTER 4. CONFRONTATION

1. M. H. Berkun, Bialek, H. M., Kern, R. P., and Yagi, K., Experimental studies of psychological stress in man, *Psychol. Monogr.* 76, #534 (1962).

2. The verb *to cope with* means to confront and combat with success. The term *coping* designates either the action of struggling against the problems confronting the individual or the result of such action, the condition attained by those who have successfully mastered their problems.

3. Richard S. Lazarus of the Department of Pschology, University of California, Berkeley, is one of the leading scholars of the psychology of coping and has published a great deal on the subject. Readers will find it profitable to consult such basic works as R. S. Lazarus, *Psychological stress and the coping process* (New York: McGraw-Hill, 1966) and A. Monat and R. S. Lazarus, eds., *Stress and coping: An anthology* (New York: Columbia University Press, 1985).

4. J. Speisman, Lazarus, R. S., Mordkoff, A., and Davidson, L., Experimental reduction of stress based on ego-defense theory, *J. Abnorm. Soc. Psychol.* 68 (1964): 367–74.

5. R. C. Kessler, Price, R. H., and Wortman, C. B., Social factors in psychopathology: Stress, social support and coping processes, *Ann. Rev. Psychol.* 36 (1985): 351–72.

6. R. M. Yerkes, and Dodson, J. D., The relation of strength of

stimulus to rapidity of habit formation, *J. Comp. Neurol. Psychol.* 18 (1908): 459–82.

7. C. L. Hull, *Principles of behavior* (New York: Appleton-Century-Crofts, 1943).

8. E. A. Duffy, The psychological significance of the concept of "arousal" or "activation," *Psychol. Rev.* 64 (1957): 265–75; D. Bindra, A motivational view of learning, performance, and behavior modification, *Psychol. Rev.* 81 (1974): 199–213. For a general review of motivational systems, see F. Toates, *Motivational systems* (Cambridge, UK: Cambridge University Press, 1986).

9. A. Hugelin, L'activation: Physiologie des états de veille et de sommeil, électro-encéphalogramme, in C. Kayser, ed., *Physiologie,* vol. 2 (Paris: Flammarion, 1976), 1193–1265; J. D. French, The reticular formation, in *Psychobiology: The biological bases of behavior* (San Francsico: Freeman, 1967), 232–38.

10. S. Schachter and Singer, J., Cognitive, social, and psychological determinants of emotional state, *Psychol. Rev.* 69 (1962): 379–99.

11. J. M. Weiss, Psychological factors in stress and disease, *Sci. Am.* 226 (1972): 104–13.

12. J. V. Brady, Ulcers in "executive" monkeys, *Sci. Am.* 199 (1958): 95–100.

13. R. Dantzer, Neuroendocrine correlates of control and coping, in A. Steptoe and E. Appels, eds., *Stress, personal control and health* (London: Wiley, 1989).

14. J. Joffe, Rawson, R., and Mulick, J., Control of their environment reduces emotionality in rats, *Science* 180 (1973): 1383–84.

15. S. Mineka and Henderson, R. W., Controllability and predictability in acquired motivation, *Ann. Rev. Psychol.* 36 (1985): 495–529.

16. M. R. Gunnar, Contingent stimulation: A review of its role in early development, in S. Levine and H. Ursin, eds., *Coping and health* (New York: Plenum 1980), 101–19.

17. J. Rodin, Aging and health: Effects on sense of control, *Science* 233 (1986): 1271–76.

18. S. F. Maier, Seligman, M. E. P., and Solomon, R. L., Pavlovian fear conditioning and learned helplessness: Effects on escape and avoidance behavior of (a) the CS–US contingency and (b) the independence of the US and voluntary response, in B. A. Campbell and R. M. Church, eds., *Punishment and aversive behavior* (New York: Appleton, 1969), 299–342.

18a. Seligman and Maier use the term *learned helplessness* to designate the inability of preliminarily shocked animals to attempt to find a solution to a difficult situation. This terminology is not descriptive but profoundly interpretive. The term *helplessness* is very strong and designates a feeling of powerlessness toward external events. The qualifier *learned* attributes this feeling of helplessness to prior experience; the animals are thought to have learned that they have no control over the shocks to which they are subjected. This instruction in the ineffectiveness of action is at the root of their sense of powerlessness. From it derives resignation and passive submission to all eventualities.

19. M. E. P. Seligman, *Helplessness: On depression, development, and death* (San Francisco: Freeman, 1975).

20. M. E. P. Seligman, Abramson, L. Y., Semmel, A., and von Baeyer, C., Depressive attributional style, *J. Abnorm. Psychol.* 88 (1979): 242–47. See Mineka and Henderson (note 15) for a recent survey of criticisms of Seligman's theories.

21. The origin of this difference between species is not easy to explain. I have attempted to discuss this point with people like Overmier and Maier but have never received an entirely satisfactory explanation. Levine suggested, more or less in jest, that a dog normally has such confidence in his keeper that when he receives a treatment as harshly unpleasant as inescapable electric shock, he loses all faith in human goodness. I myself have spent a lot of time vainly trying to reproduce the phenomenon of learned helplessness in pigs, but I, unable to endure their cries, abandoned the attempt. My colleagues and I, as others have done, resumed our experiments with rats. This is much more comfortable for the researcher(!), but achieving the phenomenon with any regularity is far from simple.

22. T. R. Minor, Jackson, R. L., and Maier, S. F., Effects of task-irrelevant cues and reinforcement delay on choice escape learning following inescapable shock: Evidence for a deficit in selective attention, *J. Exp. Psychol. Animal Behav. Proc.* 10 (1984): 543–56.

23. J. M. Weiss and Glazer, H. I., Effects of acute exposure to stressors on subsequent avoidance-escape behavior, *Psychosom. Med.* 37 (1975): 499–521.

24. M. Tiggeman and Winefield, A. H., Situation similarity and the generalization of learned helplessness, *Quart. J. Exp. Psychol.* 30 (1978): 725–35.

25. H. Anisman and Zacharko, R. M., Depression: The predisposing influence of stress, *Behav. Brain Sci.* 5 (1982): 89–137.

26. A. J. Sherman and Petty, F., Neurochemical basis of the action of antidepressants on learned helplessness, *Behav. Neural Biol.* 30 (1980): 119–34; A. D. Sherman and Petty, F., Additivity of neurochemical changes in learned helplessness and imipramine, *Behav. Neural Biol.* 35 (1982): 344–53.

27. A. J. MacLennan and Maier, S. F., Coping and stress-induced potentiation of stimulant stereotypy in the rat, *Science* 219 (1983): 1091–93.

28. J. M. Weiss and Goodman-Simson, P., Neurochemical mecha-

nisms underlying stress-induced depression, in T. M. Field, P. M. McCabe, and N. Schneiderman, eds., *Stress and coping* (Hillsdale, NJ: Lawrence Erlbaum, 1984), 93–116.

29. S. M. Antelman and Chiodo, L. A., Stress and its effects on biogenic amines and role in the induction and treatment of disease, in L. L. Iversen, S. D. Iversen, and S. H. Snyder, eds., *Handbook of psychopharmacology,* vol. 18 (New York: Plenum Press, 1984), 279–341.

30. T. R. Minor and LoLordo, V. M., Escape deficits following inescapable shock: The role of contextual odor, *J. Exp. Psychol. Animal Behav. Proc.* 10 (1984): 168–81.

31. For a description of attachment processes, see H. Montagner, *L'attachement: Les débuts de la tendresse* (Paris: Odile Jacob, 1988).

32. G. L. Engel and Schmale, A. H., Conservation-withdrawal: A primary regulatory process for organic homeostatsis, in *Physiology, emotion, and psychosomatic illness* (Amsterdam: Ciba Foundation Symposium #8, Elsevier, 1972).

33. C. Trevarthen, Emotions in infancy: Regulators of contact and relationships with persons, in K. Scherer and P. Ekman, eds., *Approaches to emotion* (Hillsdale, NJ: Lawrence Erlbaum, 1984), 129–57.

CHAPTER 5. THE MISFORTUNES OF INDIVIDUALITY

1. M. R. Goldfried, Strickler, G., and Weiner, O. B., *Rorschach handbook of clinical and research applications* (Englewood Cliffs, NJ: Prentice-Hall, 1971).

2. H. J. Eysenck, *The biological basis of personality* (Springfield, IL: Thomas, 1967).

3. J. A. Gray, *The psychology of fear and stress* (Cambridge, UK: Cambridge University Press, 1987).

4. J. P. Henry and Stephens, P. M., *Stress, health, and the social environment: A sociobiologic approach to medicine* (New York: Springer-Verlag, 1977); J. P. Henry, Neuroendocrine patterns of emotional response, in T. Plutchik and H. Kellerman, eds., *Emotion: Theory, research and experience,* vol. 3. (Orlando, FL: Academic Press, 1986), 37–60.

5. A. Steptoe, Ruddell, H., and Neus, H., eds., *Clinical and methodological issues in cardiovascular psychophysiology* (Berlin: Springer-Verlag, 1985).

6. M. Frankenhaeuser, Psychobiological aspects of life stress, in S. Levine and H. Ursin, eds., *Coping and health* (New York: Plenum, 1980), 203–23.

7. H. Ursin, Baade, E., and Levine, S., *Psychobiology of stress: A study of coping men* (New York: Academic Press, 1978).

8. R. F. Benus, Koolhaas, J. M., and Van Oortmeerssen, G. A., Individual differences in behavioural reaction to a changing environment in mice and rats, *Behaviour* 100 (1987): 105–22; R. F. Benus, Koolhaas, J. M., and Van Oortmeerssen, G. A., Aggression and adaptation to the light-dark cycle: Role of intrinsic and extrinsic control, *Physiol. Behav.* 43 (1988): 131–37.

9. G. Mittleman and Valenstein, E. S., Ingestive behavior evoked by hypothalamic stimulation and schedule-induced polydipsia are related, *Science* 224 (1984): 415–17.

10. R. Dantzer, Behavioral, physiological and functional aspects of stereotyped behavior: A review and reinterpretation, *J. Animal Sci.* 62 (1986): 1776–86.

11. M. Meyer-Holzapfel, Mouvements stereotypes chez les animaux domestiques, expression de malaises phsychiques, in A. Brion and H. Ely, eds., *Psychiatrie animale* (Paris: Desclée de Brouwer, 1964), 295–98. The description achieves full flavor when one knows that schizophrenia is supposed to be characterized by ambivalence!

12. M. Lyon and Robbins, T. W., The action of central stimulant drugs: A general theory concerning amphetamine effects, in W. Essman and L. Valzelli, eds., *Current developments in psychopharmacology,* Vol. 2 (New York: Spectrum, 1975), 81–163.

13. K. A. Miczek, *Ethopharmacology: Primate models of neuropsychiatric disorders* (New York: Alan R. Liss, 1983).

14. S. M. Antelman, Eichler, A. J., Black, C. A., and Kocan, D., Interchangeablility of stress and amphetamine in sensitization, *Science* 207 (1980): 329–31; G. Mittleman and Valensrein, E. S., Individual differences in non-regulatory ingestive behavior and catecholamine systems, *Brain Res.* 348 (1985): 112–17; G. Mittleman, Castaneda, E., Robinson, T. E., and Valenstein, E. S., The propensity for nonregulatory ingestive behavior is related to differences in dopamine systems: Behavioral and biochemical evidence, *Behav. Neurosci.* 100 (1986): 213–20.

15. G. C. Goddard, McIntyre, D. C., and Leech, C. K., A permanent change in brain function resulting from daily electrical stimulation, *Neurology* 25 (1969): 295–330.

16. The sensitization of dopaminergic neurons under the effects of stress depends on cerebral peptides like the endorphins. In fact, a local microinjection of enkephalins at the level of cell bodies of dopaminergic neurons sensitizes the response to amphetamine and to substances with morphinic activity. Conversely, administration of naloxone, an antagonist of opiate receptors, hinders the development of sensitization.

17. E. R. Kandel, From metapsychology to molecular biology: Explorations in the nature of anxiety, *Am. J. Psychiatry* 140 (1983): 1277–93.

18. R. M. Post, Rubinow, D. R., and Ballanger, J. C., Conditioning, sensitization and kindling: Implications for the course of affective illness,

in R. M. Post and R. C. Ballanger, eds., *Neurobiology of mood disorders* (Baltimore: Williams & Wilkins, 1954), 432–66.

19. S. M. Antelman and Chiodo, L. A., Stress: Its effects on interactions among biogenic amines and role in the induction and treatment of disease, in L. L. Iversen, S. D. Iversen, and S. H. Snyder, eds., *Handbook of psychopharmacology,* Vol. 18 (New York: Plenum, 1984), 279–341.

20. J. P. Boulenger, ed., *L'attaque de panique, un nouveau concept?* (Chateau-du-Loir: Éditions Jean-Pierre Goureau, 1987).

21. D. Sheehan, Current concepts in psychiatry: Panic attacks and phobias, *New Engl. J. Med.* 15 (1982): 156–58.

22. M. Friedman and Rosenman, R. H., *Type A behavior and your heart* (New York: Knopf, 1974).

23. R. H. Rosenman and Chesney, M. A., Type A behavior and coronary heart disease, in C. D. Spielberger, I. G. Sarason, and P. B. Defares, eds., *Stress and anxiety,* vol. 9 (Washington, DC: Hemisphere, 1985), 207–29; C. D. Jenkins, Rosenman, R. H., and Zysanski, S. J., Prediction of clinical coronary heart disease by a test for coronary-prone behavior patterns, *N. Engl. J. Med.* 290 (1974): 1271–75; R. H. Rosenman, Brand, R. J., Jenkins, C. D., Friedman, M., Strauss, R., and Wurm, M., Coronary heart disease: A critical review, *Circulation* 63 (1981): 1199–1215; K. A. Matthews and Haynes, S. G., Type A behavior pattern and coronary disease risk: Update and critical evaluation, *Amer. J. Epidemiol.* 123 (1986): 923–60.

24. S. Booth-Kewley and Friedman, H. S., Psychological predictors of heart disease: A quantitative review, *Psychol. Bull.* 101 (1987): 343–62. The methodology used in this review and the conclusions to be drawn as to the importance of Type A characteristics in coronary disease are discussed in K. A. Matthew, Coronary heart disease and Type A behaviors: Update on an alternative to the Booth-Kewley and Friedman (1987) quantitative review, *Psychol. Bull.* 104 (1988): 373–80.

25. D. R. Ragland and Brand, R. J., Type A behavior and mortality from coronary heart disease, *N. Engl. J. Med.* 318 (1988): 66–69.

26. R. B. Williams, Lane, J. D., Kuhn, C. M., Melosh, W., White, A. D., and Schanberg, S. M., Type A behavior and elevated physiological and neuroendocrine responses to cognitive tasks, *Science* 218 (1982): 483–85.

27. D. C. Glass, Krakoff, L. R., Contrada, R., Hilton, W. H., Kehoe, K., Manucci, E. G., Collins, C., Snow, B., and Elting, E., Effect of harassment and competition upon vascular and plasma catecholamine response in Type A and Type B individuals, *Psychophysiology* 17 (1980): 453–63.

28. J. P. Kahn, Gully, R. J., Cooper, T. B., Perumal, A. S., Smith, T. M., and Klein, D. F., Correlations of Type A behavior with adrenergic receptor density: Implications for coronary artery disease pathogenesis, *Lancet* ii (1987): 937–39.

29. J. Archer, Rodent sex differences in emotional and related be-

havior, *Behav. Biol.* 14 (1975): 451–79; J. A. Gray, Emotionality in male and female rodents: A reply to Archer, *Br. J. Psychol.* 70 (1979): 525–40.

30. M. Frankenhaeuser, Challenge-control interaction as reflected in sympathetic-adrenal and pituitary-adrenal activity: Comparison between the sexes, *Scand. J. Psychol.* suppl. 1 (1982): 158–64.

31. O. R. Floody, Hormones and aggression in female mammals, in B. B. Svare, ed., *Hormones and aggressive behavior* (New York: Plenum, 1983): 39–90.

32. N. J. MacLusky and Naftolin, F., Sexual differentiation of the central nervous system, *Science* 211 (1981): 1294–1303; B. S. McEwen, Neural gonadal steroid actions, *Science* 211 (1981): 1303–11; H. H. Feder, Hormones and sexual behavior, *Ann. Rev. Psychol.* 35 (1984): 165–200.

33. F. S. vom Saal, The intrauterine position phenomenon: Effects on physiology, aggressive behavior and population dynamics in house mice, in K. Flannelly, R. Blanchard, and D. Blanchard, eds., *Biological perspectives on aggression* (New York: Alan R. Liss, 1984), 135–79.

34. I. L. Ward and Weisz, J., Maternal stress alters plasma testosterone in fetal males, *Science* 207 (1980): 328–29.

35. E. A. Kravitz, Hormonal control of behavior: Amines and the biasing of behavioral output in lobsters, *Science* 241 (1988): 1775–81.

36. R. J. Andrew, Attentional mechanisms and animal behavior, in R. A. Hinde and P. P. G. Betson, eds., *Growing points in ethology* (Cambridge, UK: Cambridge University Press, 1976), 95–113; J. Archer, Testosterone and persistence in mice, *Animal Behav.* 25 (1977): 479–88.

37. J. M. Koolhaas, Fokkema, D. S., Bohus, B., and Van Oortmeerssen, G. A., Individual differentiation in blood pressure reactivity and behavior of male rats, in T. M. Dembroski, T. H. Schmidt, and G. Blumchen, eds., *Biobehavioral bases of coronary disease,* vol. 3 (Basel: Karger, 1986), 517–26.

38. D. M. Camp and Robinson, T. E., Susceptibility to sensitization: I. Sex differences in the enduring effects of chronic d-amphetamine treatment on locomotion, stereotyped behavior, and brain monoamines, *Behav. Brain Res.* 30 (1988): 55–68; D. M. Camp and Robinson, T. E., *Susceptibility to senitization:* II. The influence of gonadal hormones on enduring changes in brain monoamines and behavior produced by the repeated administration of d-amphetamine or restraint stress, *Behav. Brain Res.* 30 (1988): 69–88.

39. F. Alexander, *Psychosomatic medicine: Principles and applications* (New York: Norton, 1950).

40. P. Marty, de M'Uzan, M., and David, C., *L'investigation psychosomatique* (Paris: PUF, 1953).

41. T. W. Smith and Anderson, N. B., Models of personality and disease: An interactional approach to Type A behavior and cardiovascular risk, *J. Personal. Soc. Psychol.* 50 (1986): 1166–73.

42. S. A. Corson and O'Leary-Corson, E., Constitutional differences in physiologic adaptation to stress and distress, in G. Serban, ed., *Psychopathology of human adaptation* (New York: Plenum, 1976), 77–94.

CHAPTER 6. MIND AND IMMUNITY

1. D. Felten, Felten, S. Y., Carlson, S. L., Olschowka, J. A., Livnat, S., Noradrenergic and peptidergic innervation of lymphoid tissue, *J. Immunol.* 135 (1985): 755s–65s.

2. D. A. Weigent and Blalock, J. E., Interactions between the immune and neuroendocrine systems: Common hormones and receptors, *Immunol. Rev.* 100 (1987): 79–96.

3. H. O. Besedovsky, Del Rey, A., Sorkin, E., DaPrada, M., and Keller, H. H., Immuno-regulation mediated by the sympathetic nervous system. *Cell. Immunol.* 48 (1979): 346–55; J. M. Williams, Petersen, R. G., Shea, P. A., Schmedtje, J. F., Bauer, D. C., and Felten, D. L., Sympathetic innervation of murine thymus and spleen: Evidence for a functional link between the nervous and immune systems. *Brain Res. Bull.* 6 (1981): 82–89.

4. N. E. S. Sibinga and Goldstein, A., Opioid peptides and opioid receptors in cells of the immune system, *Ann. Rev. Immunol.* 6 (1988): 219–49.

5. L. Berci and Kovacs, K., eds., *Hormones and immunity* (Lancaster, PA: MTP Press, 1987).

6. R. S. Lewis and Calahan, M. D., The plasticity of ion channels: Parallels between the nervous and the immune systems, *Trends Neurosci.* 11 (1988): 214–18.

7. G. Forni, Bindoni, M., Santoni, A., Belluardo, N., Marchese, A. E., and Giovarelli, M., Radiofrequency destruction of tuberoinfandibular region of hypothalamus permanently abrogates NK cell activity in mice, *Nature* 306 (1983): 181–84.

8. M. Stein, Schiavi, R. C., and Camerino, M., Influence of brain and behavior on the immune system, *Science* 191 (1976): 435–44; T. L. Roszman, Cross, R. J., Brooks, W. H., and Markesbery, W. R., Neuroimmunomodulation: Effects of neural lesions on cellular immunity, in R. Guillemin, M. Cohn, and T. Melnechuk, eds., *Neural modulation of immunity* (New York: Raven Press, 1985), 95–108.

9. N. Geschwind and Behan, P. Left-handedness: Association with immune diseases, migraine, and developmental learning disorder, *Proc. Natl. Acad. Sci. USA* 79 (1982): 5097–5100.

10. K. Bizière, Guillaumin, J. M., Degenne, D., Bardos, P., Renoux, M., and Renoux, G., Lateralized neocortical modulations of the T-cell lineage, in R. Guillemin, M. Cohn, and T. Melchenuk, eds., *Neural modulation of immunity* (New York: Raven Press, 1985), 81–94.

11. P. J. Neveu, Cerebral neocortex modulation of immune functions, *Life Sci.* 42 (1988): 1917–23; P. J. Neveu, Barneoud, P., Vitiello, S., Betancur, C., and Le Moal, M., Brain modulation of the immune system: Association between lymphocyte responsiveness and paw preference in mice, *Brain Res.* 457 (1988): 392–94.

12. R. Glaser, Rice, J., Stout, J. C., Soeicher, C. E., and Kiecolt-Glaser, J. K., Stress depresses interferon production by leukocytes concomitant with a decrease in natural killer cell activity, *Behav. Neurosci.* 100 (1986): 675–78; J. K. Kiecolt-Glaser, Garner, W., Speicher, C. E., Penn, G., and Glaser, R., Psychosocial modifiers of immuno-competence in medical students, *Psychosom. Med.* 46 (1984): 7–14; R. Glaser, Rice, J., Sheridan, J., Fertel, R., Stout, J., Speicher, C., Pinsky, D., Kotur, M., Post, A., Beck, M., and Kiecolt-Glaser, J. K., Stress-related immune-suppression: Health implications, *Brain Behav. Immunol.* 1 (1987): 7–20; J. K. Kiecolt-Glaser, Kennedy, S., Malakoff, S. Fisher, L., Speicher, C. E., Glaser, R., Marital discord and immunity in males, *Psychosom. Med.* 50 (1988): 213–29.

13. B. Dorian and Garfinkel, P. E., Stress, immunity and illness: A review, *Psychol. Med.* 17 (1987): 393–407.

14. M. Stein, Keller, S. E., and Schliefer, S. J., Stress and immuno-modulation: The role of depression and neuroendocrine function, *J. Immunol.* 135 (1985): 827s–33s; Depression, stress and immunity, *Lancet* i (1987): 1467–68.

15. S. Levy, Herberman, R., Lippman, M., and d'Angelo, T., Correlation of stress factors with sustained depression of natural killer cell activity and predicted prognosis in patients with breast cancer, *J. Clin. Oncol.* 5 (1987): 348–53.

16. S. S. Chang and Rasmussen, A. J., Jr., Stress-induced suppression of interferon production in virus-infected mice, *Nature* 205 (1965): 623–24; G. F. Solomon, Levine, S., and Kraft, J. K., Early experience and immunity, *Nature* 220 (1968): 821–22; R. J. Wistar and Hildeman, W. H., Effect of stress in skin transplantation immunity in mice, *Science* 131 (1960): 159–160.

17. W. B. Gross, Effect of social stress on occurrence of Marek's disease in chickens, *Am. J. Vet. Res.* 33 (1972): 2275–80.

18. F. Blecha, Barry, R. A., and Kelley, K. W., Stress-induced alterations in delayed-type hypersensitivity to SRBC and contact sensitivity to DNFB in mice, *Proc. Soc. Exp. Biol. Med.* 169 (1982): 247–52.

19. L. Sklar and Anisman, H., Stress and coping factors influence tumor growth, *Science* 205 (1979): 513–15; M. Visintainer, Volpicelli, J., and Seligman, M., tumor rejection in rats after inescapable or escapable shock, *Science* 216 (1982): 437–39.

20. M. L. Laudenslager, Ryan, S. M., Drugan, R. C., Hyson, R. L., and Maier, S. F., Coping and immunosuppression: Inescapable but not escap-

able shock suppresses lymphocyte proliferation, *Science* 216 (1982): 437–39.

21. P. Mormède, Dantzer, R., Michaud, B., Kelley, K. W., and Le Moal, M., Influence of stressor predictability and behavioral control on lymphocyte reactivity, antibody responses and neuroendocrine activation in rats, *Physiol. Behav.* 43 (1988): 577–83.

22. A. Raab, Dantzer, R., Michaud, B., Mormède, P., Taghzouti, K., Simon, H., and Le Moal, M., Behavioral, physiological, and immunological consequences of social status and aggression in chronically coexisting resident-intruder dyads of male rats, *Physiol. Behav.* 36 (1986): 223–28.

23. C. L. Coe, Rosenberg, L. T., and Levine, S., Immunological consequences of psychological disturbances and maternal loss in infancy, in C. Rove-Collier and L. P. Lipsitt, eds., *Advances in infancy research* (Norwood: Ablex Publications, 1987).

24. G. Croiset, Heijnen, C. J., Veldhuis, H. D., De Wied, D., and Baillieux, R.E., Modulation of the immune response by emotional stress, *Life Sci.* 40 (1987): 775–82; G. Croiset, *The impact of emotional stimuli on the immune system* (Ph.D. diss., University of Utrecht, 1989).

25. R. M. Sapolsky and Donnelly, T. M., Vulnerability to stress-induced tumor growth increases with age in rats: Role of glucocorticoids, *Endocrinology* 117 (1985): 662–66.

26. S. E. Keller, Weiss, J., Schliefer, S. J., Miller, N. E., and Stein, M., Stress-induced suppression of immunity in adrenalectomized rats, *Science* 221 (1983): 1301–4.

27. B. Crary, Hauser, S. L., Borysenko, M., Kutz, I., Hoban, C., Ault, K. A., Weiner, H. L., and Benson, H., Epinephrine-induced changes in the distribution of lymphocyte subsets in peripheral blood of humans, *J. Immunol.* 131 (1983): 1178–81; R. M. A. Handmann, Muller, F. B., Perini, C. H., Wesp, M., Erone, P., and Buhler, F. R., Changes of immunoregulatory cells induced by psychological and physical stress: Relationship to plasma catecholamines *Clin. Exp. Immunol.* 58 (1984): 127–35.

28. R. Fujiwara and Orita, K., The enhancement of the immune response by pain stimulation in mice: I. The enhancement effect on PFC production via sympathetic nervous system in vivo and in vitro, *J. Immunol.* 138 (1987): 3699–3703.

29. Y. Shavit, Terman, G. W., Martin, F. C., Lewis, J. W., Liebeskind, J. C., and Gale, R. P., Stress, opioid peptides, the immune system, and cancer, *J. Immunol.* 135 (1985): 834s–37s.

30. K. W. Kelley, Growth hormones regulate the activities of lymphocytes and macrophages, *Biochem. Pharmacol.* 38 (1989): 705–13.

31. E. W. Bernton, Meltzer, M. S., and Holaday, J. W., Suppression of macrophage activation and T-lymphocyte function in hypoprolactinemic mice, *Science* 239 (1988): 401–3.

32. P. C. Hiestand, Mekler, P., Nordmann, R., Grieder, A., and Per-

mongkol, C., Prolactin as a modulator of lymphocyte responsiveness provides a possible mechanism of action for cyclosporine, *Proc. Natl. Acad. Sci. USA* 83 (1986): 2599–2603.

33. W. C. Koff and Dunegan, M. A., Modulation of macrophage-mediated tumoricidal activity by neuropeptides and neurohormones, *J. Immunol.* 135 (1985): 350–54.

34. S. Métalnikov, *Rôle du système nerveux et des facteurs biologiques et physiques dans l'immunité* (Paris: Masson, 1934).

35. R. Ader and Cohen, N., COS-immune system interactions: Conditioning phenomena, *Behav. Brain Sci.* 8 (1985): 379–426.

36. M. Russell, Dark, K. A., Cummins, R. W., Ellman, G., Callaway, E., and Peek, H. V. S., Learned histamine release, *Science* 225 (1989): 733–34.

37. G. MacQueen, Siegel, S., Marshall, J., Perdue, M., and Bienenstock, J., Pavlovian conditioning of rat mucosal mast cells to secrete rat mast cell protease II, *Science* 243 (1989): 83–85.

38. K. W. Kelley and Dantzer, R., Is conditioned immunosuppression truly conditioned? *Behav. Brain Sci.* 9 (1986): 758–60; R. Dantzer and Crestani, F., Conditioning of immune responses, in J. Delacour and J. C. S. Levy, eds., *Systems with learning and memory abilities* (Amsterdam: Elsevier, 1988), 213–25.

39. According to the British Medical Association, hypnosis is a transitory condition of modified attention that can be produced by another person and during the course of which various phenomena may appear, either spontaneously or in response to verbal instructions. These phenomena include changes of both consciousness and memory, a heightened sensitivity to suggestion, and ideas that are not customary in the subject's normal frame of mind. Phenomena like paralysis, anesthesia, muscular rigidity, and vasomotor modifications may also be presented, or suppressed, under the influence of hypnosis. There is no strict relationship between sensitivity to hypnosis and suggestibility.

40. A. H. C. Sinclair-Gieben and Chalmers, D., Evaluation of treatment of warts by direct suggestion under hypnosis, *Br. Med. J.* 6 (1963): 1649–52.

41. N. P. Spanos, Stenstrom, R. J., and Johnston, J. C., Hypnosis, placebo, and suggestion in the treatment of warts, *Psychosom. Med.* 50 (1988): 245–60.

42. S. Black, Inhibition of immediate type hypersensitivity response by direct suggestion under hypnosis, *Br. Med. J.* 6 (1963): 925–29; S. Black, Humphrey, J. H., and Niven, J. S. F., Inhibition of Mantoux reaction by direct suggestion under hypnosis, *Br. Med. J.* 6 (1963): 1649–52.

43. G. R. Smith, Jr., and McDaniel, S., Psychologically mediated effect on the delayed hypersensitivity response by direct suggestion under hypnosis, *Psychosom. Med.* 45 (1983): 65–69.

44. T. J. Luparello, McFadden, E. R., Jr., Lyons, H. A., and Bleecker,

E. R., Psychologic facts and bronchial asthma: Laboratory model for investigation, *NY State J. Med.* (1971, Sept. 15): 2161–65.

45. H. Kotses, Rawson, J. C., Wigal, J. K., and Creer, T. L., Respiratory airway changes in response to suggestion in normal individuals, *Psychosom. Med.* 49 (1987): 536–41.

46. R. Dantzer and Kelley, K. W., Stress and immunity: An integrated view of relationships between nervous and immune systems, *Life Sci.* 44 (1989): 1995–2008.

47. H. Besedovsky and Sorkin, E., Network of immune neuroendocrine interactions, *Clin. Exp. Immunol.* 27 (1977): 1–12; H. Besedovsky, del Rey, A. E., and Sorkin, E., What do the immune system and the brain know about each other? *Immunol. Today* 4 (1983): 342–46.

48. H. Besedovsky, Del Rey, A., Sorkin, E., and Dinarello, C., Immunoregulatory feedback between interleukin-1 and glucocorticoid hormones, *Science* 233 (1986): 652–54; F. Berkenbosch, Van Oers, J., Del Rey, A., Tilders, F., and Dinarello, C., Corticotropin-releasing factor-producing neurons in the rat activated by interleukin-1, *Science* 238 (1987): 524–26; E. W. Bernton, Beach, J. E., Holaday, J. W., Smallridge, R. C., and Fein, H. G., Release of multiple hormones by a direct action of interleukin-1 on pituitary cells, *Science* 238 (1987): 519–22; R. Sapolsky, Rivier, C., Yamamoto, G., Pitolsky, P., and Vale, W., Interleukin-1 stimulates the secretion of hypothalamic corticotropin-releasing factor, *Science* 238 (1987): 522–24.

49. J. E. Blalock and Smith, E. M., Human leukocyte interferon: Structural and biological relatedness to adrenocorticotropic hormone and endorphins, *Proc. Natl. Acad. Sci. USA* 77 (1980): 5972–74.

50. E. M. Smith, Meyer, J. W., and Blalock, J. E., Virus-induced corticosterone in hypophysectomized mice: A possible lymphoid-adrenal axis, *Science* 218 (1982): 1311–13.

51. A. J. Dunn, Powell, M. P., and Gaskin, J. M., Virus-induced increases in plasma corticosterone: A possible lymphoid-adrenal axis, *Science* 218 (1982): 1311–13.

52. M. J. Kluger, *Fever: Its biology, evolution and function* (Princeton, NJ: Princeton University Press, 1979).

53. B. L. Hart, Biological basis of the behavior of sick animals, *Neurosci. Biobehav. Rev.* 12 (1988): 123–37.

54. C. A. Dinarello, Biology of interleukin-1, *FASEB J.* 2 (1988): 108–15.

55. M. Iriki, Fever and fever syndrome: Current problems, *Jap. J. Physiol.* 38 (1988): 233–50.

56. D. O. McCarthy, Kluger, M. J., and Vander, A. J., Effect of centrally administered interleukin-1 and endotoxin on food-intake of fasted rats, *Physiol. Behav.* 36 (1986): 745–49; I. G. Otterness, Seymour, P. A., Golden, H. W., Reynolds, J. A., and Daumy, G. O., The effects of contin-

uous administration of murine interleukin-1 alpha in the rat, *Physiol. Behav.* 43 (1988): 797–804; S. Shoham, Davenne, D., Cady, A. B, Dinarello, C. A., and Krueger, J. M., Recombinant tumor necrosis factor and interleukin-1 enhance slow wave sleep, *Am. J. Physiol. Regul. Integr. Comp. Physiol.* 253 (1987): R142–R149; A. Tazo, Dantzer, R., Crestani, F., and Le Moal, M., Interleukin-1 induces conditioned taste aversion in rats: A possible explanation for its pituitary-adrenal stimulating activity, *Brain Res.* 473 (1988): 369–71.

57. N. W. Kasting, Veale, W. L., and Copper, K. E., Vasopressin: A homeostatic effector in the febrile process, *Neurosci. Biobehav. Rev.* 6 (1928): 215–22.

58. B. Beutler and Cerami, A., Cachectin (tumor necrosis factor): A macrophage hormone governing cellular metabolism and inflammatory response, *Endocr. Rev.* 9 (1988): 57–66.

59. S. Pestka, Langer, J. A., Zoon, K. C., and Samuel, C. E., Interferons and their actions, *Ann. Rev. Biochem.* 56 (1987): 727–77.

60. C. D. Breder, Dinarello, C. A., and Saper, C. B., Interleukin-1 immunoreactive innervation of the human hypothalamus, *Science* 240 (1988): 321–24; W. L. Farrar, Kilian, P. L., Ruff, M. T., Hill, J. M., and Pert, C. B., Visualization and characterization of interleukin-1 receptors in brain, *J. Immunol.* 139 (1987): 459–63: J. E. Merrill, Macroglia: Neural cell responsiveness to lymphokines and growth factors, *Immunol. Today* 8 (1987): 146–50.

61. J. M. Krueger, Rosenthal, R. S., Martin, S. A., Walter, J., Davenne, D., Shoham, S., Kubillus, S. L., and Biemann, K., Bacterial peptidoglycans as modulators of sleep: I. Anhydro forms of muramyl peptides enhance somnogenic potency, *Brain Res.* 403 (1987): 249–57.

62. M. Lotz, Carson, D. A., and Vaughan, J. H., Substance P activation of rheumatoid synoviocytes: Neural pathway in pathogenesis of arthritis, *Science* 235 (1987): 893–95.

63. J. D. Levine, Dardick, S. J., Roizen, M. S., Helms, C., and Basbaum, A. I., Contribution of sensory afferents and sympathetic efferents to joint injury in experimental arthritis, *J. Neurosci.* 6 (1986): 3423–29; J. A. Todd, Acha-Orbea, J., Bell, H. I., Chao, N., Fronek, Z., Jacob, C. O., McDermott, M., Sinha, A., Timmerman, L., Steinman, L., and McDevitt, H. O., A molecular basis for MHC class II–associated autoimmunity, *Science* 240 (1988): 1003–9.

64. M. Lotz, Carson, D. A., and Vaughan, J. H., Effect of neuropeptides on production of inflammatory cytokines by human monocytes, *Science* 241 (1988): 1218–21.

65. A. Smith, Tyrell, D., Coyle, K., and Higgins, P., Effects of interferon alpha on performance in man: A preliminary report, *Psychopharmacology* 96 (1988): 414–16.

CHAPTER 7. THE EXPERIENCE OF ILLNESS

1. I. Illich, *La némésis médicale* (Paris: Seuil, 1975).
2. A. De Sedouy, *De quoi souffrez-vous, docteur?* (Paris: Olivier Orban, 1989).
3. G. Canguilhem, *The normal and the pathological,* Carolyn R. Fawcett, trans. (New York: Zone Books, 1989).
4. M. Foucault, *Naissance de la clinique* (Paris: PUF, 1966).
5. J. Ruffié, *Vers une médecine predictive, Le Monde,* 1 Feb. 1989.
6. A. Gide, *Si le grain ne meurt* (Paris: Gallimard, 1920).
7. There are in fact two kinds of behaviorism. Radical behaviorism totally denies the existence of mental states. Methodological behaviorism, more pragmatic, considers objective study of these states unattainably difficult and directs its attention, therefore, to objects and quantities that can be measured directly.
8. For a deeper analysis of pain and pain-affected behavior, see the excellent work edited by François Boureau: *Pratique du traitement de la douleur* (Paris: Doin, 1988).
9. For a more thorough analysis of these aspects, see R. Fitzpatrick, Hinton, J., Newman, S., Scrambler, G., and Thompson, J., eds., *The experience of illness* (London: Tavistock, 1984).
10. N. Hodgkinson, *Will to be well: The real alternative medicine* (London: Hutchinson, 1984).
11. J. C. Smuts, *Holism and evolution* (New York: Macmillan, 1926).
12. For further details, see *Examining holistic medicines* (Buffalo, NY: Prometheus, 1984), an excellent work edited by D. Stalker and C. Glymour. The book describes not only the various practices claiming to be "holistic" and their unbridled proselytism, at least in the United States, but also the vacuity of their content. For the French scene, readers will consult with profit F. Laplantine and Rabeyron, P. L., *Les médecines parallèles: Que sais-je,* #2395 (Paris: PUF, 1987).
13. J. C. Eccles, *The neurophysiological basis of mind* (Oxford, UK: Clarendon Press, 1953).
14. M. Bunge and Ardila, R., *Philosophy of psychology* (New York: Springer-Verlag, 1987).

CONCLUSION: TO DISPEL THE ILLUSION

1. E. Morin, *Le grand dessein, Le Monde,* 22 Sept. 1988.
2. As A. R. Feinstein, an eminent professor of epidemiology, states without hesitation, epidemiology has undoubtedly fostered progress in the identification of the classic pathogenic agents—viral, bacterial, or parasitic; see A. R. Feinstein, Scientific standards in epidemiologic studies

of the menace of daily life, *Science* 242 (1988): 1257–63. But as regards the multiple factors of daily life that contribute to the outbreak and development of illnesses, including foods and medical treatments, the balance sheet is notably uneven. Fundamental methodological progress would seem to be mandatory!

3. Action is not limited to setting out with the intention of doing something. Acting (as opposed to reacting) involves having a mental representation of the intended objective as well as the capability of correcting this representation in the light of the results obtained. Cognitive psychology is interested in how the brain processes information, from perception to the formation of mental images. Devoted entirely to the thinking brain and wishing at all costs to see it as an intelligent machine, this science introduces an insidious neo-dualism into its consideration of the way the mind works.

4. Conference of Nobel laureates in Paris, *Promesses et menaces à l'aube du XXIe siècle* (Paris: Editions Odile Jacob, 1988).

AUTHOR INDEX

Abbott, D. H., 62
Ader, R., 172–73, 174
Alexander, F., 3–4, 152, 193
Amsel, A., 96
Anderson, N. B., 153
Andrews, R. V., 58
Anisman, H., 85, 86, 164
Antelman, S. M., 137
Arnone, M., 97
Axelrod, J., 38

Behan, P., 160
Benus, R. F., 127
Bernard, C., 6, 198, 199
Besedovsky, H., 182, 183
Bizière, K., 161
Blalock, J. E., 184–86
Bolles, R. C., 54, 56, 201
Bourgeois, M., 14
Brady, J., 77, 78
Bunge, M., xiv, 207, 208
Burchfield, S., 110

Camp, D. M., 151
Canguilhem, G., 198, 199, 200
Cannon, W., 5, 6, 7, 10, 43, 74
Chalmers, D., 176
Chapman, J. P., 21
Chapman, L. J., 21
Chorine, V., 171, 172
Cohen, N., 174
Coley, W., 190
Cousins, N., xiv, xvi, 210
Croiset, G., 167

Da Costa, J. M., 139
Dantzer, R., 97, 129, 131, 132, 181
David, C., 4
de M'Uzan, M., 4

Derogatis, L. R., 27
de Sedouy, A., 198
de Wied, D., 47
Dodson, J. D., 72
Dollard, J., 94
Donnelly, T. M., 169
du Gard, R. M., 115–16
Dunbar, F., 3
Durkheim, E., 23–24

Eccles, J. C., 207
Eikelboom, R., 114
Eysenck, H. J., 120, 121–22, 152

Fanselow, M. S., 54, 55, 56, 201
Felten, D. L., 158
Foucault, M., 205
Frankenhaeuser, M., 124, 125, 148, 152
Freud, S., 2, 139
Friedman, M., 28, 142, 143–44, 145, 146, 152

Gaddini, R., 91
Galen, xiv
Garcia, J., 17, 18
Geschwind, N., 160
Gisler, R. H., 170
Glaser, R., 163
Glass, D. C., 147
Goodman-Simson, P., 88
Gray, J., 9, 121–22
Groddeck, G., 2–3

Hall, N., 176
Hart, B. L., 190
Henry, J. P., 123, 152
Hofer, M., 90

SUBJECT INDEX